The Media Moguls

Other Books by Dana L. Thomas

The Plungers and the Peacocks—150 Years of Wall Street
The Money Crowd—Who They Are and How They Operate in
    Our Financial Revolution
Lords of the Land—The Triumphs and Scandals of America's
    Real Estate Barons
The Story of American Statehood
Crusaders for God
Let the Chips Fall—A Political History of New York (written
    with Newbold Morris)

THE MEDIA MOGULS

*From Joseph Pulitzer
to William S. Paley:
Their Lives and Boisterous Times*

Dana L. Thomas

G.P. Putnam's Sons
New York

Library of Congress Cataloging in Publication Data

Thomas, Dana Lee, date.
  The media moguls.

  Bibliography: p .
  1. Press—United States—History.
I. Title.
PN4855.T5 1981   302.2'3   81-8502
ISBN 0-399-12218-4   AACR2

Contents

Foreword

Any book that deals seriously with the media must take into account one towering irony. The newspaper publishers who pry so ruthlessly into the shortcomings of other people express little enthusiasm for exposing their own. If the great media moguls were, in fact, to demonstrate the same candor that they expect from others, their disclosures would be painfully embarrassing.

Indeed the history of journalism is shot through with paradoxes. Joseph Pulitzer, a notorious peddler of demagogic articles that helped sweep Americans into a war with Spain, became after his death the patron saint of journalistic integrity, with an award given in his name for the highest quality news reporting. Joseph Patterson who founded the *Daily News,* one of the most unflinchingly conservative newspapers in American history, started out as a firebrand socialist who preached the overthrow of the capitalist system. Katharine Graham's Washington *Post,* which gained a worldwide reputation as a crusader against government corruption, served for most of its history as a mouthpiece for crooked politicians, especially for thieving officials in the scandal-ridden Harding Administration. *Esquire,* the magazine that for decades has catered to America's sophisticated elite, started out as a trade magazine for the rough-and-tumble Seventh Avenue garment industry. David Sarnoff, who more than any other fostered the technological innovations that made possible America's radio and television industries, was a cultural snob who looked down his nose at the values of the untutored audiences his pocketbook fattened on.

But in addition to addressing this impressive irony, *The Media Moguls* takes into account the teeming variety of journalistic experiences. It deals with the development of ethnic journalism in America, exemplified by Abraham Cahan's *Daily Forward,* which was launched as a newspaper for Jewish immigrants herded into the slums of the Lower East Side at the turn of the century. It explores the curious world of financial journalism, the rise of the *Wall Street Journal* and the publishing house of Dow Jones. It pays particular attention to one branch of the media that has never received adequate treatment, the field of magazine publishing. It discusses the growth of the "true confession" magazine and the phenomenon of the sex periodical culminating in the journalism of hard-core pornography. And it evaluates the emergence of the underground press, whose publishers and editors started out as a fringe group of brash bohemians only to be embraced and financially enriched by the Establishment they professed to abhor. This book also deals with an oddly persistent strain of evangelical journalism that has survived today's dehumanizing technology and pervasive cynicsm—the optimism so dauntlessly expressed by the *Reader's Digest* which for over half a century has been extracting cheery moral lessons from the agony and tragedy of daily life.

Today the media is standing at a crossroads. The battle for survival of the free press has entered a climactic stage. On the one hand automation has taken over every phase of newspaper production, and the completely televised newspaper that will be routinely flashed to readers on their home video screens is just around the corner. On the other hand, thanks to major advances in video and information-retrieval technology, AT&T, IBM and other communications giants are threatening to challenge newspaper publishers in their traditional role as disseminators of news, advertising and vital statistics. The outcome of this struggle will have a vast impact on our society. Historically the press has flourished under the protection of the First Amendment guaranteeing freedom of speech. But as one observer puts it, "AT&T and its colleagues who, with their huge capital assets and nationwide communications networks are in the strongest possible position to merchandise tomorrow's electronic newspaper, are hardly ideal trustees for making the editorial decisions and inspiring the discussions of ideas that are the lifeblood of democracy."

While traditionally the press has thrived on diversity of expression, the emergence of television as today's preeminent communicator has drastically changed the dynamics of journalism. Television has homogenized the taste of its audience, creating a monolithic culture that is the hypester's delight. Accordingly, a writer on the media must conclude with a cautionary note. If America, under the pressure of runaway inflation and severe political turmoil, ever abandons democracy and succumbs to a dictatorship, a major reason may well be that the media has become so dangerously adept at peddling demagoguery that it will need very little persuasion to transform itself at the nod of a Man on Horseback into an enthusiastic dispenser of poisonous totalitarianism.

With regard to the preparation of this book, the author, besides exploring the essential material indicated in the bibliography, has interviewed numerous people in the field. Thanks to twenty-two years' service as an editor and writer for *Barron's National Business and Financial Weekly,* the Dow Jones publication, he has gathered much valuable information about the press and its leading personalities. His affiliation was especially helpful in obtaining material for the chapter on the *Wall Street Journal.* The writer was one of the first to explore the career of William Paley, head of CBS, in a previous book he authored entitled *50 Great Modern Lives,* and ever since he has been an avid student of developments in Paley's career. Important information about Bernarr Macfadden, the legendary pioneer of true confession journalism, was obtained from Lewis Copeland, who was a close friend of Macfadden's as well as of the writer's.

Unfortunately, the people who were helpful in the course of the research are too numerous to be mentioned individually, but the writer expresses his thanks to each and every one of them. He is especially grateful to his wife, Melba, whose devotion, encouragement and counsel have been indispensable during the ordeal of writing.

DANA L. THOMAS
New York City, 1981

Part One

The Rise of
"Front Page" Journalism

1

Jimmy Bennett of the New York *Herald* Springs a Leak

From Clipper Ships to the Birth of the Associated Press

THE GREATEST NEWS story of all is the one the American press rarely discusses—the story of itself. Yet its rivalries and power struggles, the fortunes of its rising superstars and falling titans make far more exciting reading than much of the news it so diligently reports. With a headline the press can catapult a nobody into celebrity, or topple the mighty from their roost of power. That is undoubtedly why investigative reporters who are so effective in bringing down presidents, cabinet ministers and international bankers are loath to probe into the operations of the newsgathering business and of the publishers who pay them their salaries.

Some owners of America's newspapers have been operating labor plantations where slavery and the auction block have persisted long after the destruction of the Southern Confederacy. While publishers have made a religion of talking about a "free press," thanks to the First Amendment nobody can tell them what or what not to print. Although there are—and have been—high-principled publishers, many press lords have never permitted their reporters to tell readers the whole truth and nothing but the truth when it affected their own private interests.

American newspaper publishers are the only captains of industry who, thanks to a guarantee of freedom of speech, are exempt from the prohibitions placed upon other entrepreneurs. The law prohibits other American corporations from engaging in subterranean dealings in politics, but newspapers, under the credo of "the people's right to know," are allowed to dispatch reporters to break bread, fraternize, peddle influence with congressmen, cabinet officials and occupants of the White House. Years ago, even before the media had attained its current influence, Walter Lippmann marveled at the astounding immunity the press enjoys from the government scrutiny imposed on other private profit-makers. "In a few generations it will seem ludicrous to historians that a people professing government by the will of the people should have made no serious effort to guarantee [the integrity of] the news without which a governing opinion cannot exist . . . and then they will recall the Middle Ages during which the [Catholic] Church also enjoyed immunity from criticism. And perhaps they will insist that the news structure of secular society was not seriously examined for analogous reasons."

The dilemma newspaper publishers constantly struggle with is how to reconcile their public service role with their private venality. The search for the truth in the news is frequently at odds with the desire to maximize profits. A. J. Liebling, a perceptive critic of the newspaper industry, once observed, "Freedom of press is reserved for those who own one." Liebling proposed that a new prize be established alongside the Pulitzer. "I propose that the American Society of Newspaper Editors sponsor an annual award to an American newspaper for lying, which would, I suggest, inspire far more interest than Pulitzer prizes, the latter having by now attained all the prestige of bean-bags tossed to good little newspapers by other papers that had them last year."

The compulsion of newspapers to conceal the truth about their own activities is endemic. *Editor & Publisher,* the trade journal, several years ago described the efforts of David Shaw, a writer for the Los Angeles *Times* who apparently had not caught the common virus and who sought to interview reporters about themselves for an article he was preparing. "When you interview members of the press," Shaw discovered, "you learn they are no different from lawyers, policemen or anyone else. They keep telling you that this or that is off the record, or after they read what you write, they insist they didn't know they were talking for publication and that they were misquoted."

Shaw found that journalists were unwilling to divulge even the least controversial news items—the kind they expect other people to reveal to them as a matter of course. A spokesman for the United Features Syndicate, for instance, refused to disclose how much UFS had charged the New York *Daily News* for the rights to buy the comic strip *Peanuts* from it—a harmless enough disclosure one would think. Shaw was informed that the United Features Syndicate has a policy "of not talking to the press."

If this penchant for secrecy is to be found among hirelings, it is even more conspicuous among the top honchos. Washington *Post* owner Katharine Graham, whom Arthur Schlesinger, the historian, has called "possibly the most powerful woman publisher on earth," is fiercely secretive about her own affairs. She is a public figure who wields immense influence, and while it would seem that the American people have as much right to know about her sources of power as they have to learn about the individuals her newspaper so relentlessly exposes, Mrs. Graham is highly reluctant to give interviews.

Similarly, the Chandler family which runs the powerful Los Angeles *Times* that helped launch the political career of Richard Nixon, and which for a hundred years has played a pivotal role in the political and economic history of California, has been loath to permit historians or journalists to study the family records. Rupert Murdoch, the feisty publisher of a global network of newspapers including the New York *Post*, who has made a career raking up scandals about other people, doesn't behave as though the public's right to know applies to an examination of his own operations even though this might provide a most illuminating insight into the power he exercises against others. "Punch" Sulzberger, publisher of the New York *Times*, sends his sleuths around the world to unearth stories for his readers, but several years ago the *Times* was reluctant to let United States government health officials enter its printing plants to investigate the possibility that chemicals it used might be hazardous to its workers; and Sulzberger's newspaper didn't think this news was "fit to print."

15

The lack of social responsibility displayed by many publishers has nowhere been more strikingly expressed than by Lord Thomson, the Canadian press lord: "I buy newspapers to make money to buy more newspapers to make more money. As for editorial content, that's the stuff you separate the ads with."

Lord Thomson's pronouncement is in bizarre contrast to the attitude of those who toil in the industry's vineyards. Most working reporters regard their trade with awe, as if, like the mystery of the Catholic Mass, the transubstantiation of news into the printed word cannot be expressed in simple human terms. When an airplane or a toy manufacturer goes into bankruptcy, the newspapers report that their business "went broke." But when a newspaper ceases to publish, newsmen refer to this as if it were a death in the family. Reporters talked in hushed tones about the "death" of Pulitzer's New York *World,* the "death" of the New York *Herald Tribune,* the "death" of the Brooklyn *Eagle* as though Albert Schweitzer had passed to sainthood in the Great Beyond.

But if newsmen have a mystical sense of their trade, their bosses regard their mission more pragmatically. In the spring of 1978 one of America's last newspapers with a grand historic tradition, the 102-year-old Chicago *Daily News,* folded. Such celebrated reporters as John Gunther, Edgar Ansel Mowrer and Bill Stoneman had cut their eyeteeth on the *News.* Carl Sandburg had once been its movie critic. Ben Hecht had toiled for it, accumulating the experiences which he later turned into his play *The Front Page.* Over the years, the *News* garnered fifteen Pulitzer prizes. The Mowrer brothers, Ed and Paul, won theirs for covering the rise of Hitler and Mussolini. George Weller won his for describing an emergency appendectomy performed by an amateur sailor aboard a World War II submarine. Keyes Beech won a Pulitzer for his reporting of the Korean War.

True to tradition Mike Royko, a *News* columnist, referred to the folding of his newspaper as a "death in the family." But the honchos at Marshall Field Enterprises who ran the *News* looked upon it in a different light. When a veteran reporter, typing the lead story on the newspaper's final day, asked why the paper "couldn't have been kept alive as an act of civic responsibility," James Field, an executive, retorted, "It seems to be strange logic that we have an obligation to fund an entity that is not viable in the marketplace." So much for one publisher's attitude towards his "holy profession."

Winston Churchill once remarked during a trip to the United States, "Your toilet paper is too thin and your newspapers are too thick." Whether overly thick or not, American newspapers in their haphazard fashion manage to faithfully reflect the nation's prevalent life-style. Newspaper editors learned early in the game that two themes were especially enticing to their readers: sex and death. Oddly enough, one of the most widely read sections of the daily newspaper, regardless of region or ethnic group, is the obituary column. Surveys have shown that more readers turn to the obituary columns to learn who has died than turn to the sports, the entertainment or the gossip pages to learn about the living.

One of the major status symbols for a public leader is to be chosen as a subject of a New York *Times* obituary while he is still alive, the article being filed for release against the grand event. There is a story told at the *Times* about an irreverent editor who used to put the names of a hundred subjects of obituaries into a hat and pass them around to the rest of the staff, selling chances at a dollar each. The editor who drew the name of the celebrity to become the first to die received the top prize. When his death occurred, another name was put into the hat for another drawing, and so on.

Sex is the other big theme. It has been a bread-and-butter product from the days of Hearst and Pulitzer to the era of Rupert Murdoch. Murdoch, an Australian publisher, moved onto the American scene after causing a bitter controversy in Britain when he introduced as a feature in his London *Sun* a topless woman selected for the gigantic size of her breasts—an innovation that outraged some British highbrows and leaders of the women's liberation movement, but delighted the great mass of readers who care nothing for tilted-nose morality. Murdoch insists that he isn't merchandising sex to debase the tastes of his readers. "Newspapers don't change tastes. They reflect tastes. We don't want to be pretentious. We don't want to be full of aging columnists who suck pipes and pretend that they're great prophets about everything."

Not only do other overachieving capitalist publishers feel this way, but at least one left-wing newspaper owner who

17

bristles with "social concern" for the masses has said amen to Murdoch. She is Dorothy Schiff, the socialite publisher, who several years ago sold her New York *Post* to Murdoch. The dowager publisher of a newspaper populated by a bevy of journalistic pundits headed by that incomparable father figure, Max Lerner, confided to a reporter after the sale of the *Post* that she was certain she had placed the fortunes of the paper in safe hands (Murdoch's). "You know," twittered Mrs. Schiff, "we have the same birthday, March 11—and neither of us believes in astrology, but I love coincidences!" Asked whether she was uncomfortable with the possibility that Murdoch might turn the *Post* into a sex sheet like those he publishes elsewhere, Mrs. Schiff snorted, "I've always been a mass-circulation person myself . . . I have very common tastes." And she added as a pungent afterthought, "I find that intellectuals are more interested in gossip than anybody else—Arthur Schlesinger [the historian] is the biggest gossip in the world!" And indeed, it is mankind's unquenchable thirst for gossip that has kept the newspaper industry alive and prosperous.

The media did not always have the overwhelming influence that it enjoys today. The meat that the Caesars of the press feed on was not always as nourishing. A century and a half ago, newsmen were held in contempt, along with actors and prostitutes. James Gordon Bennett, Sr., the founder of the New York *Herald,* once remarked bitterly to a friend, "You asked me who the Five Hundred in American society are? I'll tell you. They're the sons-of-bitches who are too snippity to invite me to their dinners."

In those benighted days Mrs. Nixola Smith, the granddaughter of publisher Horace Greeley, called on Mrs. Astor, the doyenne of Manhattan's high society, to obtain an interview for her column. Mrs. Astor kept her cooling her heels in an anteroom for an hour, and then sent a maid with a two-dollar bill along with a note: "Since you work for a living and have apparently taken pains to come, here is some money for your efforts." Mrs. Smith returned the money with a message of her own. "Tell your mistress she has forgotten not only who she is but who *I* am. Remind her that when John Jacob Astor was skinning rabbits my grandfather was publishing the New York *Tribune*."

Manners have changed considerably since Mrs. Smith's day. The insolence of America's nineteenth-century oil and steel barons, the lust for power of the Medicis and the other *condottieri* of the Italian Renaissance, can hardly compare with the arrogance of the great American publishing clans that have played a dominant role in shaping the affairs of our nation. Even today, although the industry is permeated by chain publications run by outside management, a number of powerful newspapers are still family-owned and operated like feudal fiefdoms. The tyranny of overbearing fathers, the Oedipal ties of mothers and sons, the rivalries of paranoid siblings have in many cases had a much greater impact on the editorial positions adopted by family-run newspapers than the needs of the communities they are supposed to serve.

Newspaper founders have by and large been insuperable egotists, and they have passed their regnancies onto heirs who, if possible, were even more self-involved. To cite one case, James Gordon Bennett, Sr., a benevolent despot, was a founding father of the mass circulation press. He showed up in Manhattan in 1835 and launched the *Herald* on a five-hundred-dollar shoestring. Thanks to his overwhelming success, he passed on to his son James, Jr., an income of a million dollars a year.

Before he was sixteen, Jimmy had lost his physical and mental chastity. During rounds of ubiquitous brawling, he was thrown out of the fanciest bistros in Paris, Vienna and the Riviera. As one boon companion observed, "Like many of the upper classes, Jim loved the sound of smashing glass." When Bennett turned thirty-five, he decided to quit bachelorhood, and he became engaged to Miss Caroline May, a Maryland socialite. News of the prospective wedding was played up in Manhattan's society columns. It was fashionable among the Five Hundred to hold open house on New Year's Day, and Miss May's parents invited New York's fanciest nabobs and their ladies to a reception to meet their daughter and her fiancé. The drawing room of the Mays' Fifth Avenue mansion was thronged with lavishly coiffed dowagers and debutantes chatting with escorts attired in Prince Albert cutaways, who smoked Coronas while a fifty-piece orchestra played Strauss waltzes.

The gathering was warming up with brandy and eggnogs

when Bennett, who had been whetting his pipes at a downtown bar before joining the festivities, drew up to the mansion in his barouche and sauntered into the drawing room. He kissed the hand of his fiancée and bowed to her parents who were standing regally at her side. Then he snatched a tumbler of bourbon from a servant, tossed off one drink and then another as he made his way among the guests.

In the midst of a jaunty bon mot, the inebriated publisher suddenly felt an urge to respond to the call of nature. He made his way as if dancing an elaborate minuet toward a fireplace at one end of the hall. Behind its wrought-iron grille a fire roared, warming the chilly room. Swaying a trifle to leeward, the publisher of the New York *Herald* unbuttoned his fly and urinated into the flames.

There was a sudden hush. The fifty-piece orchestra stopped playing as the conductor's baton froze in midair. Maidens and dowagers hid behind their fans and shrieked. The publisher was hustled by servants out of the grand salon and deposited on the sidewalk; his overcoat and cane were hurled after him.

Eyewitness reports of Bennett's spectacular leak were bandied that evening around scores of dinner tables along Park and Fifth avenues. The only newspaper that didn't carry an account of the event was the New York *Herald*.

The morning after, the sobered-up publisher set out for the august Union Club to assay the reaction of his colleagues. When he stepped from his barouche, Frederick May, Caroline's younger brother, was waiting for him brandishing a horsewhip and shouting that he was determined to avenge his sister's honor. Bennett wrestled him to the sidewalk as the superannuated members of the Union Club craned their heads excitedly from the windows to watch the bloodletting. The police broke up the scuffle and escorted Bennett home. The publisher dispatched a message to Frederick May, challenging him to a duel. Bennett recruited Charles Longfellow, the son of the venerated poet and a boon drinking companion, for his second.

The duel, the most celebrated to be fought outside the South since the match between Alexander Hamiliton and Aaron Burr, took place two days later at a spot in Maryland appropriately called Slaughter's Gap. By this time, however, tempers had considerably cooled. Young May had no stomach for taking the life of the *Herald*'s publisher even if he had mistaken a fireplace for a urinal, and Bennett was reluctant to add the crime of killing to the folly of indecent exposure. The duelists fired over each other's heads, shook hands and went home.

Though Bennett escaped with his life, the outraged public had no intention of letting him escape with his honor. Caroline May's parents broke off their daughter's engagement and the publisher was ostracized from the nation's drawing rooms and social clubs. With an imperious gesture of defiance Bennett left America and went into exile in Paris, where he continued to run the *Herald* for the next forty years. The Parisians weren't as stuffy about urinals as Bennett's Victorian countrymen. And they were only too happy to help the newspaper potentate spend his million-dollar-a-year income among them. Until his death Bennett ran the New York *Herald* as effectively as if he were on the spot, making only occasional trips to America.

While the newspaper profession was dominated in its early years by uninhibited, freebooting males, a sprinkling of enterprising journalists emerged from the distaff side. One of the most flamboyant scribes covering Washington in the early days of the nation was Anne Royal, a free-lance journalist who, in the 1820s, wangled an exclusive interview with the President of the United States. She accomplished this in a most unorthodox fashion. John Quincy Adams had a habit of sneaking to the banks of the Potomac River at dawn, shedding his clothes and plunging into its icy waters for an early morning swim before tackling a busy day in the executive suite.

One morning Anne trailed the President to the river and, when he dived into the water naked as a bluejay, she sat down on his pants and called out to him that she wished to interview him and wouldn't stir from her perch until he answered her questions. The astonished Adams meekly submitted to her inquiries, his bald head bobbing up and down as he treaded water.

Another resourceful woman who managed to achieve a solid reputation in journalism was Maria Morgan.

One morning in the late 1860s, just after the Civil War, this strapping lass, over six feet two inches, walking with a pronounced limp and wearing cowboy boots with a six-shooter strapped around her waist, showed up in the office of John Bigelow, the editor of the New York *Times,* and announced in a thick Irish brogue that she was looking for a job as a reporter. Bigelow regarded her with astonishment mingled with amusement. There was no job available, he replied. Then he added mischievously, as an afterthought, "except for a livestock reporter."

"I'll take it," rasped the Brobdingnagian female. In this fashion Maria (Midy) Morgan, a wench born in the 1820s near Cork, joined the staff of the stately New York *Times* and launched one of the most bizarre careers in the newspaper business. Limping badly as a result of a riding accident, trudging through the mud of the cattle yards and riding freight trains packed with hogs, dressed in high rubber boots and carrying a Colt revolver, Midy became an authority on America's livestock markets. Her passion for animals was all-consuming; she wrote as enthusiastically about her cattle and horses as the *Times'* society reporter wrote about the comings and goings of the Beautiful People. Once Midy traveled on a cattle boat crossing the Atlantic and penned a series of angry articles describing the inhumane conditions under which the livestock were crowded into the steerage. As a result of her pieces, the treatment of cattle shipped over the ocean was considerably improved.

So considerable was Midy's reputation as a judge of horse-flesh that leading Americans sought her opinions on their horse-breeding activities. Ulysses Grant consulted Midy on the thoroughbreds he raised on his farm. Commodore Vanderbilt sought her advice on proper training. King Victor Emmanuel of Italy, a horse lover, cabled asking her to select some prize stallions from Ireland for his stables. The Italian king was so pleased with Midy's efforts that he presented her with a watch studded with his initials in diamonds. Midy put the gift in a vault until Victor Emmanuel died, then took it out and fastened it to a chain she wore around her neck in his memory.

At her death it was found that Midy Morgan had salted away a substantial fortune. In return for her advice on horse breeding, Commodore Vanderbilt had invested Midy's money in the stock of his railroad, the New York Central. Also, acting on the Commodore's suggestions, Midy snapped up valuable real estate in New York and made a financial killing. She left an estate of over a hundred thousand dollars together with a collection of valuable jewelry which she bequeathed to the

Metropolitan Museum, the *pièce de résistance* being Victor Emmanuel's diamond-encrusted watch.

As a newsgatherer, the American journalist is unmatched. Points out Ishbel Ross, a newspaper historian:

> Over the generations the U.S. reporter has survived like a jungle cat, thanks to his cunning and the quick action of his reflexes in a crisis. Important news events strike as rapidly as a bolt of lightning. The reporter, armed with only his press card, has pushed his way through fire lines and riot squads, clambered aboard sinking ships, piled into the cockpit of crashing planes, dodged mortar shells in wartime and bullets during strikes, descended into exploded mine shafts, moved through floods, traveled all over the world by every means human ingenuity can devise, to cover the rise and fall of governments, the eruption of earthquakes and revolutions, the crowning and collapse of kings—all this with the single purpose of providing copy for the city room where, under glaring lights, an army of copy readers and rewrite men move like restless bugs as the phones ring and the tickers click, continually beating out the heart of the news.

The first newspapers in America were political pamphlets and scientific journals issued for a handful of upper-class readers. After the Civil War, however, the waves of immigrants to the New World, coupled with the influx of rural Americans into the cities, generated new mass markets for publishers. At the same time, landmark developments in printing and production technology made possible large enough printings to supply the rapidly expanding audience of readers. As Americans continued to pour into metropolitan centers, the writing of the news became increasingly geared to the interests of the masses. Immigrants from Central and Eastern Europe as well as the Mediterranean countries who poured into the slums of the New World were highly susceptible to the enticement of sensational journalism that provided an escape from their impoverished lives.

One leading peddler of mass journalism was, fittingly enough, a Hungarian immigrant who had landed penniless on these shores and ended up amassing a fortune by shrewdly merchandising brash hyperbole. Joseph Pulitzer made a splash publishing newspapers that were a paradigm of yellow journalism—an ironic fact often overlooked by aspiring news scriveners and authors who have salivated at the prospect of receiving the prize for journalistic and literary excellence given in his name.

Pulitzer was an odd mixture of the idealist and the charlatan. He crusaded editorially for America's working classes while manipulating them with the rankest sensationalism. He campaigned against the extravagant life-style of the rich while building himself a yacht that rivaled in elegance the boats owned by Morgan and Astor. He wrote editorials castigating President Cleveland for secretly awarding a gold contract to the banking house of Morgan while calling for taxes to be levied on large incomes and inheritances, yet he himself cavorted in his villa on the Riviera and his townhouses in London and New York, hiring the New York Philharmonic to play at lavish supper parties. He denounced the huge profits reaped by Wall Street insiders at the expense of the American public, but he was exultant when his own son married into the wealthy Vanderbilt family. While posturing as a champion of the oppressed, writing and fighting editorially for better working conditions and a higher standard of living for the poor, Pulitzer vied with William Randolph Hearst in the peddling of war-mongering journalism. He planted propaganda lies to push America into war with Spain in 1898, sending a number of his countrymen to their deaths. An aristocrat by now to his fingertips—Pulitzer married Kate David, a cousin of Jefferson Davis, the ill-fated president of the Confederacy—the publisher was nevertheless strangely out of tune with the social world he moved in. Six feet two, thin as a beanpole, he looked like an undernourished anthropoid with a bulbous head, a huge eliptical nose and tiny narrow chin. To the end of his life he spoke with a heavy foreign accent.

Born to an impoverished Jewish family in Hungary in 1847, Pulitzer ran away as a teenager to enlist in the British Army in India, but was rejected because of poor eyesight and a sickly constitution. Emigrating to America, he joined the Union Army during the Civil War, became a newsman, had a fling at politics and eventually bought at auction an evening newspaper that had just gone bankrupt—the St. Louis *Dispatch*. He merged it with the *Post*, a morning paper, acquired the New York *World* from its owner Jay Gould for $346,000 and was soon on his way to launching a publishing empire.

As Pulitzer grew increasingly rich, he suffered from ailments that robbed him of the enjoyment of his wealth. His nerves became shattered and he developed an abnormal sensitivity to noise. He soundproofed his apartment, pursuing his journalistic duties in a veritable fortress of silence. When an editor who consulted him thoughtlessly crumpled paper or dropped a pencil, it was enough to send the publisher into a paroxysm of pain. His eyes, always poor, became dangerously worse. One day as he was sailing aboard his yacht in the Mediterranean, he turned to his secretary. "How dark it's suddenly become." "It's not dark at all," the other replied. "Well, it is to me." And indeed, before long it became midnight for Pulitzer. Before he passed away in 1911, Pulitzer, in an effort to elevate the helter-skelter standards of news reporting, donated two million dollars to Columbia University to start the well-known school of journalism.

Despite his greed and demagoguery, the fits of war hysteria during his early days, this tortured, curiously ambivalent publisher stubbornly fought for the economic betterment of America's working man, supported labor strikes and social legislation and strove in his years of maturity for excellence in the reporting of the news. If Pulitzer had chosen to write the complete, confidential story of his own progress from poverty to wealth, from cynicism to idealism, from physical well-being to total blindness, the result could have been fascinating enough to have won for him the first prize for literature awarded in his name.

Another virtuoso manipulator of journalism for the masses and a contemporary of Pulitzer was William Randolph Hearst, the first publisher to bring big inherited money and big business methods into the newspaper industry. Thanks to a thirty-million-dollar fortune inherited from his father's mining operations, Hearst, in the closing years of the nineteenth century, entered a field that had been dominated by working newsmen who had started in their shirt-sleeves, and he proved that a multimillionaire who had no newspaper experience whatsoever could push experienced rivals to the wall with massive outlays of money. Hearst ran a whorehouse of journalistic enterprise. When he moved into New York to buy the *Journal* he debated, in the words of Henry Villard, "as to whether he should found the best or the worst newspaper in the city." Brandishing a "very big bankroll in a very small crap game," Hearst bought up the best editors, cartoonists, syndicate writers and production men by the carload. He froze out the "ribbon clerks," making it so costly to get into the field that no working newspaperman has since been able to launch a major daily from scratch and survive.

The publisher was the only son of George Hearst, a mining prospector who had struck it rich in the Comstock Lode, amassing vast ranchlands and mining properties that employed thousands of economic peons. Willie Hearst was a pampered Little Lord Fauntleroy who grew up in the cocoon of a protective boyhood. A *bon vivant* with a penchant for lascivious jokes, he was thrown out of Harvard when he sent several professors chamberpots with their names engraved on them. He played around in the world's fanciest bistros and then, seized with the impulse to enter the business world, he asked his father to let him handle the San Francisco *Examiner,* a newspaper that the elder Hearst had taken over on the verge of bankruptcy for a bad debt. Hearst, Sr., couldn't imagine why young Willie would want to run a faltering old newspaper instead of one of his ranches, but he acceded. Willie nursed the newspaper along, preventing further losses, and when Hearst, Sr., died, his widow sold the family stock in Anaconda for $7.5 million and handed the cash to her son.

Hearst used his grubstake to move into the turbulent world of New York journalism, buying up the *Journal* and plunging into a bitter circulation fight with Joseph Pulitzer's *World.* In the 1890s both publishers cranked their propaganda machines, whipping up a public frenzy for war with Spain. Hearst chartered a boat, sailed to Cuba, rushed ashore brandishing a six-shooter and captured six unarmed Spanish sailors half-drowned on the beach. He ordered them to kneel and kiss the American flag that one of his editors had conveniently brought along while a Hearst photographer snapped pictures for the readers back home. Hearst falsified documents and faked news trying to create an incident that would push Americans into still another war, with Mexico. But he failed.

Meanwhile, leveraging his cash like a gambler shooting hot

dice, Hearst grabbed up more newspapers than anyone else in the business. He plunged into politics and in 1905 was elected Representative from New York. The night he won, he presented a display of fireworks outside Madison Square Garden to celebrate his victory. Mortars were tossed into the crowd by Latin American terrorists furious at Hearst's imperialism. A hundred people were killed, but the news didn't appear in the Hearst papers.

The publisher wasn't destined to go very far in politics. Observed John Dos Passos, "the limp handshake, the solemn eyes, set close to the long nose, the small, flabby, scornful smile were out of place among the Washington backslappers." Hearst failed to win the presidency and went back to his newspapers, those weapons of patriotic propaganda, featuring red, white and blue borders on the masthead with a tiny American flag at either end of the dateline.

Using his newspaper revenues for investments outside the field, Hearst moved into New York real estate, snatching up the Ziegfeld Theater, the Warwick Hotel, the Ritz Tower, and other Gotham landmarks. However, despite his money and entrepreneurial shrewdness, Hearst stumbled badly in the end as the newspaper business underwent drastic changes. Other chain owners, aping his business methods, began competing with him; his papers grew less and less profitable as operating costs skyrocketed. He held on to some of his papers too long to wangle an advantageous sale. During the Depression of the 1930s Hearst almost went under. Heavily in debt, his position extremely shaky, he was forced to take out a mortgage on his lavish residence, San Simeon, to keep possession of it. The mortgage money was provided ironically by a competitor, Harry Chandler, publisher of the Los Angeles *Times* who, in a further gesture of sportsmanship, refused to foreclose the mortgage when Hearst was unable to keep up with his payments.

Hearst not only made serious misjudgments in his newspaper operations but made them in his other investments as well, notably his art collection. He had prided himself that he was as successful a collector as J. P. Morgan, but during the Depression when the rest of his assets crumbled, the worth of his art collection nose-dived even more spectacularly. In a distress sale held at Gimbels, some of Hearst's Oriental and

Mideastern works went to bargain-seekers for under a dollar and a medieval abbey, which the publisher in his halcyon days had ordered transferred stone by stone from Spain at a cost of half a million dollars, was knocked down by a bidder to under twenty-thousand dollars.

When the publisher died in 1951 amidst a squabble between his heirs and his mistress over the disposition of his estate, observers could hardly have foretold the final indignity that would be heaped upon the memory of the roguish old patriarch who had made a career waving the American flag. Who could have foreseen that a generation later his great-granddaughter, Patty Hearst, would break into more sensational headlines than even the old maestro of yellow journalism had dreamed up, for being kidnapped and consorting with the revolutionary underground and becoming the cult heroine of America's counterculture guerrillas?

Hearst and Pulitzer were able to profit handsomely by manipulating the mass audience because the news merchandising techniques of the American press had reached a highly sophisticated level. Initially, in the days of the clipper ships before the introduction of the telegraph, publishers along the Eastern seaboard, to ferret out news and transmit it from Europe and other foreign areas as rapidly as possible, sent their reporters north to Halifax, Nova Scotia, equipped with carrier pigeons. When a ship bound for the United States hove into view, the newsmen boarded launches to meet it, climbed aboard and stayed with it for the final leg of the journey. While on board they scanned the latest foreign newspapers, wrote a digest of the important news developments on tissue paper, rolled it into pellets which they tied to the legs of the pigeons, and released the birds from the deck of the ship to fly to their shore-based editors for the quickest possible printing and distribution.

During the 1840s a half-dozen publishers from New York state formed an association to further facilitate the acquisition and distribution of news. They pooled their money to buy a fleet of tender ships stationed in New York harbor to carry reporters out to meet incoming vessels and peruse the latest news from abroad. This rudimentary association of publishers was destined to evolve into the Associated Press. After the Civil War, a rival organization was launched to vie with the AP in serving newspapers from coast to coast, the Scripps-Howard United Press. And a third competitor, Hearst International News Service, made its bow in 1909. Forty-nine years later it merged into the Scripps-Howard organization and was renamed United Press International.

Ironically, it took national catastrophes like wars to serve as a catalyst for the major improvements in newspaper operations. The outbreak of the Civil War, for example, generated an unprecedented hunger for the latest news developments. American publishers met the challenge by dispatching several hundred war correspondents to the fighting fronts. Since millions of readers found themselves on edge waiting from Saturday to Monday for the latest developments concerning their loved ones in the combat zones, the need arose to put out special weekend editions in addition to the traditional daily ones; hence the first Sunday newspapers in the history of the industry were launched. Moreover, the use of eye-catching headlines to dramatize the happenings on the battlefield paved the way for the even more skillful employment of headlines during the slick tabloid era that followed the war. In addition, while previously publishers had concentrated their efforts on turning out morning newspapers, the time element involved in covering the latest news from the fronts suggested the advantage to be gained by publishing evening editions, and the industry began to print evening newspapers.

After the Civil War, the power struggle between newsgathering agencies intensified. By the 1890s the most powerful press association, gathering and transmitting to a family of subscribing publications articles of national and international importance, was the Associated Press of New York. This agency had emerged as a quasimonopoly. Not only was it beyond the means of most independent newspapers to duplicate the news coverage of the New York AP, but even if they had the resources to do so, there was a formidable obstacle in their path. For some years the Western Union Telegraph Company had been providing its wires to the New York AP at special rates thanks to the volume of business the AP gave it, and it refused to undermine the profitability of this association by giving equally low rates to outside newspapers. Moreover, Western Union had virtual control of the wire systems across the nation.

Under these monopolistic conditions, the Associated Press of New York fattened its revenues while expanding its operations. The first leased telegraph wire it used for carrying the news was one strung from Washington to New York in 1879. Five years later, a news wire was installed from New York to Chicago. By this time the Associated Press of New York consisted of seven newspapers which sold their services to a number of regional subscribers, and these groups in their turn followed the policy of their giant leader by restricting their own memberships arbitrarily. Newly started newspapers and all others that had not been original members were kept out. Member rates were boosted arbitrarily, but no member paper dared object for fear of being thrown out of the club.

Meanwhile one AP subgroup, located in the Middle West and calling itself the Western Associated Press, was becoming increasingly frustrated by what it considered to be its second-class citizenship vis-à-vis the "arrogant" New York City members who made the major decisions and set the prices for the entire Association. At first the Western AP was unable to effectively press its claims for equal power with the New York group, but in the early 1880s it gained a powerful ally in its campaign. Western Union quarreled with the New York City group which insisted on lower wire rates and threw its weight behind the efforts of the Western AP, encouraging it to secede and promising to help the Westerners become a major competitor with the New York group.

The threat was enough to cause the New York members to back down. In 1882, to prevent outright secession, they offered to set up with their Midwestern colleagues a new joint executive committee that would divide the power of decision making and control of operations equally between New York and the Midwest. The Western AP members accepted this compromise, and for the next seven years an uneasy truce prevailed between the two factions.

Then in 1889 a disaster occurred which not only traumatized the nation but, since it took place in Pennsylvania, the home grounds of one of the Western Associated Press's major bureaus, provided a once-in-a-lifetime opportunity for news coverage. The Western AP's prestige with the American public was boosted to such an extent that it was finally able to prevail in its power struggle with the New York branch of the Association. The agency was reorganized and the modern Associated Press was born.

Johnstown was a town in the western valley of Pennsylvania. Fourteen miles above it was a giant reservoir where the waters of South Fork Run and a dozen crystal-clear creeks and forks were restrained behind a wall of earth and masonry. This body of water, three miles long and more than a mile wide in places, was called Lake Conemaugh, and was the largest artificial lake in the country.

The South Fork Reservoir had originally belonged to the Pennsylvania Railroad Company, but in 1879 it had been sold to a real estate investment group that decided to stock the reservoir with fish and build a summer resort. Nestling high in the Allegheny Mountains, affording a magnificent view, the resort became frequented by a clique of wealthy families from Pittsburgh—the Carnegies, the Mellons and the Fricks among others—who turned the resort into an exclusive hunting and fishing club for themselves, their wives and children.

While the Pittsburgh nabobs relaxed and played along the shores of the lake, many inhabitants of the valley below were worried over living within stone's throw of a huge, rickety reservoir that stored twenty million tons of water, especially since local engineers had insinuated that the dam was a faulty structure and it could burst its seams at any moment. If this happened, a tidal wave of water equivalent to the amount that cascaded over Niagara Falls every thirty minutes would pour into the valley.

At the end of May 1889 a vicious storm arose and the most tremendous rain ever recorded fell in western Pennsylvania. Beginning on May 30 and continuing until June 1 the rain poured down continuously for thirty-six hours. Long before the downpour had ended the rivers, streams and lakes of the Allegheny mountain area were overflowing dangerously. Three inches of rainfall in this mountain area ordinarily produced a threat of a flood. Six inches threatened a catastrophe.

Fourteen miles to the south of the Lake Conemaugh Dam lay the community of Johnstown, a lively industrial town, the

31

site of a large iron foundry and numerous taverns where the folk relaxed after a hard day's toil. As the rain continued to increase in strength and poured down without cessation, the residents of Johnstown became increasingly worried. Two rivers flowed through the town and while the rising waters still remained in their channels, some anxious people, fearing the worst, began moving their furniture out of their homes on boats and rafts.

Then, suddenly, the South Fork Reservoir gave way. Awash since before noon, the great wall could no longer withstand the pressure that four thousand accumulated gallons of water was exerting. Tearing away at the rocks and soil, the world's largest mass of water to be confined behind an earthen wall pushed the center of the dam ahead of it and rushed through Johnstown.

The devastation was complete, the death toll set at over twenty-two hundred people. In many cases there was no identification of the victims except by guesswork or recognition of the locality where they were found. The disaster at Johnstown sent shock waves through America. In Pittsburgh, the largest city near the scene of the tragedy, many of whose inhabitants had relatives and friends in the stricken town, crowds besieged the newspaper bulletin boards, rendering the streets impassable. They demanded to know if their kinfolk were among the survivors, but no names could be given. The flood had destroyed all means of communication with Johnstown.

It was under these seemingly insurmountable conditions that the Western Associated Press, operating out of its bureau in Pittsburgh, through sheer enterprise and pluckiness launched an epochal news coverage of the disaster. The first reporters who managed to reach Johnstown were sent by the Western AP. A special one-car train was chartered to rush the general manager of the Western AP and two crack reporters, Owen Wetmore and Bill Orr, to the disaster area.

The reporters battled their way through the swirling waters that flooded the railbed leading into the ravaged town. Tom Connelly, the general manager of the AP, twisted his ankle. He attempted to continue, limping, but the pains shooting up his leg prevented him from doing so. Wetmore and Orr supported him over their shoulders up a hill to a farmhouse, then continued slogging their way into Johnstown, arriving at the outskirts. Stumbling across a telegraph lineman about to operate his Morse equipment, Wetmore persuaded him to tap out a message for the AP Bureau in Pittsburgh: "Johnstown devastated; appeals to the nation for food and shelter for thousands who are homeless and starving!" These words, the first to be flashed by an on-the-scene newsman, would be followed in the next few weeks by millions of words sent by reporters to newspapers all over the world.

Wetmore and Orr pitched AP headquarters in a crumbling old grain storehouse that hadn't been used for years. Several hours later, Connelly hove into view hobbling on a pair of crutches a farmer had given him. His ankle was still swollen and painful, but he had made his way three miles into Johnstown, and as the ranking newsman, he took charge of the operation. The reporters salvaged boards from the debris around them to use as writing desks. Wetmore and Orr rambled over the disaster area interviewing survivors, and met the first relief train sent in from Pittsburgh, while Connelly, his bandaged leg immobilized, sat on the ground, using a board resting on two whiskey barrels for a desk, and began writing his first dispatches. Several hours later that afternoon, telegraph wires for general news dispatches were strung into Johnstown and Connelly began transmitting his messages to the Pittsburgh office of the AP.

Far beyond changing the fortunes of any single newsman, the Johnstown Flood had repercussions in the upper echelons of the newspaper industry. It reshaped the future of newsgathering in America by forcing a shift of influence in the power struggle between the Western Associated Press and the New York branch. It was the Western branch that had scooped the nation with the first stories on the Johnstown Flood, and it was this same enterprising team that led the way in probing the cause of the tragedy, namely the South Fork Fishing Club's failure to properly maintain the dam. Thanks to the prestige it had won as a result of its performance during the Johnstown disaster, the Western branch of the Associated Press became the most publicized newsgathering agency in the nation and its officials, who had been treated as second-class colleagues by the Eastern branch located in New York, now demanded and won a ruling voice in its councils. Two influential New York newspapers, the *Tribune* and the *Sun,* withdrew from the New York Associated Press and joined the uprising of their Midwest-based colleagues. A complete reorganization of the agency was effected, reflecting the new power and influence of America's Midwestern members.

In 1893, four years after the Johnstown Flood, a new Associated Press, incorporated as the Associated Press of Illinois, was set up with the nucleus of the old Western AP but including the New York *World,* influential newspapers in Baltimore and Philadelphia and other powerful members of the Western press. Thus was born the modern Associated Press which has continued to grow in power and influence to this day.

Meanwhile, as the American society developed, the fortunes of the newspaper industry underwent some surprising and spectacular changes. Publishers were to emerge on the scene whose behavior would make the antics of Hearst, Pulitzer and James Bennett, Jr., seem positively straitlaced by comparison.

2

Bintel Briefs and Death in the Electric Chair

Captain Patterson Launches the *Daily News*

DESPITE THE ARDUOUSNESS of their trade, despite the skimpy wages and endless competitive grind, reporters stay on their job as long as they can walk and breathe, because once they have been bitten by the bug there is nothing else for them to do. Observes Ishbel Ross, a reporter during the "front-page" era of the 1920s: "Strange music sings in the ears of the newsgathering tribe. Visions haunt them as they stalk the streets. They fall asleep with the sound of the rumbling presses in their heads. Newsmen cannot resist the chance to be thrust into the middle of things, to be given a front seat at the spectacle of world events, to be placed on the spot where tragedy, exultation, victory and defeat unfold."

The Johnstown Flood not only triggered the reorganization of the press associations to strengthen the distribution of the nation's newsgathering efforts, but, coupled with these developments, a wide, popular audience emerged ready and eager to consume the accelerated output of the news. One constituency that provided a steadily expanding supply of enthusiastic readers resulted from the waves of immigrants that landed on the shores of America after the Civil War. Indeed, a significant offshoot of the mass press was the development of a series of ethnic newspapers serving numerous foreign groups that had moved into the American community. Since the immigrants were generally the poorest of the poor, their participation was made possible only because of landmark technological developments that brought down the costs of producing and distributing newspapers.

Although a free press was guaranteed under the United States Constitution, it took two generations before American newspapers actually began serving the man in the street. For a long time, due to the primitive printing equipment in use, the expense of putting out a paper was so excessive that the average American couldn't afford the luxury of buying one. The first newspapers were political pamphlets edited for the intellectual elite and the rising class of merchants who depended on receiving news from the four corners of the world to conduct their shipping business. Papers were sold by subscription and cost eight to ten dollars a year, which amounted to an entire week's salary for a skilled mechanic.

However, a series of technological developments took place that dramatically reduced costs of publication, making newspapers available at a price almost everybody could afford. During the 1820s Richard Hoe, a manufacturer of printing equipment in Manhattan who had been using the primitive Gutenberg flatbed press, invented a greatly improved press driven by steam cylinders that boosted the speed of printing newspapers to an incredible four thousand copies an hour. Hoe, a highly resourceful fellow, continued to come up with technological improvements. In 1847 he developed a press that held type on a cylinder instead of a flatbed and speeded up the rate of printing to twenty thousand copies an hour. In 1861 Hoe converted his bed of type into a curved stereotyped plate, and within two years he was printing rolls of paper instead of single sheets, accelerating his production even more dramatically. Furthermore, the introduction of Samuel Morse's telegraph after the Civil War speeded up the transmission of news. In 1866 the Mergenthaler linotype was introduced, enormously cutting the time and labor involved in converting words into type, while the introduction of wood pulp into the newsprint manufacturing process had the result of lowering publishing costs even further.

All this reduced the price of a newspaper to a few pennies,

well within the means of the working and immigrant classes. The inexpensive new American newspaper set the model for a host of foreign language newspapers, which, written in the native tongue of the populations they served, benefited from the new technological economics achieved by American papers to make their own publications available for a few cents.

One restless, volatile group especially hungry for the blessings of communication consisted of Jewish immigrants who at the turn of the century poured into America, settling in particular on New York's Lower East Side. It was a dreary, sterile life they lived. They huddled into freezing tenements, worked in sweatshops fourteen hours a day or begged in the streets. These "suffering masses" immortalized in Emma Lazarus' inscription on the Statue of Liberty had arrived in the land of freedom only to be dumped into slums choked with garbage and rats.

One of these embattled immigrants was Abraham Cahan, the son of a Hebrew teacher who had been born on the outskirts of Vilna, Russia. Like many young Jewish intellectuals, Cahan had been radicalized by the novels and pamphlets of Tolstoy, Turgenev and Kropotkin. He joined the revolutionary underground and barely escaped arrest by the Czarist police following the assassination of Alexander II. Leaving the turmoil of East European politics, Cahan went to America in 1882 and quickly learned the English language. He tried his hand at two novels, *Yepl* and *The Rise of David Levinsky*, delineating the social progress of an East Side Jewish immigrant.

Meanwhile, he veered into journalism. So well had he mastered English that he got a job as a cub reporter on the New York *Sun,* then the *Evening Post* and, finally, he was hired by Lincoln Steffens for the *Commercial Advertiser*. Through these stints, Cahan cut his teeth on the racy American style of human-interest journalism. He applied this experience to the task of publishing a Jewish language newspaper for a community of newcomers on the Lower East Side.

The Jews take their politics seriously. The newspaper Cahan was to publish, the *Daily Forward,* was founded by socialists in the Jewish community who wanted to express their political views. The Lower East Side in the 1890s bristled with impoverished intellectuals who worked by day in the sweatshops

37

of the garment industry and spent their nights debating heatedly over how to build a better world.

Abe Cahan became a mover and shaker in socialist politics. But he split with a faction that veered far to the left, and when the extremists started a newspaper to expound their views, he and several associates founded a competing newspaper to propound a more temperate line. The *Jewish Daily Forward,* which made its bow in 1897, was organized in a highly unconventional manner. Nine managers headed a board of two hundred people, each of whom put up a small amount of cash to provide the financing. The money was not contributed as an investment, and no dividends were expected. Abe Cahan was elected publisher and editor by a vote of the board managers. For the first decade or so the *Forward*'s profits, as noted, were not distributed as dividends but were used to improve the paper's editorial and news coverage. Some of the earnings went into launching an edition in Chicago, and some to help the socialist labor movement in America. The *Forward* refused to accept advertising.

Cahan, whose first love was writing fiction, quickly became restless in his position. He left the *Forward* and the paper was plunged into a bitter struggle to survive. Its editors crammed the paper with Marxist polemics and turgid editorials that incessantly attacked capitalism. Not one iota of human-interest journalism or entertainment was provided, nothing to appeal to the immigrant masses who desperately wanted to escape the bitterness of their daily lives. Bogged down by its own weight, the *Forward* sputtered along with only seven thousand readers until it seemed on the verge of going under; only then did the board plead with Cahan to quit writing novels and return as publisher.

Cahan reluctantly agreed. But he insisted to his associates they drop their Marxist polemics and enliven the newspaper with a strong dose of American-style journalism, the snappy colorful writing that other New York newspapers were using so successfully to attract readers. Reminiscing in later years, Cahan told how he brought grass-roots journalism to New York's East Side. "We went out after human interest stuff and played it up. We started a sports page. What a hullaballoo that raised! We made the paper as lively as possible. It was a complete metamorphosis from the dry, political tract it had been."

Cahan and his reporters went into the streets of the East Side, found out how the people were living, what they were thinking and doing. The *Forward* became a repository of the shared problems of a community struggling to survive. Responding to the needs and aspirations of his fellow immigrants, Cahan, in a stroke of inspiration, launched a letters column, "Bintel Briefs," which became the paper's most popular feature. These were the days before psychiatrists ministered to the masses, and the quickest, cheapest way for a Jewish immigrant to get advice was by writing about his problems to the editor of the *Forward*. Questions were asked about marriage and divorce. Was it right to marry outside the faith, or divorce one's faithful wife who had followed her husband all the way from Europe to America in steerage? Writers endlessly debated what constituted proper Jewish behavior in the new Gentile world.

Cahan's reporters made the rounds interviewing people and writing articles that became a treasure trove of sociological data. They wrote about Jewish children taking violin lessons in the hope they would be discovered as musical prodigies. They wrote about Jewish girls thrown out of work and forced to take up prostitution, of a handful of nouveaux riches who were moving uptown to the Bronx. One editorial triggered a lively controversy by urging Jewish mothers to show their children how to use handkerchiefs. Several of Cahan's more humorless associates were scandalized. What was a socialist newspaper doing giving such trivial, bourgeois advice as using a handkerchief, they wanted to know? Cahan retorted, "Since when has Socialism been opposed to clean noses?"

So popular were the "Bintel Briefs" that poor, uneducated Jews, newly arrived from Eastern Europe and unable to write Yiddish, trekked to the editorial offices of the *Forward* to have their musings put into letters. A lively trade grew up as people calling themselves "Bintel Brief" scribes went around preparing letters at a price. In the early days Abe Cahan replied personally to each letter until the flood of material became so great that a staff of editors was assigned to handle it.

In addition to promoting human-interest journalism, Cahan continued his campaign for Socialism, inveighing editorially against the sweatship conditions that existed in the garment industry. Activist, journalist and an important agent of assimilation, Cahan was one of a handful of immigrant Jews who

39

released an explosion of creative energy that poured in the early part of this century beyond the newspaper field into the mainstream of American culture.

Catering to the masses by persuasive media operators reached its zenith during the era of the American tabloid, a bantam-sized newspaper packed with lurid headlines and sensational pictures that epitomized front-page journalism following the First World War.

The publisher who pioneered the tabloid newspaper in America was Joseph Medill Patterson and his history-making journal was the New York *Illustrated Daily News,* later shortened to the *Daily News.* Patterson's tabloid became, as *Time* magazine has put it, "an expert, irritating, irreverent, gamey newspaper with the biggest circulation in the U.S."

The strange, enigmatic, fearsome individual who ruled his publishing caliphate with an iron will was a tall, slim fellow with a leathery face, a bristling mane of salt-and-pepper hair, gnarled hands and two thin slits for eyes. He walked with a brisk military air, but there his formality ended, for he dressed in a shabby, offhand manner that embarrassed his friends and amazed even his most carelessly attired reporters.

When the *News* went over a million readers, Patterson built a ten-million-dollar thirty-six-story skyscraper on East Forty-second Street to house his burgeoning business, and he had a quotation from Lincoln carved over the entrance: "The Lord Must Have Loved the Common People . . . He Made So Many of Them." The lobby of this skyscraper was designed like a giant compass with a revolving globe in the center, lit from underneath to give it a mysteriously effulgent flow. Like the balloon Charlie Chaplin tossed up and down in his movie *The Great Dictator,* the globe in Patterson's lobby was his planetary plaything—the symbol of his power, acquired through his virtuosity at manipulating the mind of Lincoln's common man.

As with other benevolent despots, this multimillionaire publisher bristled with eccentricities. In order to find out what his public wanted to read he became a one-man research team. He descended into the Manhattan subways to peer over the shoulders of straphangers and discover what news articles appealed to them. He rode out to Coney Island, in the dress of a workingman, buying hot dogs, drinking beer and rubbing shoulders with laborers, their wives and children. He visited the Bowery disguised as a hobo, staying overnight in flophouses and eavesdropping on the conversations of tramps.

He bummed around for days on end with the riffraff of the city. Once, after emerging from an orgy of slumming, the publisher dined with wealthy friends in the elegant Oak Room of the Plaza Hotel. A taxicab driver who had gone into the hotel to have a dollar bill changed saw Patterson and rushed over to him, slapping him on the back. The maître d'hôtel grabbed the cabbie by the arm and prepared to evict him. "Joe is an old friend of mine," protested the driver. "We were together on the Bowery drinking Sneaky Pete. Isn't that right, Joe?" Patterson rose, put his arm around the driver and invited him to dinner. The cabbie stared at his friend in his white tie and tails. "Joe, you son of a bitch," he exclaimed, "you always knew how to go out panhandling and come back with fifty cents. But what the hell's your racket now?"

Patterson was a grandson of Joseph Medill, a ruthless powerhouse publisher who started out by studying the law, then became active in politics, throwing his support behind Abraham Lincoln's presidential candidacy. That was Medill's first and last gesture of liberalism. He bought the Chicago *Tribune* and established it as a relentless spokesman for right-wing politics. During violent labor strikes in Chicago, where the unions were fighting for a foothold at the end of the nineteenth century, Medill called for the lynching of labor leaders. He also suggested that the best way to deal with unemployment was to put poison in the food the Salvation Army doled out to hoboes. This, Medill explained, would bring about a quick death and discourage other bums from asking for handouts. Medill's daughter, Eleanor, married Robert Patterson who became the publisher of the Chicago *Tribune,* and Joe and Eleanor, or Cissy as she was nicknamed, were two children of this marriage. Another daughter, Catherine, married Robert McCormick, heir to the reaper fortune. Their son, Robert Rutherford McCormick, together with his cousins, Joe and Cissy Patterson, eventually formed the triumvirate that became the journalistic spearhead of America's radical right: Joe Patterson as publisher of the New

York *Daily News,* Cissy as head of the Washington *Times-Herald,* and Robert McCormick as owner of the Chicago *Tribune.*

Joe Patterson was educated in private schools in America and on the Continent, and he married the daughter of a partner of Marshall Field, the department store tycoon. But he displayed early in life the virus of rebelliousness and promptly veered into radical politics. He became active in a political municipal reform movement in Chicago, was appointed Commissioner of Public Works, and then he stunned his family by proclaiming that he had become a socialist dedicated to the overthrow of the capitalist system. This unlikely convert to socialism issued a personal manifesto that must have sent old Joseph Medill spinning in his grave.

"The whole body of our laws as presently framed is ridiculous," insisted young Patterson. "They are designed always to uphold capital at the expense of the community. . . . Money is power and domination. It is wine and women and song. . . . It is warmth in winter and coolness in summer. It is clothing and food. . . . It is horses and automobiles, and silks and diamonds. . . ." And Patterson concluded his verbal thunderbolt: "As I understand it, I am a Socialist. I have never read a book on Socialism, but that which I have enunciated I believe in general to be their theory. If it is their theory, I am a Socialist."

In addition to speechifying, Patterson turned out a proletarian novel, *A Little Brother of the Rich.* The book was an immediate best seller, but the literary critics were less warm, taking the author to task for his crude polemics and lack of literary taste. Even the critics on the left failed to rally to Patterson's support. They condemned the novel, notwithstanding its social message, for its lack of professional skill.

Hell hath no fury like a rejected author and Patterson's ego was devastated. The first seeds of disenchantment with the proletarian revolution were planted. The internecine squabbles among the Socialists, the oratorical bombast by theoreticians who were long on theory and short on action, made him increasingly skeptical that socialism, despite its utopian message, was a program for meaningful reform.

While Patterson wrestled with his doubts, his family affairs took a turn that changed the course of his career. In 1910, his father, who had been the publisher of the Chicago *Tribune*, died. If the paper was to continue to prosper it was necessary for the next generation to take over. Patterson and his cousin Robert McCormick were the logical candidates and the duo moved into the *Tribune*'s executive suite, assuming financial and editorial control.

For the next six years the cousins worked in harmony, but the *Tribune* was too small an arena for two outsized egos to coexist permanently. The rift deepened after World War I. Joe Patterson, who had gone overseas as an artillery captain, during a leave from his military duties met Lord Northcliffe, the resourceful British press magnate who had amassed a fortune introducing a new kind of newspaper into England—a tabloid spiced with pictures and headlines that exuded sex and violence.

Patterson was impressed with Lord Northcliffe's *Daily Mirror* and decided to launch an American tabloid of his own. On a battleground in France, within earshot of an artillery bombardment, he met with his cousin, Robert, an army colonel. Patterson told his relative that when the war was over he wanted to start a tabloid in New York.

Colonel McCormick agreed to the project and after the armistice was signed, Patterson launched the New York *Illustrated Daily News*, which like the Chicago *Tribune* was organized as a corporate subsidiary of the parent Tribune company. The Medill trust, of which Patterson and McCormick were the sole trustees, controlled the majority of the corporation's shares; thus Colonel McCormick had a financial interest in his cousin's publication.

The inaugural edition of America's pioneer tabloid came out in June 1919. The initial months were a struggle for survival; the wily publisher William Randolph Hearst, sensing that a tabloid would reap a tremendous fortune in the frenetic atmosphere of postwar America, offered Patterson $500,000 in cash if he would fold his newspaper and let the Californian move into Gotham with his own tabloid. Patterson turned the offer down although during the first months the circulation of the *News* fell below 30,000 readers. But the paper rallied. In twelve months the daily readership went over 240,000. Within six years it soared to over one million. By the 1930s the *News* was enjoying a daily circulation of 1.7 million and 3 million on

Sundays. It had become America's most widely read newspaper.

Indeed, Joe Patterson, the erstwhile socialist, proved to be one of the smartest converts to free enterprise the newspaper field has ever known. Once, Patterson had yearned to improve the world by exhorting the underprivileged to revolt. Now he figured the least he could do was to feed them fantasies while they toiled on the plantation. "I keep the masses happy," he told a fellow publisher, "while you fellows milk them."

Patterson's tabloid made its debut at an opportune time. The *Daily News* flourished on the public's insatiable appetite for sensational journalism during the madcap, gin-soaked nineteen twenties. But Joe Patterson's success was not achieved overnight. The struggle of the *Daily News* to establish itself was a painful one. While it caught on with the public relatively rapidly, many of New York's retail merchants and other prime advertisers refused to deal with a newspaper that pandered to the "vulgar" tastes of the working classes, not for any reasons of morality, but because they reasoned that the slum dwellers who read the *Daily News* didn't have enough money to buy the goods they peddled. Outside of the Help Wanted section, the *News'* advertising was painfully skimpy.

Patterson's promotional team, hoping to convince advertisers they were missing a golden opportunity, embarked on an intensive market research project that turned up interesting results. The lower classes, alleged the *News,* were far different from what they had been at the turn of the century. Foreign-born citizens had been caught up in the American syndrome of "wanting to make it" and were enjoying a rapidly expanding purchasing power. The *News* published dollars-and-cents studies to prove that these lower-class New Yorkers were positively panting for the material goodies of life.

A series of advertisements launched by Patterson's crew shouted "Tell It to Sweeney; the Stuyvesants Will Take Care of Themselves." It was the Sweeneys who were flocking en masse to see Rudolph Valentino and Theda Bara, the new movie sex symbols; who were cheering Babe Ruth at the baseball park and Jack Dempsey in the prize ring. The purchasing power of the Sweeneys was beginning to dominate the American economy and set the standards of taste that would influence the nation's cultural patterns for years to come.

Catering meticulously to the desires of the Sweeneys, the *News* bristled with service articles and giveaway contests; an army of readers raised on the paper became fanatic supporters. The telephone wires of the *News* hummed with calls from people seeking advice: young couples inquiring where they could get married without waiting for a blood test; forlorn wives complaining that their husbands had left them or were out playing all-night poker; unemployed workers asking for assistance in obtaining a job; would-be suicides pleading for help before turning on the gas. The *Daily News* became a counselor-at-large for the millions.

Captain Patterson's headlines crackled and sizzled, his pictures were masterfully conceived, his news stories were concise and to the point, exhibiting a clever mixture of color and raw vulgarity. Patterson thought up the ideas for comic strips that served as powerful circulation builders. He developed the concept for *Andy Gump*. (The name "Gump" was suggested to Patterson by his own mother's continually saying "By gum.") Patterson hit upon the character of Dick Tracy and hired a cartoonist to put the finishing touches to his conception. Little Orphan Annie, one of his biggest hits, was jointly launched by the New York *Daily News* and the Chicago *Tribune*. Patterson paid his cartoonists record sums for the day; cartoons, he felt, were contemporary parables for the common folk and they deserved the best talent money could buy. Sidney Smith, the artist for the Gumps, received $120,000 a year at a time when dollars were really dollars.

But it was in the pioneering of pictorial journalism that Patterson's paper discovered its major forte and made its heaviest contribution in an era before the advent of *Life, Look* and television. Patterson's hardy band of news photographers began snapping pictures long before the development of today's high-speed precision cameras and stroboscopic flashlights.

The early *News* photographer carried a cumbersome camera with glass plates, a bottle of magnesium powder and a flash pan. He couldn't take a picture in a fog. Although his flash gun was activated by powder which drove a piston down to trigger the shutter, more often than not the shutter didn't go off at the same time as the powder and the picture couldn't be snapped. It was especially dangerous for the photographer to try taking flash pictures of a fire at night. If a spark from the flames touched the powder on his spread pan, it could trigger an explosion. A number of *News* photographers were badly burned in the face and arms in the line of duty.

News photographers were the first to snap pictures from the air, operating dangerously from the primitive, open-cockpit biplanes then in use. John Chapman, an early *News* photographer who subsequently became the paper's drama critic and wrote about those early days, describes how in order to take a photo he had to slip to his knees on the rear seat, face backwards from the direction the plane was flying and shoot over its tail as the pilot banked down on the scene. All this was accomplished without modern safety belts. Photographers, when flying over the ocean, carried a primitive inflated tube in case they fell into the water.

The 1920's were tailormade for Captain Patterson and his crew. Hardly had the publisher settled into his executive suite when Joseph Elwill, a nationally known bridge expert, was found murdered in his Manhattan brownstone, sitting upright in a chair with blood spurting from a gaping wound in his head. The case abounded with the stuff "Front-Page" editors gloried in: rich, beautiful women, racetrack gamblers, bootleggers, a Cairo princess, a Parisian Café dancer, a Brazilian newspaper magnate, a mysterious duchess, a cuckolded husband—and in the forefront, Elwill, the enigmatic bridge virtuoso whose liaisons were so numerous and difficult to unravel, his murder was never solved. Hard on the heels of the Elwill crime, "Dot" King, a showgirl called the "Broadway Butterfly," was found slain in her apartment, chloroformed.

But the coverage that brought Captain Patterson the biggest single jump in readership involved another fantastic murder. In 1927 Ruth Snyder, a mother and housewife in Queens, New York, and her paramour, Henry Judd Gray, a corset salesman, got rid of Ruth's husband in the tradition of a cheap detective thriller: Ruth drugged her spouse with chloroform, then Gray put on rubber gloves and strangled him.

No editor exploited this murder case more aggressively than Captain Patterson. He ordered his reporters to dog the Snyder and Gray households and interview the families of the accused. His newsmen set up a constant watch, keeping the bereaved relatives prisoners inside their homes, afraid of emerging to be bombarded with questions.

46

As soon as the lovers were arrested it became obvious they would be found guilty, and in fact they were convicted and sentenced to die in the electric chair.

It would be an unprecedented scoop if the *Daily News* were able to snap a picture of Ruth Snyder being shriveled to death by thirty thousand volts of electricity. True, it would be formidably difficult to get such a picture. The State would take every precaution to prevent an invasion of the condemned woman's privacy. Only a handful of newsmen would be allowed in and they would be frisked from head to foot to be sure they carried no cameras with them.

But these obstacles didn't deter the Captain. Shortly after the verdict of guilty was handed down, he called in his top editors. "If Ruth Snyder goes to the chair, you fellows are going to get me a picture of her—or else!" When the lovebirds were admitted to the Sing Sing Death House, the publisher hatched a scheme for carrying out his scoop.

Ruth Snyder went to her death thirty minutes before Gray, at ten-thirty on the night of January 12, 1928. Before the start of the ceremony thirty-six official witnesses, including a dozen newsmen, filed into the death chamber where the electric chair stood in front of wooden benches.

Precisely on time, Ruth Snyder entered through a door to the rear, walked to the Chair and sat down. When the attendants had finished strapping Ruth down, a guard slipped a black hood over her head. The warden gave the signal, the executioner pulled the switch and thirty thousand volts surged through Ruth Snyder's body. Two minutes later, the attendant physician applied his stethoscope to the young woman, still braced upward in the chair and pronounced her legally dead.

Among the reporters who rushed off to file their stories was a photographer for the *Daily News* who had carried out Captain Patterson's mission to the letter. It had been meticulously planned. With the anxiety of a pilot flying blindly at midnight from an open-cockpit biplane, photographer Tom Howard had walked into Sing Sing carrying a small German Inca camera fastened under his trousers to his ankle with a cable release wire that ran up his leg through a hole he had cut in his trouser pocket. The camera worked on a bulb exposure. It would have been fatal to use any other device, since the clicking of a shutter would have sounded like a cannon in the stillness of the execution chamber.

Moments before the executioner pulled the switch, Howard surreptitiously lifted the cuff of his trouser barely enough to expose the lens, praying that it was pointing squarely at the woman in the chair and not at the ceiling or the stretcher. Then, he squeezed the cable release, snapping the picture.

The following morning Captain Patterson splashed over the front page of the *Daily News,* under the headline DEAD, the macabre picture of Ruth Snyder caught in her death shudder in the electric chair. When horrified members of Patterson's promotional staff saw the photograph, they phoned the boss warning him that advertisers would protest this grisly exhibition by boycotting the *News* in droves. But Joe Patterson knew his readers better than they did. A quarter of a million copies of the *News* were gobbled up as soon as they hit the stands.

Then, despite the protests of his business advisors who were afraid of tempting fate further, the feisty publisher ordered the picture to be reprinted on the front page of the Sunday edition of the *News* which was distributed nationally. Although 350,000 additional copies were issued, the demand couldn't be met. The appetite of the nation's voyeurs was insatiable. The obliging Captain printed the picture a third time, in a center-fold spread for the following Sunday's edition, and almost a half million more copies of the *News* were snapped up. This single photograph of Ruth Snyder perishing in the electric chair brought Captain Patterson over a million additional readers. It was the most sensational example of pictorial journalism up to that time and it launched a new era of gamey journalism disguised as "truth-in-the-news" reporting.

The era of calculated pandering to Americans' appetite for violence had arrived.

Part Two

The Games Twentieth-Century Press Lords Play

3

Lady Galahad
in a Wicked World

Katharine Graham and the Buried Scandals
of the Washington *Post*

SINCE THE COLORFUL, halcyon days of the nineteenth and
early twentieth centuries, the newspaper industry has changed
strikingly. Once one of the nation's bastions of family enterprise, the business in recent decades has been revolutionized
by the emergence of publicly owned newspaper chains. Until
the 1950s the field was still dominated by family dynasties, but
the line of descendants willing to operate their family paper
has run thin, forcing the sale of scores of newspapers to
outside interests. The strong commitment to publish that
existed in the first generation often vanishes by the third or
fourth generation, and the squabbles of heirs over their
patrimony so cripples the paper's operations that the only
answer is to sell it to outsiders. Furthermore, the galloping
advances of production technology and the rising costs of
doing business have made it increasingly urgent to raise huge
sums of capital, compelling even those owners desirous of
holding onto their property to issue stock to the public,
diluting their control.

Along with the enormous new capital investment that has
poured into newspapers a breed of outside managers has
emerged compelled to answer to stockholders instead of

operating as private owners according to their own caprices. The new corporate managers have been putting the operations of the industry into alignment with other businesses in terms of production and merchandising efficiency. Moreover, over the last twenty years heavily capitalized newspaper chains have been steadily taking over smaller independents, boosting their profitability with infusions of money and professional expertise.

The advantages to a chain operator of snapping up the last remaining newspaper in an area and converting it into a monopoly are substantial. Otis Chandler, the current publisher of the Los Angeles *Times,* observes, "If a newspaper is uncompetitive it gives you a franchise to do what you want. . . . You can engineer your profits. You can control expenses and generate revenues almost arbitrarily." One major incentive to snapping up an independent newspaper is the chain operator's favorable treatment under the Internal Revenue Code which permits publishers to set aside a portion of their profits at special tax advantages in order to buy other newspapers, claiming this as a necessary cost of doing business.

In establishing a monopoly and eliminating competition a publisher can effect huge operating economies: through merging the plants of his former competitor into his own and consolidating the two staffs into a single one, he becomes the sole recipient of all the advertising revenues in the community. These heady advantages enable the would-be buyer to offer the seller a price for his paper far above what the intrinsic net worth of the newspaper is in terms of its current assets. The purchaser is able to do this because of the inflated profits his money-making machine can turn out once he buys the independent and establishes a monopoly position. Moreover, the chain operator's big accumulation of reserves often enables him to provide highly advantageous tax-free deals to the seller to sweeten his offer. Currently, almost 60 percent of America's dailies are owned by the chains. The twelve largest chains account for 40 percent of the nation's circulation. The top four—Newhouse, Knight-Rider, The Tribune Company and Gannett—enjoy 20 percent of this.

Not among the Big Four newspaper chains, but nevertheless one of the single most influential communications conglomerates in the United States, is Katharine Graham's Washington Post Company.

Today Washington is, as it has been for generations, the center of American political journalism. In this power-obsessed city by the Potomac press lords dine with presidents and seek to buttress their influence by extending their reach into the throne room of governmental power.

Washington has always been an especially opportune arena for the perceptive, aggressive journalist. The most powerful personality in the Washington press corps today is Katharine Meyer Graham, the owner of the Washington *Post*. The paper she runs has grown from shabby origins to become an instrument of formidable influence. The daughter of Eugene Meyer, a Wall Street banker who bought the *Post* during the Depression, Katharine took over the newspaper after her husband, Philip Graham, a brilliant but emotionally tortured individual, committed suicide.

Eight years ago, the Watergate scandal that toppled Richard Nixon from the presidency transformed the Washington *Post* into the most-talked-about newspaper in America, a development that irked the top brass at the New York *Times* no end. The *Times* had achieved its reputation step by step over seventy years of dogged effort; and virtually every other newspaper of note has won its spurs only over the long haul. But the Washington *Post*, thanks to the investigative efforts of Bernstein and Woodward, was transformed overnight into the major rival of the *Times* for the nation's press leadership.

Ironically, for a newspaper whose chief claim to recognition has been its incorruptibility, Katharine Graham's publication, for most of its history, has behaved with the utmost cynicism. Its publishers have served as lackeys for notoriously corrupt presidents and its reporters have jumped slavishly for dollar bills waved by the politicians whose collars they wore. The paper began as a Democratic daily launched by Stilson Hutchins, a young newspaper man from New Hampshire, with a readership of 6,000 when Washington was a city with only 130,000 residents, and over the year its allegiance has swung like a weathervane in the political winds. John McLean, who had entered the newspaper business by acquiring the Cincinnati *Enquirer* on a shoestring and building it into a paper of major influence, purchased the Washington *Post* from a successor of Hutchins' and proceeded to turn it into a scandal sheet that obtained information embarrassing to powerful politicians and used it to twist their arms for favors. McLean's son, Edward, who took over management of the *Post* from his father in 1905, was a roisterer and a ne'er-do-well who had augmented his inherited wealth by marrying Evalyn Walsh, the daughter of a prospector who had made millions striking silver in the Comstock Lode.

After the marriage ceremony, the fathers of the newlyweds handed them $250,000 to splurge on their honeymoon. To go through a quarter of a million dollars in three weeks of nuptial celebration requires considerable ingenuity, but the couple was equal to it. Evalyn picked out a $50,000 chinchilla coat in Paris and bought a Mercedes when they arrived in Holland; then, frustrated because she had only one Mercedes, she returned to Paris to buy a second one. Returning home, the McLeans continued their euphoric spending. Evalyn paid $5,000 for a pair of bed sheets because, she explained, "Any woman knows restful sleep will wipe away her wrinkles."

The young publisher of the Washington *Post* continued his exuberant frolics between putting out editions of his newspaper. Once, in a heady mood induced by a liberal intake of bourbon, "Ned" hired a locomotive, jumped into the cab and drove it from Washington to New York in the wee hours of the morning, blowing the whistle full blast to rout sleepy citizens from their beds along the way. Ned gave lavish parties for the elite of Congress, the Cabinet and the Supreme Court, hiring call girls to strip and pose as Greek statues on his lawn. He kept a pet seal, which he called Colonel George H. Harvey, and ordered his valet to deliver a daily bottle of whiskey to slake the animal's thirst. Once during a diplomatic reception at the White House, Ned unbuttoned his fly and urinated down the leg of the Belgian ambassador. In the final stage of a drinking binge, as his hands shook with delirium tremens, the publisher of the Washington *Post* would put his head into the noose of a pulley rope, tie a towel around his wrist and jerk his hand up to his mouth for still another sip of bourbon.

The publisher's wife was as madcap as her mate. She began, out of sheer boredom with her life of acquisition and consumption, to take morphine, and as her addiction grew, she became increasingly more cunning in obtaining and hiding her supplies. She bribed druggists to send her the dope through the mail, addressed to the Washington *Post* to throw physicians off the scent. She squirreled it into the stuffing of chairs and sofas; and when the doctors grew hot on her trail, she hid it inside the family pipe organ.

One of Evalyn McLean's most troublesome acquisitions was the celebrated Hope Diamond. According to legend, the centuries-old diamond had called down a curse on all who had worn it. Evalyn's lust for the jewel was sufficient to overcome her uneasiness over its melancholy story, but to make sure she wasn't tempting fate, she visited a church to have the diamond blessed by a priest. While the clergyman was robing himself for the ceremony, a storm broke and lightning struck a tree which narrowly missed wrecking Evalyn's Mercedes, parked next to it.

The McLeans made their most prestigious acquisitions, however, not in diamonds but in presidents of the United States. Warren G. Harding was one of the slickest baubles in American political history; he was just the type to win Ned's addlepated devotion. This man, who in 1921 succeeded Woodrow Wilson in the White House, had a strikingly handsome appearance and a voice that was as resonant as a trumpet—no mean asset for a politician on the hustings in the days before the invention of the loudspeaker. But Harding received his intellectual nourishment from a lifetime reading of Wild West stories, and his speeches were larded with homilies designed for an audience that kept its mouth open and its mind shut. Observed William Allen White, the editor, "Our dramatic theory seems to be based on the proposition that if you put one red shot and two hundred black ones in a double barrel shotgun and fire both barrels at a National Convention of Elks, the man hit by the red shot will make a good president."

Ned first met Harding, then a senator from Ohio, at one of the poker parties Alice Longworth held for her Washington friends. The McLeans found Harding irresistibly attractive: "A stunning man," Evalyn reminisced in her autobiography, "he chewed tobacco, biting from a plug, and he did not care if the whole world knew he wore suspenders."

The McLeans became very chummy with Harding and the publisher of the *Post* performed yeoman service when the senator ran for the presidency in 1920. Harding's career was progressing smoothly until a rumor spread in Democratic circles that the candidate had Negro blood in his veins. The story originated from a genealogical study prepared by a Professor William Chancellor of the College of Wooster, Ohio. The professor, a self-styled expert in genealogical research, came after prodigious researches to the conclusion that "Warren Gamaliel Harding is not a white man," and added piously, "May God save America from international shame and from domestic ruin." In the primitivist America of the 1920s, permeated as it was with virulent racism, such information could certainly spell political ruin for the presidential nominee.

In this extremity, the publisher of the Washington *Post* came gallantly to Harding's support. Ned McLean had heard about Professor Chancellor from Harry Daugherty, Harding's close political advisor, and McLean spearheaded the efforts by Harding's friends to stifle all gossip about the Senator's Negro lineage. When Harding became President, his administration launched a determined effort to obliterate Professor Chancellor's genealogical findings, along with the professor himself. The Department of Justice dispatched agents to Wooster College to investigate Chancellor's background, and he was expelled from the faculty when he announced that he was expanding his monograph into a full-fledged book. The Federal Bureau of Investigation located the publisher who had had the temerity to offer a contract for the volume and confiscated the entire first edition.

Having helped the President into the White House by endorsing him in the *Post*, Ned McLean and his wife continued to fraternize with the Hardings after the inauguration, but they were not present at the President's sudden end. In the summer of 1923 Harding started on a trip to Alaska to make an inspection of post offices and military bases. The President had asked the McLeans to join him but they preferred to spend the vacation at their home in Bar Harbor, Maine.

During his trip the President became increasingly fatigued. As the ship approached San Francisco on the return lap, he fell ill of what was publicly announced to be ptomaine poisoning. Complications arose and the President died in a hospital in San Francisco of what the doctors described as an apoplectic stroke.

Hardly was Harding buried when a chain of incidents involving frauds and embezzlements perpetrated by his closest aides during his regime were uncovered, and their exposure scandalized the nation. Harry Daugherty, the attorney general and former Republican political boss of Ohio where Harding's career had been launched, was revealed to have masterminded a skein of financial shakedowns; Jesse Smith, a Harding crony, was found to have served as a bag man collecting money under the table from bootleggers seeking immunity from the Prohibition laws. Secretary of the Interior Albert Fall was discovered to have been bribed to hand over the Navy's reserves of oil to private interests. Charles Forbes, the head of the Veterans' Bureau, was disclosed to have swindled the U.S. Treasury of two hundred million dollars in fraudulent contracts. In addition to all this, a woman from Ohio, Nan Britton, bobbed up claiming she had been President Harding's mistress and had engaged in sexual intercourse with him on numerous trysts in the White House, giving birth to his daughter. She demanded money from the Harding family for the upkeep of his child.

Gaston B. Means, one of Ned McLean's friends and a former FBI official close to inner circles of the White House, insisted that he had irrefutable evidence that President Harding had not died of an apoplectic stroke as claimed but had actually been poisoned by his wife who had learned of his affair with Nan Britton and had become insanely jealous.

Throughout all of these happenings, Ned McLean and his Washington *Post* stood staunchly by the memory of the dead President. The publisher not only continued to defend Harding's odoriferous memory beyond the grave, but he gave the biblical definition of friendship a heady new dimension: Greater love hath no man than that he is willing to lay down his life not only for his friend but for his friend's crooked friends.

During the Harding regime, it was subsequently disclosed, Secretary of the Interior Albert D. Fall for a hundred-thousand-dollar bribe had secretly leased the government's oil reserves which had been set aside for the use of the Navy to Harry Sinclair, president of the Mammoth Oil Company. Shortly after Harding's death, a congressional committee learned of Secretary Fall's acquisition of sudden wealth. He had been under financial duress and unable to pay his taxes, but now he was plunging into real estate speculation and flinging hundred-dollar bills around in nightclubs. When the congressional investigators discovered that the Secretary had received one lump payment of one hundred thousand dollars, they pressed him for an explanation. Searching desperately for a defense, the Secretary latched onto the publisher of the Washington *Post*, Harding's good friend Ned McLean. Fall visited McLean and asked a favor. Would the publisher be willing to tell the Committee that he had given him the hundred thousand dollars as a "loan"? McLean readily obliged. To provide credibility the two men went through the motions of arranging a "loan." McLean made out a check for a hundred thousand dollars. But it was a paper transaction; the check wasn't intended to be cashed and McLean didn't have the money on deposit to cover it.

When Senator Walsh announced in the press that he wanted to question McLean about the loan, the publisher suddenly developed a severe sinus infection which sent him scurrying off to Florida. He could no longer endure the severity of a Washington winter, he told news reporters. But the Committee insisted on subpoenaing the publisher and forced him to return to Washington where he underwent severe questioning. Afraid of being charged with perjury, McLean yielded and admitted under oath that the check he gave Fall had never been cashed and had been returned to him by the Secretary a month after it was signed.

After the congressional investigation, Ned McLean's fortunes declined precipitously. Worn out by excessive drinking and riotous living, the publisher suffered a mental breakdown and was clapped into an institution.

The fortunes of the family newspaper, the Washington *Post*, also took a fatal tumble. McLean's involvement with Secretary Albert Fall, his appearance before a congressional committee and his narrow escape from a perjury indictment had received nationwide publicity. The credibility not only of the publisher but of his newspaper, which printed flagrantly dishonest reports alleging the innocence of its publisher during the investigation of his activities, utterly collapsed. Its circulation crumbled and its losses continued unchecked through the 1920s.

By 1933 the *Post* was so heavily in the red that the McLean family was compelled to put it up at a public auction to the highest bidder. (No single buyer had come up with a satisfactory offer.) The auction was conducted on a hot day in June on the stairs of the old Post Office building. From a window in an office above, Evalyn, dressed in black and wearing the Hope Diamond, looked down defiantly upon the crowd of wealthy financiers, politicians and newspaper publishers who had assembled hoping to snatch up the *Post* at a bargain.

The winning bid of $825,000 was made by Eugene Meyer, a Wall Street financier who, together with his son-in-law, was to spend $20 million more to lift this shabby newspaper out of the garbage dump and give it a thorough delousing before he handed it over to his daughter, Katharine Meyer Graham, the current publisher.

Meyer, a German Jew, had made a fortune in Wall Street operating as an investment banker, and he had had the foresight to get out of the stock market with his money intact just before the 1929 crash. During the First World War Meyer went to Washington with his friend Bernard Baruch to serve in the government as a dollar-a-year man. He became one of the first governors of the Federal Reserve Board and chairman of the Reconstruction Finance Corporation. He retired temporarily from public life when Franklin Roosevelt was President, breaking with Roosevelt over his New Deal policies. Meyer became one of Roosevelt's severest critics, referring constantly to the President as *"That* Man!"—a favorite epithet of America's conservatives.

A short, rotund, feisty individual, Meyer climbed up the social ladder and became an increasingly "assimilated" Jew. He married in a Lutheran ceremony Agnes Ernst, a strikingly beautiful blond German who had been photographed a number of times by her close friend Edward Steichen. Agnes Meyer was a cultured woman who studied Chinese art, collected French impressionists and patronized the leading intellectuals of the day. A proud aristocrat, she had thrown in her lot with a man who came from a line of distinguished Jews. Several of Meyer's ancestors were rabbis. His great-great-great-grandfather had been the administrative head of the Jewish population in the kingdom of Louis XIV. Yet Agnes remained continually sensitive about the relationship. "My own marriage," she observed, "has helped me to realize what a tolerant, universal religious spirit could arise in our country if there were more intermarrying between the feuding sectarian groups, especially between Christians and Jews; so my husband's far more intense spirituality has been a constant challenge to me, and a constant reminder that the Jews made the covenant with God, whereas Christians, as a rule, have more complaisant souls because they merely inherited it."

And Agnes complained about experiencing "the Jewish problem from within. . . . I too occasionally suffer the cruelty meted out to the Jews by anti-Semites. It hurts to discover what it means to be treated not as an individual human being, but as a nameless member of a race. There is no doubt that the Jew, for example, has to be twice as good as the average non-Jew to succeed in many a field of endeavor."

The Meyers led an exciting intellectual life. Eugene told his wife, "You have often irritated me, but I confess you have never bored me." And Agnes conceded in her reminiscences that "the lighting flashed and the thunder reverberated in our household." Paul Claudel, the French poet, after spending a weekend with the Meyers wrote that he felt "like a cat that had been thrown into an electric fan."

Katharine Graham, the current publisher of the *Post*, was the second of the five children born to the Meyers and the only one who showed the slightest interest in becoming a newspaper reporter. She worked as a teenager on the *Post*, and on graduating from Vassar briefly became a reporter for the San Francisco *News*. In June 1940 she married Philip Graham, a rising young lawyer prominent in New Deal circles. At the end of the war when Graham returned from the army, Eugene Meyer tapped his son-in-law to take over the *Post*. Meyer was preparing to leave the paper and become the director of the World Bank; his only son had become a psychiatrist and Meyer, who was highly impressed with Graham, installed him as publisher at the age of thirty. Graham, a brilliant ambitious young Southerner and a Harvard graduate, had served as law clerk to Justice Felix Frankfurter of the U.S. Supreme Court, becoming at twenty-six the leading legal counsel in the President's Lend-Lease program, then joining the Army intelligence corps.

Upon taking over the *Post*, Graham embarked on a program of flamboyant expansion, buying *Newsweek* magazine for fifteen million dollars, acquiring television and radio stations in Washington and in Jacksonville, Florida, and purchasing

Washington's *Times-Herald* to forge with the *Post* the number one position in Washington readership.

Philip Graham, reminisces historian Arthur Schlesinger, "was fascinated by power and by other men who were fascinated by power." Spurred by a curious amalgam of ambition and idealism, Graham plunged into the civil rights movement giving legal and political counsel that helped resolve the crisis at Little Rock, Arkansas, when Governor Faubus refused to permit black children to enter "white" schools. At the time Lyndon Johnson was majority leader of the Senate and Graham worked closely with the Senator to win support for the Civil Rights Act of 1957. During their collaboration Graham developed a deep respect for Johnson and became committed to his candidacy for President. Brilliant and gregarious, Graham showed signs as business and political pressures mounted of becoming restless and emotionally unstable. He had been raised in the South in genteel poverty and he carried deep feelings of insecurity into his later life, especially after he married into the wealthy Meyer clan. He was in the habit of joking on the Washington cocktail circuit that the best way to get ahead in life was to marry the boss's daugther. But it was evident that the jest was seasoned with bitterness. Graham resented the fact that he had achieved his position as a publisher by marriage, and he tried feverishly to prove himself on his own.

As time went on he plunged into spells of increasingly profound depression. Psychiatrists diagnosed him as a manic-depressive, and Graham dragged on for several years alternating between spells of depression and euphoria. He would plunge exuberantly into a round of business and social activities and then suddenly retreat into a fit of melancholy. During his periods of psychotic behavior he would turn furiously on Katharine and make sneering innuendoes about her "Jewish blood." He took a mistress and traveled around the country telling everybody he was going to divorce his wife and marry her.

His close friends were appalled by the disintegration of this brilliant mind. John Kennedy, who had been very close to Graham and who, as President, relied on his advice, was especially disturbed. On one occasion Graham phoned the

President and began to berate him over a fancied insult. "Do you know who I am?" Graham shrieked. And Kennedy replied, "I know you are not the Phil Graham I have always admired."

Finally the tortured publisher found release. Katharine received permission from her husband's psychiatrist to take him out of the institution he was in and bring him home to their farm in Virginia for a weekend. As she was upstairs attending to something, Graham picked up a shotgun and killed himself. He was forty-eight.

The burden of running the Washington *Post* was suddenly thrust on a middle-aged widow who had maintained a low profile playing the housewife to her flamboyant husband. She could have sold the newspaper but she was determined to hold on to it. She could not part with it "after the way I'd seen my father and then my husband struggle to keep it alive." At the age of forty-six she took over the *Post* and its affiliated businesses "in a state of absolute terror."

Totally unprepared for leadership, Katharine Graham turned to Fritz Beebe, the family's lawyer and its chief financial adviser, to learn the rules of corporate finance. She was a quick study, becoming a highly enthusiastic strategist. According to some associates, Katharine seems keener today on playing the financial game of expanding her corporate empire, leveraging acquisitions and massaging the capital strucutre than she is interested in the day-to-day editorial operations of the *Post*. But when she first took over the newspaper, Katharine had the virginal innocence of the very rich about money matters. Upon being introduced to one of the *Post*'s European correspondents she is said to have remarked after learning about his relatively meager salary, "Oh dear, you don't have to live on your *salary*, do you?"

Tall and slim, with iron-gray immaculately coiffed hair, a superstar of Washington's high society, Katharine is a stockholder in *Ms.*, the Women's Liberation house organ, having invested twenty thousand dollars to help launch the first issue; despite her identification with the feminist movement, however, she prefers to be called *Mrs.* Graham instead of *Ms.* A top-seeded, Vassar-bred member of Washington's horsey set, she can be blunt and earthy. She has posted approvingly on a wall of her office a directive one of her editors distributed to her reporters, "Ambiguity is bullshit."

And yet, the publisher can occasionally display a patrician snobbery in her personal behavior. According to one associate, "She really can't identify with the chauffeur who drives her limousine, or the mechanic who fixes the tires and tunes up the engine." Observes another, "You couldn't exactly call her a traitor to her class. If you don't talk her kind of Piping Rock Lockjaw, you're never sure she remembers who you are. You have the feeling she's saying to herself: 'Who the hell is this? I know he's one of my people but what in Christ is his name?' There's a caste system both here and at *Newsweek*. She only breaks bread with her social equals."

The publisher moves freely in the world of the arts, literature and politics. One of her closest friends is Truman Capote, the novelist and café society celebrity, who gave a masked ball in her honor. Among her escorts have been publisher Clay Felker, composer William Walton, historian Arthur Schlesinger, and economist John Kenneth Galbraith.

Katharine has fully exploited her powerful political position. After her husband's death, she remained a close friend of Lyndon Johnson, and when he became President his first major address was written at Katharine's Georgetown residence. Yet she broke with Johnson as he led America deeper and deeper into the Vietnam War. When she told the President that he could not count on the Washington *Post*'s support for his reelection, Johnson's eyes filled with tears.

At the time Eugene Meyer purchased the *Post* for less than a million dollars, it had a readership of fifty thousand. For years, it plodded along as a well-intentioned, liberally oriented but extremely dull newspaper, one of the most uninspired in the nation. With the advent of the 1960s and the rise of the counterculture, the *Post* performed clever plastic surgery on its image. It recruited witty young writers from the school of the "New Journalism." It hired Maxine Cheshire as gossip columnist, engaged Nicholas von Hoffman, an incisive writer on American mores, unleashed Sally Quinn as a sharp social observer and built a reputation for trendy, "elitist journalism."

Like other newspapers, the *Post* remained strongly biased in its editorial stance, but biased in a fashion designed to please the chic liberal establishment. It went relentlessly after Richard Nixon but offered relatively inadequate coverage of the Chappaquiddick incident involving Senator Ted Kennedy. When Nixon appointed Agnew as his running mate at the 1968 Republican Convention, the *Post* ran an editorial saying that Nixon's choice of Agnew was "perhaps the most eccentric political appointment since the Roman emperor Caligula named his horse a consul."

At the same time, the *Post* corporation has permitted divergent editorial opinions within its own household. While Katharine Graham and the *Post* were still defending President Johnson's handling of the Vietnam War, *Newsweek,* its affiliated publication, was bitterly attacking Johnson and the war. (Subsequently, the *Post* changed its position.) Also while WTOP, a radio station owned by the *Post* Corporation, bitterly opposed Nixon's nomination of Clement Haynsworth to the Supreme Court, the *Post* endorsed this nomination in its editorial page.

Of course, the *Post* rose to its current perch of eminence largely because of its exposure of malfeasance in the Nixon administration. When the *Post* purchased Cissy Patterson's *Times-Herald* in the mid-1950s and became the leading newspaper in Washington, it found that its major rival in news coverage of the capital was the New York *Times* Washington bureau. The two have been involved in a bitter rivalry ever since. The *Times* was the first paper in the nation to leak the Pentagon Papers, the top secret documents disclosing the intrigues of U.S. officialdom that led to the Vietnam War. When the *Times* published three articles based on these documents, a federal court egged on'by the government issued a temporary restraining order to stop the rest of the series from being published. The Nixon administration furiously attacked the *Times* for publicizing top-secret information. The Washington *Post* had also obtained some of the Pentagon Papers and it wrestled with the decision to suppress publication or to publish on its own, ignoring the legal trouble that the *Times* encountered and exposing itself to the wrath of the Nixon government. Washington *Post* lawyers argued against publication. The *Post* Corporation was about to make its first public offering to raise money in Wall Street and a prospectus for the thirty-three-million-dollar issue was already being processed by the SEC. The cautious *Post* attorneys argued that publishing the Pentagon Papers and locking horns with the government could be fatal to the outcome of its offering. Mrs. Graham, displaying conspicuous courage, brushed aside her doubts and ordered the Papers printed.

The New York *Times* received the Pulitzer Prize for being the first with the Pentagon exposé, but the *Post* shortly afterward struck back. Katharine Graham turned loose two of her reporters, Bob Woodward and Carl Bernstein, when Nixon conspirators were jailed for breaking into the Democratic National Committee headquarters at Watergate. In turn, the *Post* and Katharine Graham have benefited from the public deification that two bright young reporters underwent as a result of their investigative journalism. In the opinion of some observers, Mrs. Graham and her writers received far more credit for exposing the malfeasance of Watergate than they deserved. The investigations that actually broke the scandal, it is pointed out, were conducted by the FBI, federal prosecutors, a grand jury and a congressional committee. The prosecutors and grand jury had developed an open-and-shut case against the five burglars who were arrested after the Watergate break-in considerably in advance of the *Post* articles written by Bernstein and Woodward. The case had also been presented fully to the grand jury and would have been widely publicized during the subsequent trial. But Bernstein and Woodward managed to obtain leaks about the case the prosecutor was presenting and they published them in advance of the trial.

In the final analysis, Judge Sirica, the grand jury and the committee of Congress, putting pressure on the five conspirators, were the forces chiefly responsible for the Watergate exposure. When the defendants were finally convicted, they faced long jail sentences unless they cooperated with the Ervin Committee investigating the case. Nixon was toppled primarily by agencies within the government itself. Bernstein and Woodward were, in effect, beneficiaries of a massive power struggle within the FBI. After the death of Hoover, the FBI was plunged into bitter internecine warfare waged between old guard conservatives, the followers of J. Edgar Hoover and a relatively more liberal faction. Patrick Gray, appointed by Nixon as the new head of the Bureau, was considered a liberal by the right-wingers and bitterly opposed by them. This old guard faction leaked information to Bernstein and Woodward, not because they cared about exposing the Watergate cover-up but because they were bent on discrediting Patrick Gray. By exposing the Bureau's inefficiency under Gray's leadership, they hoped to destroy him professionally. However, these facts have been obliterated by the tidal wave of acclaim that swept Bernstein, Woodward and Mrs. Graham of the *Post* to international eminence.

Ever since it was purchased by Eugene Meyer, the Washington *Post* has merchandised itself as a liberal publication, espousing all the "socially right" causes. However, Katharine Graham, in fraternizing with the super-rich and the mighty in high places, may be experiencing the fate of other over-achievers. She is suspect in certain quarters of having lost her crusading zeal since arriving at the pinnacle of power. Furthermore, the *Post* serves a city whose population is over 60 percent black, where poverty and hopelessness are rampant. And there are critics who complain that the newspaper is currently not providing the leadership in covering social causes that is its obligation; that it is more interested in stylish chitchat than in crusading. (Significantly, since 1975 the *Post*, after successfully smashing a strike of its printers, has been operating with nonunion pressmen.)

Katharine Graham and her crew are highly sensitive to allegations that the *Post* has lost its virtue as well as its poverty. Her deputy managing editor, Dick Harwood, bristles at the suggestion that the *Post* has sold out to the Establishment. Perhaps, he retorts, the social concerns of the 1980s have changed. The battles of the 1960s are over, he insists. The civil rights movement has won most of its basic goals. "Have we created an egalitarian society?" asks Harwood. "No, I'm not saying that. But we have changed the terms of the debate. It's not whether there should be food stamps. We have that legislation. Now the story is who cashes them and makes money off the program."

Moreover, Bob Woodward, the lowly reporter who became rich via his Watergate articles, is equally belligerent in maintaining that the *Post* has not wavered one iota in its social commitment. Woodward, who has become wealthy enough to launch his own conglomerate, has chosen to remain an editor with the *Post,* providing an intriguing example of one reporter's inability to get the scrivener's ink out of his bloodstream. He still cares very deeply about the misery of the poverty-stricken in our country, Woodward insists. "Fundamentally," he told a recent interviewer, "a lot of us around here are bleeding hearts. . . . I've never been poor, but I've had that sense. It's an emotional thing to some of the editors and reporters here."

Several years ago, Time, Inc., decided to challenge Katharine Graham's Washington operation by buying the financially ailing Washington *Star* and converting it into a powerful rival of the *Post.* For the first time in her career, Mrs. Graham was faced with serious competition in her own backyard.

Upon acquiring the Washington *Star,* Time undertook drastic reorganization. It created five-zone local editions in place of the paper's original single section in order to merchandise the *Star* more effectively in the suburbs. Moreover, Time brought in editors and reporters with glittering backgrounds to replace the seedy crew that had been mishandling the paper for years. Among the newcomers were the former editor of the Boston *Herald-American* and the former New York *Times* financial writer Eileen Shanahan. (In July 1981 *Time* gave up the attempt to turn the newspaper around financially and announced plans to stop publishing the *Star.*)

Today the *Post* Company is a lustily thriving conglomerate that includes the Washington newspaper, *Newsweek,* television stations (in Washington, Jacksonville and Miami), radio stations (in Washington and Cincinnati), part-ownership of a paper mill in Nova Scotia, a partnership in the Los Angeles *Times*/Washington *Post* News Service to which over three hundred papers subscribe and a one-third interest in the internationally published *Herald-Tribune.*

Looking to the future, the publisher has been grooming her son, Donald Graham, to succeed her. As part of his early training he spent a number of months on the Washington, D.C., police force "to learn his city in his own way."

Early in 1979, the sixty-one-year-old publisher relinquished control of the Washington *Post* to Donald Graham, retaining her position as chairman of the board and chief executive officer of the Washington Post Company. How long she will retain this post is a matter of speculation among her associates. Even if she quits in the relatively near future, her friends are convinced that her alert, restless mind won't allow her to remain in retirement. She will continue to be active on the American scene one way or another. She herself says that when she retires "I hope to think of something really clever to do. I'll pump gas before I'll do nothing."

However, Katharine Graham will never have to pump gas any more than her notorious predecessor Evalyn Walsh McLean had to. While Mrs. Graham has made a career out of exposing the kind of malfeasance Evalyn McLean reveled in, both women have one thing in common. They have been overweening nonconformists. Their own lives make far more fascinating copy than most of the people their newspaper writes about.

4

Gadfly to the Business World

The Extraordinary Story of the
Wall Street Journal

=====

AMERICA'S PRESS HAS always mirrored the major preoccupations of our society, and that branch of journalism that has been devoted to business and financial reporting has served as an especially significant barometer, since economic forces have been a basic factor shaping the moral and social values of the nation.

Shaken by the dehumanizing process of a rampaging technology and a revolution in moral and ethical standards, America is currently buckling under overwhelming economic pressures. Thanks to its mighty industrial and technological muscle, the nation has been providing unprecedented material wealth while piling up the problems of Job. Its factories have been pouring out autos, vacuum cleaners and deodorants. And its lakes and rivers have become increasingly poisoned by industrial chemicals. People have become wealthier in their material possessions and increasingly poorer in their capacity to enjoy them.

Of all the problems facing the nation, none is more ominous than America's inability to stabilize the purchasing power of its currency. Thanks to runaway inflation, the management of money is no longer the sole preoccupation of economic pundits but has become the "in" topic of discussion for trendy

Americans. It has even filtered down into the consciousness of that upward-aspiring symbol of feminine America, the Cosmo Girl. Exhorts a recent advertisement for *Cosmpolitan*, "How does a smart girl fight inflation? . . . You start reading everything you can put your hands on about managing money. . . . *Nobody* can afford to be a dum-dum these days. My favorite magazine calls inflation a challenge . . . says I'm to meet it like all the other challenges I've faced and come out a better, more interesting person at the other end!"

Confronted with the crucial assignment of reporting on the turbulent happenings in today's economy, the nation's corps of business and financial journalists is industriously interpreting for its readers the operations of successful investors and gamesters from the gambling tables of Las Vegas and Atlantic City to the oil fields of Bahrain, from the gold bullion marts of Zurich to the cattle ranches of Argentina. Financial reporters have informed their readers about the breed of offshore fund operators who have been reaping millions working out of tax-free havens; of speculators harvesting a windfall selling shaky currencies short; about the panicky flight of U.S. dollars into gold bullion, as investors from San Francisco to Kuala Lumpur trade the precious metal. They have disclosed how astute oil operators are getting rich in the energy business, grabbing up strategic supplies as the Western World desperately steps up its search for new supply sources to contest the monopoly of Arabian oil; about the rush of Americans and foreigners into United States farm land which has risen over 1,000 percent in price as America expands its role as the world's number one breadbasket. Financial scribes are also analyzing the current revolution in the stock market as sophisticated money managers vie to outmaneuver one another in a bid to grab a greater share of America's ninety billion dollars of pension fund money. These developments have placed extreme pressure on America's financial publishers to exert their utmost talents in reporting to the American people the economic story as it unfolds in all its complexity.

Historically, the nation's economic and financial news has been buried in the back pages of newspapers. Politics, wars, murders and entertainment have been headlined events. The bulk of financial news has traditionally consisted of dull corporate handouts, the stock market tables and announcements of bond offerings, referred to in the trade as "tombstones." "Financial reporters," points out one editor, "were mostly castoffs and retreads from the city room."

But today all that has changed. Thanks to the emergence of the Arab oil monopoly, the energy crisis, the explosion of inflation and the attacks by environmentalists on the waste disposal policies of U.S. corporations, economic news has suddenly turned up on the front burner. Indeed, the economy has become the number one news beat of our time. As a leading financial editor observes, "The news media's coverage of business and economics as . . . a basic social force . . . is the biggest development in American journalism since the end of the Second World War."

The financial press was founded and developed by a breed of strong-minded individuals, among them Bertie Charles Forbes, who launched *Forbes* magazine just before the First World War. Forbes was a Scotch immigrant who started out as a printer's devil. He became a financial writer for the Hearst publications and started a magazine of his own packed with rags-to-riches stories reverently chronicling the rise of America's Great Business Achievers. He grew wealthy as the Boswell for these industrial nabobs and handed over his profitable publication to his son Malcolm, who even more than his father enjoys the elegant life-style of the people *Forbes* magazine writes about.

Malcolm, who has been unsuccessful in politics (he lost the race for the governorship of New Jersey), consoles himself with a château in Normandy, a cattle ranch in Montana, a plantation in the Fiji Islands, property in the Far West, a yacht, a private airplane and a 50 percent interest in the *Social Register*. In addition to these diversions, Malcolm is a passionate balloonist. Not only has he attempted to navigate the Atlantic Ocean by balloon, but he maintains the only museum in the world featuring a collection of balloons from the time of Jules Verne to the present. Malcolm has also indulged in the luxury of buying himself a private island in the Pacific. Asked why he has the yen to own one, he replies, "Doesn't everyone?"

Another family-held financial publishing house whose descendants enjoy a hefty chunk of the patrimony founded by their grandfather is McGraw-Hill, which owns *Business Week, Standard & Poor's Investment Advisory Service* (the issuer of widely accepted bond ratings), as well as over fifty other magazines and newsletters and a book publishing division.

Begun in the late nineteenth century as a small business and technical books publisher, the firm has grown into a conglomerate that generates almost three-quarters of a billion dollars in annual revenues. The three grandsons of John McGraw, the founder, were locked for years in a bitter power struggle. Donald, one of the cousins, resigned as a group president in 1977, and another cousin, Harold, has emerged as the top man, firmly in control.

However, the McGraws, who are estimated to own over 20 percent of the company's stock, have been threatened by corporate gunslingers lusting after their lucrative empire. Just a few years ago, American Express, the nation's third largest financial holding company with revenues of over three billion dollars annually, made a tender offer to McGraw-Hill's shareholders in an effort to snare the firm. Harold McGraw turned down this overture. He resisted it, he claims, to maintain the independence of financial publishing. American Express, a peddler of credit card and insurance operations, presumably would find McGraw-Hill's financial and statistical research capabilities ideal for its own expansionist activities. But if the publisher of *Business Week* and *Standard & Poor's* were gobbled up by American Express, how could it write objectively about the multifarious activities of its parent?

By far the most influential chronicler of today's business and financial doings is the Dow Jones empire whose headquarters are located just north of Wall Street, that thoroughfare running from the Trinity Church graveyard to the East River, and whose flagship publication, the *Wall Street Journal,* is currently America's most widely read daily newspaper and its only national one.

For almost a century, the *Journal* has been the leading reporter on the rise and fall of America's robber barons, one whose influence has been appreciated by everybody who reads the business news. Millions of television and radio listeners are familiar with the statistics of the Dow Jones stock averages provided by the ticker tape affiliated with the corporation. These averages have been accepted for generations as the leading barometer of the rise and fall of the nation's stock

72

prices (even though in recent years indexes more comprehensive and more up-to-date have been developed). What the *Wall Street Journal* chooses to publish or ignore can trigger tremendous changes in stock values, the rise or fall of financial reputations, the exchange of millions from one man's pocket to another's. Since it first began publishing in 1889, the *Journal* has tried to alert the public to stock manipulators who depend heavily upon the gullibility of the unwary to make their schemes succeed. The prices of stocks over long periods have not been based on the intrinsic worth of the companies they represent, but on what people *think* they are worth. In the heyday of Daniel Drew, Jay Gould, Vanderbilt and other market manipulators, a wide assortment of public relations handouts and word-of-mouth gossip was used to bamboozle the public. There were no financial reporters of any consequence to expose the scams being perpetrated on the trustful. Indeed, the few existing business writers were commonly bribed to serve as shills for stock syndicate jugglers.

In 1880, two reporters, Charles H. Dow and Edward D. Jones, both in their late twenties, who worked on newspapers in Providence, Rhode Island, quit their jobs and went to New York City. Dow was the first to arrive and he became a reporter on mining stocks, then having a big play on Wall Street. (A strike had been made in the Comstock Lode in Nevada and stocks of silver mines had skyrocketed.)

A rapid writer who jotted down statistics on the cuffs of his shirt during interviews, Charlie Dow quickly achieved a reputation on the Wall Street beat. He joined the Kiernan News Agency which dispatched financial news bulletins—"flimsies," as these were called—to the leading brokerage houses and the stock exchanges. Shortly after he came to work for Kiernan, his fellow reporter from Providence, Ed Jones, also joined up. The two young scribes were ambitious men and soon they decided to form their own company to provide news for clients. In the fall of 1882 they joined with a third partner, Charles M. Bergstresser, who worked at Kiernan, to organize Dow Jones and Company.

Dow Jones opened its offices in the shabby basement of a building next to the New York Stock Exchange. The room had no windows nor any covering for its bare wooden walls. The news desk was crammed behind a soda fountain run by the owner of the premises who had rented out the office space to the fledgling firm. The method of transmitting the financial news was primitive. Stringers brought their shorthand notes to Charlie Dow who, acting as a rewrite man, dictated the finished copy to four scribes writing the material on tissue paper between every two sheets and providing twenty-four copies at a time, which were then delivered by messenger boys to the brokers, market operators and other subscribers to the Dow Jones service.

In 1887 Dow Jones purchased a simple rotary machine that printed its "flimsies" from hand-set type, speeding up the process and making it more efficient. The customer list grew and revenues burgeoned so handsomely that the three partners decided to make their bow with a full-fledged financial newspaper. The first issue of the *Wall Street Journal* came out on July 8, 1889. It consisted of four pages and in addition to financial news carried an article on a boxing match that the highly popular John L. Sullivan had just engaged in with a contender for his crown. The match went seventy-five rounds (those were the heroic days of fisticuffs). The *Journal* meticulously reported this fight along with the financial news for the price of two cents a copy.

At the turn of the century the partners sold their business to Clarence Walker Barron, a newsman who for years had operated the Boston News bureau and who had also served as the *Wall Street Journal*'s New England correspondent. Before Barron, a handful of editors and writers (like Charlie Dow and Ed Jones) had laid the groundwork for efficient financial reportage, but it was Barron who raised this to a true profession. The new owner of the *Wall Street Journal* was a bizarre man of Falstaffian girth. Only five feet six inches and weighing over three hundred pounds, with a moustache and full beard, he bore a startling resemblance to King Edward VII of England. The resemblance was not only physical: his lifestyle was much akin to the hedonist monarch's.

Barron single-handedly developed the art of the financial interview by sniffing around with the exuberance of a latter-day Samuel Pepys, hobnobbing with the Rockefellers, Rothschilds, Carnegies and other magnificoes, becoming privy to their smoldering rivalries, serving up journalistic tidbits larded with spicy gossip about the greats' coups and countercoups. A

74

whirlwind reporter, Barron exhausted an army of secretaries with his perpetual dictation. He dictated in bed in the morning before dressing, while taking a bath, while having a haircut, between rounds of playing poker. Barron's contacts extended into the social stratosphere. He was friendly with Queen Marie of Rumania and rumors persisted that he was her lover.

Barron turned the *Wall Street Journal* into a hard-hitting, influential paper functioning during the early 1900s as a major communicator between the titans of finance and the American public. The publisher established strict guidelines for publicizing a business enterprise in his newspaper. The corporation had to demonstrate to him that its asset value was in reasonable proportion to its claims, or he refused to write favorably about it. Barron wasn't always right in his assessments, and in retrospect some of them are highly amusing. In the 1890s a lively debate erupted as to whether the new-fangled trolley cars then being introduced in American cities would drive horse-cars out of circulation. Barron, with his obsession for facts, made a thorough investigation. He checked the costs of the upkeep of the horses that hauled the cars, the hay the nags consumed, the expense of bedding them, and comparing these with the cost of building and running the trolley cars, he arrived at the conclusion that since the former were much less expensive to maintain, they were bound to survive the trolleys.

However, Barron didn't miss the mark very often. He served as an industrious watchdog alerting his readers to pitfalls as well as profits, and he achieved enormous successes in hard-nosed investigative reporting, including the probing of one spectacular scandal that erupted in his own backyard.

By 1920 Boston, the city where Barron began his career and which he still made his home, was no longer the exclusive preserve of Beacon Hill society. Thousands of immigrants from Europe had crowded into tenements on the fringes of aristocratic Louisburg Square, opened fruit stands within the shadow of the Old North Church, cobbled shoes and carried bricks, mixed cement and fixed watches, where hitherto only shipbuilders and witch hunters had carried on their trade. Along the Common the pale, proper faces of Beacon Hill debutantes mingled with the exciting complexions of dark-haired women from the Mediterranean countries and soft-eyed belles from County Cork. Austere Symphony Hall vibrated with music played by passionate Russians and Poles. The Titians that hung in the Boston Art Museum were appreciated by the artist's own countrymen. Boston was a lady of Puritan upbringing who, at middle age, was ready at last for a flirtation with the devil. The devil appeared in the person of a young Italian stockbroker's clerk. He took the lady for a dizzy fling and cleaned her out of fifteen million dollars.

Charles Ponzi was born in Parma, Italy. The immigrant came to America at the age of seventeen and took a series of menial jobs struggling on the fringes of existence. He washed dishes, worked as a clerk, and finally, thanks to a fertile imagination, became a millionaire.

He told a few friends he had developed a scheme for investment that would make them wealthy beyond their dreams if they would just follow his advice. He divulged that he had made a study of the U.S. postal system and if they allowed him to invest small sums for them in postal coupons he would guarantee them a 50 percent return on their money in forty-five days.

Word passed, igniting the greed of Ponzi's friends. The dapper little man from Parma quit his job as a clerk and rented a one-room office at 27 School Street within a stone's throw of hallowed ground where the patriots of the American Revolution lay buried. Opening for business on December 20, 1919, Ponzi collected on the first day two hundred and fifty dollars from excited clients, mostly impoverished countrymen who seized upon the idea of becoming rich quickly without doing anything for it. Three weeks later, Ponzi turned over to his charter clients three hundred and seventy-five dollars.

The news spread quickly. Agents knocked on the door asking to work for Ponzi, whispering the glad tidings to toilers in offices and factories. The stream of people swelled to a torrent. Clerks, stenographers, immigrants who dreamed of amassing enough money for a villa in Italy, small businessmen, peanut peddlers, organ-grinders, pushcart operators, kept ladies, burlesque girls at the Old Howard, colored folk from Columbus Avenue, all hurried up one of the narrowest streets in Boston, through an entrance marked by a sign and an arrow: "To Charles Ponzi, Head of the Securities Exchange Company." They were ushered into a room conspicuous for its simplicity. Absent were the broadloom rugs, cashmere upholstery and all the other furnishings of the big-time financial operator. Ponzi worked his miracles in the humble surroundings of an anchorite. A pine partition separated him from his public. At the teller's desk a young man paid out greenbacks, while close by a comrade watched every movement alertly, a revolver by his elbow. Free coffee and frankfurters were served to the people as they waited in a line that extended along Washington Street to hand in their money.

By the spring of 1920 Ponzi was collecting two hundred and fifty thousand dollars a day. His chief assistant, John S. Dondero, an ex-butcher's helper, was earning seven thousand dollars a week. The money came in so fast that it spilled over the dingy desk and drawers into a dozen wastepaper baskets and reached the ceilings of closets. Sixteen clerks were hired merely to keep an eye on the cash. Ponzi established branch offices in New Hampshire, Connecticut, Maine and Rhode Island to take care of the flow of money in these states. The Boston bankers looked on with consternation as their savings accounts diminished. One bank, to salvage some of its money, had the temerity to advise in the pages of the Boston *Post* a new alluring interest of 5.5 percent. But what was the 5.5 percent the bank offered compared to "fifty percent in forty-five days—double your money in six months!"

When some diehards doubted whether Ponzi was actually amassing profits on postal reply coupons as he claimed, he squelched them, explaining that he had agents in countries all over Europe making the necessary currency conversions. "I buy hundreds of thousands, even millions, of postal coupons," he announced to the press. "My scheme can be tried by anyone, except for one little thing. How I exchange these coupons for cash in America is my secret."

These were palmy days. In a little less than eight months this thirty-eight-year-old ex-dishwasher had collected ten million dollars and his name had become a byword from coast to coast. He acquired large holdings of Boston real estate. He purchased the controlling stock of the venerable Hanover Trust Company. He bought out the J. P. Poole brokerage firm which had employed him as a stock boy. He became one of Boston's financial giants, wined and dined by men who were leading figures in politics and finance when he had ridden the rails looking for odd jobs.

77

Ponzi drove around town in a custom-built blue limousine. And whenever he alighted from it in his jaunty sports suit, with a cane on his arm and a carnation in his buttonhole, he was cheered to the skies. When he walked along Tremont Street on his way to work, swarms of Irish, Italians and Jews mobbed the dapper little man, screaming, "Take my money!"

There were some cool heads in Boston, however, during that tumultuous summer of 1920. And the coolest of all belonged to Clarence Barron, the publisher of the *Wall Street Journal* and an expert analyst of the tangled mazes of high finance. Observing how Ponzism had swept the city luring money from hordes of the impoverished, Barron decided to launch an investigation to expose Ponzi for what he was certain he was, a charlatan. It required courage to attack a man who had become one of the most influential figures in the Commonwealth of Massachusetts, but Barron was willing to brave the threat of libel and other legal assaults by Ponzi's well-heeled lawyers in his conviction that Ponzi was a racketeer. Barron told his reporters, "Go the limit and get the goods on this fellow."

At first Barron's newsmen ran up against a stone wall. Ponzi was willing to talk to them; in fact he talked too readily. He showed the reporters two suitcases filled with a quarter of a million in Liberty bonds.

"This is the first installment of money I've earmarked for use against any attacks on me by your newspaper."

When the *Wall Street Journal* published an article ridiculing Ponzi's pretensions that he was paying his depositors out of profits from postal reply coupons, Ponzi replied by filing suit against Barron for five million dollars and threatened to have his property attached.

"I've forgotten more about international finance," Ponzi told the press, "than Barron ever knew."

The jaunty little man from Parma oozed confidence. But there were clouds on the horizon. Methodically, Barron kept on with his investigation. The publisher was certain that Ponzi had lied about the source of his profits. They could have been accounted for only if the issuance of postal reply coupons was limitless. The actual float of coupons, however, was not large enough to make his earnings possible. No man could have accumulated ten million dollars in a matter of months through the manipulation of six-cent stamps. A survey revealed that over the past six years the entire issue and redemption of coupons accounted for less than a million dollars. Barron sent one of his reporters to Paris where the headquarters of the International Postal League was located, and the newsman, after extensive digging into the records, confirmed that there had not been any unusual business boom in coupons over the past few years.

Barron went after Ponzi ruthlessly, with a barrage of articles and editorials. Confronted with the allegations that he was a swindler, Ponzi didn't bat an eyelash. He conceded that he hadn't actually been making his profits from postal coupons after all.

"To tell the truth," he confessed blandly, "I've just used this idea as a blind for the Wall Street boys. I didn't want them to get even a hint of what my real scheme is. And, fellows, I'm still going to keep it a secret. So long as my depositors get back their investments with profit, I don't have to account to anybody!" Ponzi took ads in Boston's newspapers in which he offered to refund money to any depositor who had cold feet. "I have five million dollars on the table and I can meet any run on me at any time," he boasted. "Yes, brothers, I may run out of blank checks, but I will never run out of cash."

Some of his brethren who had invested their life savings in him were not so sure of this. To take care of the run, Ponzi rented a second office in a former barroom over Pie Alley. For several successive days, he calmly handed out cash, meeting the run to the tune of half a million dollars a day.

When the mob of people saw fellow investors walk into the School Street office with empty hands and come out smiling with twice as much money as they had deposited, their faces reddened with shame. The run dwindled to a trickle. Those diehard pessimists who still insisted upon walking up to the cashier's office for their money were jeered at as the "faithless ones" by the army of the faithful. However, Barron and his reporters pressed on with their attack. Articles in the *Wall Street Journal* had convinced government authorities that Ponzi was running the biggest racket of the generation; that his talk of investment in postal coupons was a "song and dance" to hoodwink his investors; that actually he was using the oldest trick in the art of swindling—paying out his earliest investors

79

with the funds taken in from the recent ones.

The publisher, by now fully committed to his pursuit of Ponzi and armed with leads to track down, took a night train to Montreal where Ponzi had worked for several years before showing up in Boston. Barron called on Jean Laflamme, the Bertillon expert of the Montreal Police Department, and handed him a series of photographs taken from the files of the *Wall Street Journal.* These identified the Boston Ponzi as a clerk from the Zrossi Bank. Several years before showing up in the United States, he had served a three-year sentence for forgery in the prison of St. Vincent de Paul. That clinched matters. Two days later, United States federal agents placed Ponzi under arrest.

The little man with the carnation was charged with grand larceny and using the mails with intent to defraud. On the day of his arrest, a mob of his victims stormed the School Street office in hysteria, shrieking "Kill him!" Thousands of destitute immigrants rushed into the offices of the State Capitol under the illusion that the governor would refund their money to them.

Thanks to the probe launched by Clarence Barron and his newsmen, the swindle was halted, but not until extensive damage had been done and the collective psyche of the city had been battered. After checking the records, Barron revealed that in less than a year in business the little man from Parma had tricked over forty thousand investors into handing over more than fifteen million dollars. On the very day his business was closed, he had taken in two million dollars. No one could estimate with any degree of accuracy what his liabilities were, for he kept no books.

Although Ponzi had come to the United States several years previously, he had never bothered to take out American citizenship papers. Had he fled from this country, therefore, before Barron's investigations nailed him, he might never have been extradited. As it is, he was indicted on eighty-six counts by the federal government even before the state had its day in court. Three weeks before Christmas he pleaded guilty and was sentenced to five years in jail. He stood erect as he heard the sentence and then penciled a memorandum which he handed to the press: *"Sic transit gloria mundi."*

* * *

During his years as publisher of the *Wall Street Journal,*
Clarence Barron alerted his readers, through his skillful
investigative reporting, not only to financial boobytraps, such
as the Ponzi swindle at home, but to financial privateering
overseas. Serving as the eyes and ears for American investors
and speculators, the publisher became expert at evaluating
international news and predicting its impact upon domestic
fortunes. An obscure killing in an Istanbul alley, a sudden rise
of security prices on the Paris Bourse, the changing of one
mistress for another by a cabinet minister in Athens, the
building of a Russian super-dreadnought, the sudden, heavy
gambling of a leading left-wing journalist in Buenos Aires—
these seemingly disparate events might be links in a chain of
cause and effect with important consequences, as any crack
intelligence agent or knowledgeable foreign news correspondent appreciates. Barron microscopically analyzed the flotsam
news to ferret out a significant pattern that would enable him
to predict forthcoming financial developments.

In the years leading up to the First World War, Britain,
France and Russia had plunged into a frenetic armaments race
with the Kaiser, and the tension steadily intensified as one
military crisis after another was averted at the last moment by
frenzied diplomatic action. The economy of the United States
increasingly felt the impact of the European arms race, and to
ferret out areas of potential danger as well as havens of safety
for American investors, Clarence Barron made an intensive
investigation of the arms industry.

In 1914, on the eve of the outbreak of the war, Europe
exhibited its usual insouciance, when Barron arrived to make
an on-the-spot report on the international situation, particularly the impact of the arms race on the value of the nickel
and nitrate that fed the munitions industry. The publisher
found Europe's *haut monde* preoccupied with its typical amuse-
ments and frivolities. When he visited Vienna to meet with
Austrian bankers, he found the city steeped in spring madness.
In the cafés along the Ringstrasse journalists sipped strong
Turkish coffee and analyzed the latest gossip from Franz
Joseph's court.

The Paris that the publisher visited was also brimming with
joie de vivre. Yet Barron was fully aware that overhanging this
febrile, pleasure-loving world loomed the specter of disaster.

81

The International Brotherhood of Arms Makers had been methodically escalating their flow of supplies. Overseas commerce had started to slip noticeably. European bankers had begun to refuse to accept bills of lading as collateral. Foreign investors had commenced a heavy liquidation of their holdings and this was accompanied by an almost complete absence of buying, a condition that was sending stock prices tumbling on Europe's securities exchanges.

Barron wrote in the *Journal,* and warned his friends and fellow investors privately, that the time had come for shareholders to sell outright or go short on their stocks. He had noticed that the leading securities on the Big Board and the American Curb had begun to react under the influence of the foreign exchanges, though in a way not immediately appreciated by any but the most astute market analysts. Top-quality stocks that led the boom market that had been boiling up in recent months had suddenly stopped climbing and were falling back. Barron recommended putting out short lines on stocks that had acted the most aggressively: Mexican Petroleum, American Sumatra, Atlantic Gulf. The publisher of the *Wall Street Journal* was convinced that the next major swing in the market would be downward, and he recommended to his investors that they position themselves to take advantage of this move at the very moment that most shareholders were still locked into a bullish position.

And then, just as Barron had foreseen, trouble became evident to even the most naive trader. By the final week in July 1914, the slide of stock prices in Europe had become so precipitous that the Vienna, Brussels and Budapest exchanges were closed to prevent a further tumble; and before the end of the month, every exchange in Europe had been shut down.

On July 31, a report was flashed to the New York Stock Exchange that caused a panic. The venerable London Exchange had closed down for the first time in its history. (It had remained open even during the Napoleonic wars.) At this news, prices of stocks on the New York Exchange retreated. Steadily the selling pressure grew; the drop in prices accelerated along a broad front as layer after layer of buying support crumbled. As prices hurtled downward, there was a brief struggle by specialists and floor traders to halt the break of bellwether stocks like U.S. Steel for fear that any further drops would have a catastrophic impact on the rest of the market. But the efforts to halt the downrush were fruitless.

Within the first hour of the opening gong, the ticker had fallen fifteen minutes behind actual trading on the floor. Steadily, the time gap widened. Rumors spread from coast to coast that the price structure of stocks was utterly collapsing. The telephone lines were clogged with inquiries. By noon demoralization had set in. Sell orders were pouring in from every corner of the nation for whatever price the stocks would bring. When the gong rang mercifully to close trading for the day, an emergency meeting was held in the offices of J. P. Morgan where Big Board officials and bankers debated whether to open the Exchange the next day or shut it down for good.

The Big Board had remained open, weathering all kinds of crises over the past forty-one years, ever since the 1873 failure of J. Cook and Company, then the nation's leading banker. At first, the consensus of the J. P. Morgan conclave was to keep the Exchange open. But several brokers with extensive over-seas connections showed the board of governors a huge batch of selling orders that had just arrived from Europe. These brokers calculated that over $2.5 billion dollars' worth of American stocks were being held by overseas investors and that a massive unloading of them would cause utter disaster. Another vote was taken and it was decided to close the Exchange indefinitely. The ticker flashed the announcement that for the first time since 1873 the gong would not be sounded the next day to start trading.

Other exchanges followed the lead of the Big Board and trading in stocks came to a virtual halt throughout the nation. Not until April 1915, nine months later, was normal activity resumed on the Big Board, by which time the United States, as the leading supplier of war equipment to the Allied Powers, was enjoying a heady economic rally.

In the meantime Clarence Barron had achieved one of the most remarkable scoops in the annals of financial reporting. Not only had he accurately alerted *Wall Street Journal* readers and the investment community at large to the opportunities and pitfalls of war in Europe, but during the critical days in July just before the war erupted, he predicted that the stock market would enter a tailspin, enabling the more adventurous

83

of his friends and readers to make a financial killing by going short at precisely the right time, when the bulk of market forecasters and traders persisted in their bullish stance.

The publisher of the *Wall Street Journal* lived ten years beyond the signing of the Armistice ending the First World War, passing away in 1928 at the age of seventy-three. Emerging from a coma just before he passed away, he turned to the secretary standing by him and muttered, "What's the latest news on the ticker?"

Late in life, Barron had married Mrs. Jessie Waldron, a widow with two daughters. The marriage was a childless one, and at Barron's passing, the ownership of the Dow Jones Company passed to one of his stepdaughters, Jane Bancroft, and her husband, Hugh Bancroft, a Boston lawyer. Subsequently, the two daughters of this marriage, Mrs. William C. Cox and Mrs. A. Werk Cook, inherited the controlling interest in Dow Jones. Possessing holdings worth over $150 million, Barron's granddaughters in subsequent years were wooed by a host of aspirants eager to purchase Dow Jones, but the heiresses steadfastly refused to sell their powerful barony, fearful that outsiders might change the character of the company so meticulously fashioned by their step-grandfather. However, the Boston dowagers have been passive owners and have played no executive role. This has been reserved, since the founding of the *Wall Street Journal,* for working newspapermen who earn their spurs on the reportorial and editorial side of the business.

After the death of Clarence Barron, Hugh Bancroft, his son-in-law, took over and immediately encountered heavy weather. The Depression of the 1930s almost destroyed Dow Jones. Trading on Wall Street, which had been the *Journal*'s prime area of coverage, ground to a virtual halt, and circulation plummeted to under thirty thousand readers. Business was so sluggish Dow Jones had to fill its ticker tape with jokes to plug up the blank space between financial news bulletins.

Management was faced with a crucial decision. To stay so heavily geared to the fortunes of Wall Street and the investment community could be suicidal, since the future of the stock market was uncertain. The only way for the newspaper to survive was to broaden its appeal from that of an investment sheet to a nationally oriented economic journal covering social and political trends in addition to business developments.

The editor under whose leadership the *Journal* made the transition from a provincial into a national newspaper was Bernard Kilgore who took command just before America entered the Second World War. Kilgore, after successfully presiding over the transition period, died of cancer in 1966 at the age of fifty-nine and Bill Kerby succeeded him, serving as chairman and chief executive officer of Dow Jones until his retirement in 1977.

A short, slim man with alert steely eyes and a leathery out-of-doors tan, William Kerby sprang from a newspaper family. His father, a reporter with the Scripps Newspaper Bureau in Washington, became chief of the New York bureau during World War I.

Young Kerby went into the newspaper business, doing his stint as a reporter for United Press before joining the *Wall Street Journal* as a reporter in the Washington bureau. Kerby once explained what it was that made him become a newsman. "It's the only business I know of where you can look the world in the eye and tell it to go to hell."

When Kerby stepped down as chairman of the Board at the end of 1977, his post was taken over by Warren H. Phillips, previously the president and chief executive officer. Phillips is a handsome man in his fifties who, with his jet-black hair and meticulously groomed moustache, looks like a reincarnation of William Powell as the Thin Man. Like Kerby, Philips is a career newsman who started at the foot of the ladder. He joined the *Wall Street Journal* as a copyreader after World War II, left for a tour with the army newspaper *Stars and Stripes,* and then returned to the *Journal* as a full-time correspondent serving in West Germany. In 1950 Phillips was made chief of the *Journal*'s London bureau. He did in-depth reporting on Europe's recovery under the Marshall Plan, returned to the United States and served successively as foreign editor, managing editor, executive vice-president and, finally, president before stepping up to the post of chairman.

The *Wall Street Journal*'s editorial policies generally follow the laissez-faire line of American Big Business. Vermont Royster, one of the most colorful and provocative of the *Journal*'s editors, once put it succinctly: "We believe that the primary reason for government is to provide police power to keep me from knocking you over the head." Yet the *Journal* has taken views that have been unpopular with America's conservative community. It was one of the first major publications to argue for America's getting out of the Vietnam War, advocating this in 1968 when the view was highly unpopular with most Americans.

The panjandrums at the *Journal* have made a practice of hiring reporters straight from college, who have no training in business journalism but who show good promise as writers. The theory seems to be that if a financial crook can start at the bottom and teach himself to become an expert predator, reporters hired to expose his manipulations can also become successful sleuths by learning *their* trade on the job. The *Journal* further assumes that many of its readers are not sophisticated in financial matters and keeps its writing simple without resorting to mumbo jumbo jargon. *Journal* reporters never talk about "short" selling in the stock market without explaining just exactly what is meant by a "short" sale, even though this must be done scores of times in the course of a year. Some *Journal* rules have been instituted for purely pragmatic reasons. For instance, the risk of the printers' dropping the word "not" from the text is high; and since the dropping of it may influence transactions involving millions of dollars, *Journal* reporters are instructed to use "wouldn't" and "hasn't" as often as possible in place of "not." Also, if a *Journal* reporter is discussing a trial, instead of writing that a verdict turned in by the jury was "not guilty," he will use the word "innocent." Should the "not" be left out before "guilty," the paper would be open to substantial embarrassment. Other words are warily avoided. The word "shift" is fraught with particular peril, so *Journal* reporters use "work term" when discussing working hours and factory conditions.

A fair number of the neophytes recruited as potentially promising writers have ended up turning in landmark stories. While Barney Kilgore was head of the Washington bureau, he ferreted out the news that Henry Morgenthau, the secretary of state in the closing days of World War II when officials in Washington were discussing what peace terms to demand of Hitler's defeated nation, privately advised Roosevelt to convert Germany into a vast potato farm so that it would never rise again as a military power. This Draconian prescription triggered an uproar when Kilgore exposed it, and enlightened Americans insisted that the new Germany be given the chance to live down the mistakes of the past. Kilgore, by providing the opportunity for a healthy debate, offered a timely service.

There have been many other major scoops. Two *Journal* reporters, Stanley Penn and Monroe Kamin, won the Pulitzer in 1967 as a result of a series of spectacular articles that exposed links between the American Mafia and casino gambling in the Bahamas. The reporters demonstrated that the government of the Bahamas (constituting a clique of white politicians ruling over a predominantly black population) had close ties with the American underworld, and particularly with Meyer Lansky, the Mafia godfather, through an intermediary, a Wall Street financier named Wallace Groves. As the result of Penn's and Kamin's articles, an investigation was launched that toppled the "Bay Street Boys"—as the Bahamian ruling clique was called—opening the way for native black politicians to emerge and form a new government that terminated white rule in the Islands.

Louis Kohlmeier, another *Wall Street Journal* sleuth, won a Pulitzer Prize for coming up with a two-part article which documented in embarrassing detail how Lady Bird Johnson, the wife of the then President of the United States, had turned a $17,500 investment into a fortune, amassing a broadcasting empire in Texas by using political influence to wheel and deal with the Federal Communications Commission. Kohlmeier revealed that after Lyndon Johnson reached the White House, his family retained its ownership of the broadcasting business which was heavily dependent on federal government regulation. Time and again, Kohlmeier demonstrated, the FCC made favorable decisions to help the business interests of the President's family and Johnson did nothing to eliminate this glaring conflict of interest.

Currently, the *Journal* is growing faster than any other American newspaper. It is the country's only national newspaper and the bulk of its readers are in the thirty-five to mid-fifty age bracket, which is the fastest expanding area of the population. In the fall of 1979 the *Wall Street Journal* passed the New York *Daily News* to become America's largest daily circulation newspaper. By 1980 its daily circulation of 1.8 million was twice the size of the New York *Times,* three times that of the Washington *Post* and 80 percent that of the total combined circulation of its three major rivals in the financial field—*Fortune, Business Week* and *Forbes.*

Unlike other newspaper publishers, the Dow Jones management has succeeded in avoiding crippling labor troubles. For one thing it had the foresight to decentralize its printing plants, keeping away from heavily unionized urban centers like New York where it avoided being clobbered by the catastrophic newspaper strike in the 1970s which trimmed the city's general purpose dailies from seven to three. Management has persuaded its hired help to permit the installation of automated equipment more readily than other publishers have been able to do. As a result Dow Jones has been a pioneer of electronic journalism.

To speed up its transmission of news, the publisher, during the 1970s, expanded its network of printing plants. By 1980 thirteen widely scattered facilities were printing four regional daily editions of the *Journal,* linked by a sophisticated communications system that in seven of the plants includes the use of a space satellite positioned twenty-two thousand miles above the equator. These "mother" printing plants beam images of full pages of print to more distant facilities via satellite, a method that has enormously cut labor and production costs and improved distribution since plants could be located closer to readership markets.

In another move to avoid being bypassed by technological breakthroughs, Dow Jones has moved into the cable television industry. Beginning in 1979, the publisher launched a cable TV service providing news, information and advertising using one of the newspapers owned by its Ottaway subsidiary, the *News-Times* in Danbury, Connecticut. News Cable offers a round-the-clock telecast of national and world news from the Associated Press, as well as local news, information and sports, coupled with advertising for twenty-four thousand cable TV viewers in Danbury and other areas of Connecticut.

Thanks to News Cable service, a subscriber worried about the diet his child is receiving at school can turn to a channel and obtain a complete rundown of the day's school lunch menus. Three times a day, fifteen-second person-to-person messages are sent out to individual subscribers congratulating them on their birthdays and other domestic events.

This experiment in news cable TV is a one-way information service. Subscribers receive it on their home TV screens but cannot themselves send out a signal. In 1980 Dow Jones launched a two-way cable link experiment permitting subscribers to select the information they want and to retrieve it just when they want it. Thanks to computerized programming, a subscriber can manipulate his information for a variety of purposes. For instance, participants in the plan have immediate access to stock market prices, the financial reports of corporations, business and financial news from Dow Jones and other services, as well as entertainment schedules for local movies, classified advertising (including the sales being run in local department stores), restaurant guides and sports scores.

If a subscriber wishes to be able to compare the performance of the stocks he holds in his portfolio with the market in general, he simply presses a button on his home computer. By punching his terminal keyboard, he can ask financial questions and receive immediate answers.

In short, Dow Jones, by moving into the catbird seat of advanced technology, is striving to make certain that it will not be damaged by the revolution in communications technology that is increasingly threatening the journalism of the printed word.

While the *Wall Street Journal* is the daily transmitter of business and financial news with a breezy sociological twist, its sister publication in the Dow Jones family, *Barron's National Business and Financial Weekly,* is a hard-nosed publication directed exclusively at the investment community. *Barron's* bears the name of its feisty, irrepressible founder who launched the periodical in 1920 as an affiliate of the *Wall Street Journal.* The individual who occupies the publisher and the editorial chair today is in some ways hewn from the mold of the founder. Robert M. Bleiberg, a man with a huge moon-face on an oversized torso, is not quite as stout as Clarence Barron was, but his idiosyncrasies and oracular pronouncements are very much in the spirit of his flamboyant predecessor. In 1954, at the age of thirty, Bleiberg became the editor of *Barron's,* the youngest man to assume the post.

One of financial journalism's incomparable egocentrics, Bleiberg rules the roost with the air of the *grand seigneur.* In his college days Bleiberg is said to have flirted with liberal ideas, but this was a youthful indiscretion long since swept under the rug. Bleiberg writes in the elegant, rotund style of a latter-day Samuel Johnson and his social and political credos have the musty odor of the eighteenth century. He is a no-holds-barred proponent of undiluted, straight-whiskey capitalism.

Bleiberg's preparations for his weekly editorials are legendary. On Wednesday he starts training like an athlete, working himself into a state of fury against the man or the social target he is going to excoriate, pacing back and forth in his office, muttering a stream of imprecations. As he rehearses over and over to himself the delinquencies of his adversary, his baby-moon face grows progressively more scarlet until it seems he will have a stroke before he can pound out his evangelical message. By Thursday Bleiberg is white hot, seething with the rage of a lion ready to pounce into the arena and tear the Christians to pieces at the command of Nero. Finally, late on Friday afternoon when the last sentence of his jeremiad has been typed, he emerges limp and exhausted from his office and stumbles homeward, his journalistic orgasm spent.

On the other hand Bleiberg's chief lieutenant, Alan Abelson, who doubles as managing editor and columnist, is a wry, acerbic journalist who exudes no ideological fervor but a mood of astringent omniscience. Unlike Bleiberg, Abelson is short and wiry. The two editors exist together like Mutt and Jeff, each necessary for the nourishment of the other's ego. Abelson is one of the most publicized columnists on the American business scene. He demonstrates in striking fashion the axiom that investigative reporting isn't a profession but an obsession.

There is a popular opinion that financial writers on *Barron's,* the *Wall Street Journal* or *Forbes* can manipulate the stock market through what they write. Actually, thirty years ago Walter Winchell, the gossip columnist, was much more powerful in this respect than any financial writer of today. Winchell used to give "hot" stock tips on his weekly news broadcasts and next day the New York Stock Exchange would be so deluged with "buy orders" that officials had to send for a wagon nicknamed the "Winchell Special" to take care of the avalanche of trading slips.

Normally, today, an adverse financial story won't have a lasting effect on the stock of a major, widely held company, especially if its earnings peformance does not vindicate the writer's charges. But a journalistic attack—or boost—can have an immediate, short-term impact, especially on smaller, less widely held firms.

Alan Abelson has developed the reputation of being able to drive down the price of stocks in this category when he attacks them in his mordant fashion. As one writer notes, "Abelson's ability has brought microscopic scrutiny to his column and his reporting methods. Critics have charged that he is being used by rings of short sellers who feed him adverse information about corporations and then trade on the knowledge that a tumbling stock can be just as profitable as a soaring one. However, Abelson, while he has shown a proven ability to move the market, has never been charged with personally profiting from his column's impact on stock prices. To his critics Abelson insists 'No one uses me or has ever used me.'" And no one has ever disproved this claim.

"The life of a financial writer is fraught with danger," observes Abelson, who has been threatened by the Mafia. A partner in a brokerage house that lost money when Abelson attacked Benguet for its dubious gambling operations in the Grand Bahamas told a friend to pass word along to the columnist that if he kept writing against Benguet he would find himself at the bottom of the East River with cement blocks on his feet. One Friday afternoon Abelson received a bulky package from Railway Express. Upon opening it, he found a deerskin punctured with three big bullet holes. "I never heard from the sender again," reminisces Abelson. "He either shot himself or ran out of bullets."

One avid reader of Abelson's column who claims that he has a black belt in judo, every now and then phones the columnist threatening to walk into his office and beat him to a pulp. Another reader wrote "Dear Mr. Abelson: I'm sick and tired of your off-hand comments that knock down stock values 10–20% in a single trade. Things are bad enough already. Lay off, you son-of-a-bitch. Sincerely, A. Pissed-Off Investor."

To all such admirers Abelson sends the following missive: "Dear Sir: Some lunatic has been writing letters and signing your name to them. I just thought since I received one, you ought to know."

Abelson's sources of information are widespread. They

include outraged employees with a beef about their bosses, managers of hedge funds who find themselves locked into ruinous positions and anxious to discredit their rivals, trust officers who are scandalized about stock manipulations on Wall Street. "One of the things I found out over the years," Abelson observes, "is that the telephone is a marvelous instrument. I'm always concerned if I'm sitting in an office interviewing a guy and the next thing you know he's telling you about his disabled wife, his spastic kid, how his mother-in-law is in the hospital dying of cancer. You sit there knowing the guy's a goddamn crook, but you figure, 'Gee, can I really torture him anymore by exposing him?' On the telephone he's only a disembodied voice. You ask him why the figures of his business don't add up and no matter what he says, he's responding directly to your question. He doesn't become a full-bodied person to con your sympathy."

There are intangible satisfactions to his job, Abelson points out. He recalls how when the stock of Equity Funding, the insurance firm, was suddenly suspended on the Exchange and all week he had been hearing rumors of the firm's bogus insurance policies, he got to work, tracked down his sources and pieced together a devastating story of fraud. Abelson left the final paragraph of his story open to allow Equity to rebut his charges if they could. No officer of the firm would answer his phone calls. Finally, right on deadline, he flushed out one small game, a public relations man. Abelson recited the litany of fraudulent practices that he had uncovered. "Is it okay to write that the company flatly denies the charges?" There was a pause and a weak plaintive voice replied: "Well, we deny it—but not flatly."

"I took that," concludes Abelson, "as reasonable insurance we had the goods on Equity Funding."

Barron's under the aegis of Bob Bleiberg and his staff has been a meticulous chronicler of the major socioeconomic developments in America during the three decades following the Second World War. Shortly after Bleiberg took over as editor, Wall Street was launched on a massive bull market, the most sustained since the golden era of the 1920s. Many small investors discovered they could make money buying stocks at shoestring prices and cashing in handsomely when the stocks went up, as they seemed to do invariably. The Russians had

92

unveiled Sputnik and plunged the Kennedy Administration into a frantic race to beat the Soviets in putting a man on the moon. American industry erupted in a technology explosion. IBM, Xerox, Transitron emerged as the new glamour stocks on the Street.

Then, with economic expansion reaching a record level and prices for goods and services beginning to accelerate ominously, the nation's attention for the first time was drawn to the instability of the American dollar. The generation of Americans born after World War One had never fully appreciated the possibility of currency instability, although people living abroad had had painful experiences with the collapse of money. In America the big fear since the 1930s had been the recurrence of another major depression, not of a currency bust. However, as prices began to take off in the early 1970s and the purchasing power of the dollar deteriorated, as interest rates rose ominously and American corporations found it increasingly difficult to raise urgently needed capital, the premise of a steady-growth economy upon which this nation had been built began to be seriously questioned. A group arose, the so-called "goldbugs" who preached that man's salvation lay in accumulating the precious metal as a protection against the coming bust of the dollar. Originally, the "goldbugs" were looked upon even by sophisticated financial reporters as a fanatic breed. Their jeremiads on the catastrophic consequences that would result from runaway inflation were not taken seriously by most Wall Street experts.

Barron's was one of the few publications to soberly weigh the proposition that gold could become a major haven for panicky investors if inflation raced out of control. The burgeoning passion for owning gold, which marks the behavior of speculators who are pessimistic over the economic survival of a nation, is a highly ominous trend. The way ahead is perilous and newsmen on *Barron's*, the *Wall Street Journal* and other financial publications are burdened with the crucial responsibility of providing a journalistic radar system to warn of impending catastrophe. Perhaps the worst will happen. As all too often in the past, what has seemed mere fiction may become sober fact and journalists will be forced to take over from the novelists.

5

"Punch" Sulzberger's New York *Times* and the Incorrigible Chandlers of the "Born Again" Los Angeles *Times*

NEW YORK CITY is not only the headquarters of Dow Jones and financial journalism, but also a center of the communications industry and home to one of America's leading journals of record, the New York *Times*.

The man who launched the *Times* on its successful career was Adolph Ochs, a Jewish immigrant from Europe and a member of one of a group of German-Jewish families (the Lehman Brothers, Loebs and Seligmans were others) who settled in the American South before the Civil War. Ochs (the name in German means ox) founded a family fortune in the best Horatio Alger tradition. A street Arab, the real-life prototype of the starved urchin in a Charles Dickens novel, Ochs started work when he was eleven years old, sweeping the offices of the Knoxville *Chronicle* for twenty-five cents a day. He scraped together a few hundred dollars, married the daughter of Isaac Wise, the leading Cincinnati rabbi, and ended up buying the Chattanooga *Times*. In 1896 the ambitious young entrepreneur learned that the New York *Times*, a struggling newspaper with a circulation of ten thousand and losing a quarter of a million dollars a year, was up for sale. Ochs purchased it with seventy-five thousand dollars borrowed from the banks. Before the publisher bought the *Times,* forty-five years after it had been launched, no less than seven other owners had run it and quit under heavy losses. (At one time Leonard Jerome, Winston Churchill's grandfather and a wealthy broker, held a large block of *Times* stock.) Under Ochs, however, the *Times* gathered up its skirts like a scandalized old maid and, aloof from the street brawls of Pulitzer's *World* and the Hearst-owned *Journal,* it provided only the news "fit to print," Ochs insisting that his financial operations were as clean as a hound's tooth. When a rumor spread early in his stewardship that there was substantial British capital invested in the *Times,* Ochs made a point of publicly disclosing the details of the paper's ownership, revealing that he and his family had absolute control of the *Times* stock. Observed Oswald Garrison Villard, a contemporary publisher, "Nobody in serious journalistic circles ever believed the gossip as to foreign control of the *Times.* In the first place, the *Times* is so naturally pro-British that the British would never have had to pay money (to bribe it) even if its owner *had* been venal." Indeed, Ochs embraced the philosophy of the British upper classes with the adoration only a former office sweeper could muster.

At the turn of the century, as the *Times* grew in prestige and prosperity under his administration, Ochs decided to move its headquarters from downtown Park Row where it had been launched to Forty-second Street, which had become the heart of the Manhattan business area. But it wasn't sufficient merely to open new offices. Like the ancient Pharaohs who raised pyramids to insure their immortality, Ochs decided to build a monument of his own. He bought land between Seventh Avenue and Broadway from Forty-second Street to Forty-third to erect an office tower of brick, terra cotta and limestone. Huge crowds gathered to watch the excavation, gaping as a grandiose structure emerged.

James Bennett of the *Herald,* a major competitor of Ochs, grudgingly allowed his editors to report the story. Conceding the construction of the Times Tower to be "the most interesting engineering feat to be seen anywhere on Manhattan Island," one *Herald* article concluded, "Never before . . . has a similar undertaking been watched by so great an audience." Ochs rented a hotel room across from the construction site solely for the purpose of gazing on his mammoth ziggurat.

95

However, there was a slight hurdle to be surmounted. The splurge was costing Ochs $2.5 million. He didn't have the cash to spare, but he discovered that his friend, James Hazen Hyde, would be delighted to make him a loan. Young Hyde, upon the death of his father, had taken over the family-owned Equitable Life Assurance Company, and he dipped freely into the corporate till to live like an occidental pasha.

In January 1905, shortly after lending Ochs the $2.5 million to build his Times Tower, Hyde topped his previous flights of self-indulgence by throwing the most extravagant masquerade ball yet given in Manhattan. To regale his guests, he hired the fifty-piece orchestra and corps de ballet of the Metropolitan Opera House together with Broadway's foremost musical star, Mademoiselle Gabrielle Réjane. Manhattan's beau monde turned up in picturesque array. One dowager appeared as Marie Antoinette and was accompanied by a private detective hired to keep her diamond necklace from being pilfered. Edward Harriman, the railroad mogul, materialized as Julius Caesar. A leading Wall Street banker arrived as a Spanish bullfighter. Adjoining the dance floor was a room that had been transformed into a mammoth cavern of ice which under a hundred electric lights shimmered like a waterfall of color. At the stroke of midnight dancers from the ballet, dressed as celestial cherubim, drove translucent tennis balls across a net that glittered like a rainbow under irridescent lights.

However, the planner of these festivities, in his exuberance, committed an error that he was to regret bitterly. Hyde allowed newspaper photographers to slip in and snap pictures of the exuberant goings-on, and from eight in the evening until six the next morning when the festivities broke up, the industrious photographers took pictures which provided millions of newspaper readers with ringside seats to the event. The pictures and news accounts of the ball couldn't have been published at a worse moment. America was in the grip of a severe financial depression. Millions were out of work. Editorial writers launched a broadside demanding to know how Hyde had obtained the money to support his gaudy hi-jinks. Was it from the treasury of the Equitable Life Assurance Company? To what extent had Equitable's premium payments financed the tootling of the Metropolitan Opera orchestra and the pirouetting of the corps de ballet?

Politicians demanded that the government investigate the Equitable Life to determine if its funds were being diverted into the pockets of its owner. Pressed by the public outcry, a state legislative committee was hastily convoked, and hearings were held that resulted in the opening of a pandora's box. Witnesses testified about a labyrinth of interlocking directorships, secret rebates, reciprocal financial favors engaged in by Hyde and his board of directors.

Faced with this burgeoning scandal Adolph Ochs felt acutely uncomfortable. He had borrowed $2.5 million from Hyde's Equitable Life to build his office tower. The loan had been arranged secretly and the publisher was aware that the deal would be open to all kinds of misconstruction if it ever became public knowledge. Frantically, Ochs sought to get off the hook. He was reluctant to go to the Wall Street bankers for the money to pay back Hyde, fearing that what he told them would not be kept in confidence.

Ochs decided to call on Marcellus Hartley Dodge, the grandson of the munitions maker who had lent him one hundred thousand dollars during the early days when the *Times* was struggling for survival. Hat in hand, Ochs begged the grandson to take over the two-and-a-half-million-dollar loan from Equitable. "If the other newspapers find out that the *Times* is a debtor of Equitable, they'll have a field day smearing us." If he could get the loan and another three hundred thousand dollars for use as working capital, Ochs promised, he'd put up 51 percent of the stock of the New York *Times* as collateral.

Young Dodge agreed to the deal and Ochs pledged the *Times*' majority stock to him. Then he turned around and paid off the Equitable Company, lingering not a moment longer than he had to in the financial red light district. The transaction was carried out in the utmost secrecy. Dodge clapped the *Times* stock certificates into his personal safety vault to prevent the story from leaking out to even his closest confidants.

For the next eleven years, the *Times* remained in hock to the grandson of the munitions manufacturer, while Ochs played the role of apparent owner of the *Times* with consummate guile. However, in 1916, during the First World War, the *Times* ceased being a secretly kept woman. The Remington Arms Company, one of America's major munitions makers, had placed heavy orders with Russia. Suddenly the Czar's government collapsed and Remington, unable to collect its money, was plunged into a severe financial crisis. Marcellus Dodge, Ochs' financial good fairy, had a considerable stock interest in Remington. He turned to his friend Ochs, whose newspaper by then was solidly on its financial feet. The publisher paid off his loan to Dodge, helping him to offset his losses in Remington.

However, the *Times* didn't think that even this happy ending made the Dodge loan a story fit to print. The truth about the $2.5 million loan never found its way into the columns of Ochs' paper.

During its days of growing pains, the *Times* had its glory as well as its travail. If the occupants of the executive suite were not above indulging in peccadilloes, the hired help toiled faithfully to pick the cotton.

At the turn of the century, *Times* reporters during the night shift when the news was light were accustomed to whiling away the hours in marathon poker games with neighborhing reporters from Pulitzer's *World*. Early one morning in September 1901, the *Times* scribes played their last round of poker, took off for the Astor Bar and then headed home for bed. The only one left in the newsroom was Tommy Bracken, the office boy.

The previous day a demented assassin had whipped out a pistol and shot President McKinley, and the *Times* news staff had been busy publishing updated stories on the event. The President had rallied and the final *Times* edition reported that he was regaining his strength.

At four in the morning as Tommy Bracken sat dozing, a pneumatic tube which carried messages from the Associated Press began thumping against the wall, indicating that new information had arrived. It was abnormal for the AP to telegraph messages to a morning newspaper at 4:00 A.M. Tommy Bracken awakened, rushed over to the tube and lifted out a bulletin filed from Buffalo: "President McKinley's condition has suddenly taken a turn for the worse. The Chief Executive is sinking." Tommy took one glance at the already obsolete story put out by the *Times* reporters stating that McKinley was sleeping peacefully, having rallied his strength. As the office boy stood hesitantly, the tube again bumped against the bin. A new message had arrived. "President McKinley is growing weaker; doctors increasingly alarmed."

Bracken dashed into the composing room where several men, having cleaned the presses, were taking off their aprons and washing up. He showed one pressman the latest AP bulletin. "You've got to put out an extra or we'll look awfully foolish." The printers huddled, talked it over, then one called, "Stop the presses for a new edition." Tommy rushed back to the tube. New messages were pouring in. Bracken sat down at a typewriter and punched out a headline: "Mr. McKinley has sinking spell." It wasn't a highly skilled effort, but it did the job. Under this headline the office boy typed all the bulletins he had received, telling step by step how the President's health was declining, how doctors and members of the cabinet along with leading congressmen had been hastily summoned to the White House. Tommy handed his sheets to the pressman who cropped the headlines into the proper space. They worked until dawn to finish the job. As Tommy hopped a trolley to go home to bed, he heard newsboys shouting the *Times'* latest headlines: "President McKinley near death."

That noon Tommy returned to the newsroom. He had barely resumed his chores when the city editor barked out his name: "Tommy, get the hell over here." The editor had a newspaper spread out on his desk. "Who the devil wrote this headline?"

"I did."

"*You* did! Where the hell were the reporters?"

Tommy explained what had happened. The editor glared at him over eyeglasses perched on his nose. "Well son, you better brush up on your grammar if you want to write another story for the *Times*. Get back to your work." An hour later the editor placed a notice on the bulletin board: "I take this opportunity publicly to express my appreciation of the work of Mr. Thomas Bracken who alone and unaided this morning got out the third, fourth and fifth editions."

The following day when Tommy arrived at work, he found a twenty-dollar goldpiece in an envelope that had been personally delivered by Adolph Ochs.

During the first two decades of the twentieth century, the New York *Times* not only excelled in covering everyday events, even when it didn't have to call upon the help of its office boy, but it pioneered the practice of bringing highly specialized news into the purview of ordinary journalism.

A notable instance was the translation of highly technical developments in the world of science into language the ordinary layman could understand. Responsible for this breakthrough was Carr Van Anda who was lured from the New York *Sun* to become managing editor of the *Times* at the turn of the century. Van Anda possessed an erudition far beyond the scope of the average newsman. He was a mathematician who dabbled in physics and astronomy. Unawed by the jargon of scholars, he realized that news from the world of science could be made as exciting to the average reader as a murder or sex triangle. Van Anda led the *Times* into headlining exploits in the new fields of aviation and polar exploration. Van Anda was also responsible for making the mathematical discoveries of Albert Einstein and the man himself widely known throughout the world. When the editor learned in 1919 that the Royal Astronomical Society had confirmed Einstein's theories by examining the behavior of the sun and stars through a telescope, Van Anda translated these findings into everyday language on the front page of the *Times*.

As for Carr Van Anda's employer, even after his newspaper attained an unprecedented influence and eminence around the world, Adolph Ochs continued to remain aggressively sensitive about his racial origins, going out of his way to insure that the *Times* in no way favored Jewish interests. At the turn of the century, widespread massacres of the Jewish population in Russia took place. While most of the American press protested against these pogroms, the *Times* remained warily aloof. Oswald Garrison Villard, the socially concerned editor of the *Nation*, was bitterly critical of Ochs' editorial policies and concluded that on the Lower East Side where the masses of poor lived, "the *Times* is not worshipped."

To complicate matters, in addition to being a Jew, Ochs was a German. And when World War I broke out, he like other Americans of German origin bore the brunt of hostility as Americans, whipped into a frenzy of support for the British-French cause, unleashed bitter feelings against the Hun. What especially embarrassed Ochs was that many Jews, especially those living on the Lower East Side who had escaped from the pogroms of Russia, bitterly hated the Czar and were vociferously sympathetic towards Germany. The ambivalence displayed by the Ochs family as it grew increasingly powerful in an alien environment was further illustrated by the fact that Adolph Ochs' brother, George Washington Ochs, changed his name to "Oakes" during World War I to disassociate himself from the Germans. This branch has continued to function in the *Times* leadership; a current descendant, John B. Oakes, served until fairly recently as editorial page editor.

The *Times* supported the Allied cause unremittingly during the First World War. However, toward the end of hostilities, the government of Austria made a surprise bid to discuss "nonbinding terms for a possible truce treaty." In the face of high anti-German feeling, the New York *Times* ran an editorial advocating that the United States government consider the Austrian proposal for negotiations: "We cannot imagine that the invitation will be declined. . . . When we consider the deluge of blood that has been poured out in this war . . . we must conclude that only the madness or a soulless depravity of someone of the belligerent powers would obstruct or defeat the purpose of the conference."

Ochs' editorial aroused a storm of protest. Government leaders and people in every walk of life in America, Britain and France, bombarded the *Times* with angry letters and telegrams. Newspapers accused Ochs of hoisting the white flag of surrender. President Wilson went into a rage in the White House. The Union Club representing the civic leadership of New York announced it would hold a meeting to publicly denounce the publisher. Ochs was snubbed at parties, and old friends passed him by in the street, refusing to recognize him.

The publisher was absolutely stunned, and so humiliated that he considered the idea of retiring from the *Times* and placing its operations in the hands of a group of publicly selected trustees who had no financial stake in the newspaper. But he reconsidered and dropped the plan. When the war finally came to an end with the unconditional surrender of Germany and Austria, the outcry against Ochs died down. Nevertheless, he remained a severely shaken man.

Twelve years later, Ochs' anxiety as a Jew experienced a new twisting in the wind. The rise of Adolf Hitler and the brutal treatment of the Jews in Germany became a special nightmare, for as publisher of the *Times* Ochs had sources of information unavailable to others which provided him with the horrifying details of what was happening to the Jewish community.

At the time of Hitler's rise and the outbreak of the new pogroms, the publisher was in his seventies. He suffered a mental decline, plunging into a period of profound, almost catatonic depression. He retired as a recluse to his estate in upper New York and his once agile, resourceful mind went virtually blank. When a copy of the *Times,* now the most powerful paper in America and one of the most influential in the world, was brought to him, he stared at it uncomprehendingly.

For a time Ochs rallied, emerging from the shadows with some of his old verve. But on the afternoon of April 8, 1935, he suffered a stroke and died.

With the passing of Adolph Ochs, the last of the old-time publishing giants, who had launched their careers when the nation was still young, vanished from the scene. Henceforth, the leadership of the media would be taken over by individuals whose memories did not go back to the leisurely, genteel world that existed before the First World War, but whose personalities were conditioned by the spiritual restlessness and rampaging technological developments of the twentieth century. The death of Ochs marked the passing of an era not only for the *Times* but for the entire newspaper industry.

After the death of Ochs, Arthur Hays Sulzberger, the son of a wealthy textile manufacturer and the husband of Iphigene, Ochs' only child, took over the *Times.* He retired in 1961 and his son-in-law, Orvil Dryfoos, became publisher. Dryfoos had been a Wall Street broker, well versed in financial matters. Shortly after marrying Marian, Sulzberger's oldest daughter, he had joined the paper, working his way up. Dryfoos died at fifty of a heart ailment after serving only two years as publisher, and the job was given to Arthur Sulzberger, the first Arthur's grandson. "Punch" Sulzberger, who had been cooling his heels in a series of relatively lowly posts, was thirty-seven and serving as assistant treasurer when fate tapped him for the top job. "Punch" Sulzberger is easy-going and low-keyed in his relationships; at the same time, he can display a sharp independence, even ruthlessness in his decision making.

He has the spine of his tough old grandmother, Iphigene Ochs Sulzberger, the only daughter of Adolph Ochs and,

102

throughout the succession of *Times* publishers, a powerful presence. Iphigene, the symbol that binds the past to the present, is the queen mother, proud, witty, exuberant. She designed a family coat of arms that displays a duckbilled platypus above a motto in bold print: "Nothing is Impossible."

The feisty dowager is amused and at the same time irritated by the legend that she has been the *éminence grise,* the power behind the throne of the *Times* publishing regnancy. "I must admit that I get indignant at stories about how I'm the matriarch who runs everything." She insists that she has survived the delicate ordeal of being the daughter, wife, mother-in-law and subsequently grandmother of the publisher of the New York *Times* "by minding my own business."

Iphigene was incensed with *The Kingdom and the Power,* the book on the New York *Times* written by Gay Talese, formerly of the news staff, who disclosed the struggle that was being waged inside the *Times'* hierarchy. Mrs. Sulzberger complained that Talese interviewed her husband only once during the course of his research. When he arrived at their house, she maintains, her husband was sick. At an early stage of the interview, Sulzberger excused himself so that he could go to bed, explaining to Talese that he was certain his wife could provide the necessary information. "This seems to have made Mr. Talese think I was the power behind the throne, a role I neither occupied nor sought."

Shortly after graduating from Barnard College, Iphigene attempted to get a position on the *Times.* The managing editor hired her, but she lasted exactly fifteen minutes—until her father learned about it; he put his foot down on the notion of women in his family taking jobs. But Iphigene continued to raise her voice in an unorthodox fashion. Over the years she has written numerous letters to the editor of the *Times* on every subject under the sun, signing them with the names of long-dead uncles, aunts and cousins (a practice her grandson Arthur has adopted for his amusement). Through a family trust Iphigene has owned the controlling interest in the *Times* since her husband's death, and while "Punch" Sulzberger will ultimately inherit the fortune, even now he isn't badly off. He receives over two hundred thousand dollars a year in salary, plus a substantial bonus and annual dividends.

In recent years on the editorial side the going has been

rough. The *Times* Washington Bureau has been staffed by a group of headstrong virtuosi, who thanks to their government contacts and their coverage of important national news, have developed a powerful fiefdom and have waged an energetic struggle for independence from the New York editorial staff. This intra-family struggle which threatened to turn into an open revolt was a major crisis confronting Sulzberger when he took over. He named Abe Rosenthal, a former foreign correspondent and Pulitzer Prize winner, to be managing editor and promoted him subsequently to executive editor. Rosenthal responded by effectively stemming the revolt.

In addition to nipping the Washington uprising, Sulzberger has been expanding the *Times'* editorial and news coverage to cope with the rapidly changing demands of American society. The current situation in New York where Rupert Murdoch has taken over the New York *Post, New York* magazine and the *Village Voice,* and escalated the battle for circulation and advertising dollars, is being closely watched by the *Times* management. The *Times* doesn't attempt to reach the blue-collar masses that the New York *Daily News* and the *Post* serve so expertly, but it is very much interested in enlarging its middle-class readership. To this end, management has launched new sections packed with breezily written articles on entertainment, culture and the home couched in magazine fashion. While remaining America's "newspaper of record," the *Times* currently seems striving to outdo *New York* magazine in its reportage of gourmet living. Moreover, Sulzberger has expanded his staff of financial writers, adding broader coverage on technology and business administration to wage an even more effective battle with the *Wall Street Journal* for supremacy in business journalism.

Unquestionably, the *Times* remains the champ, and everybody delights in taking potshots at number one.

In recent years, critics have needled the *Times* over questionable practices. For example, the newspaper that has always been quick to expose the malfeasance of others has at times drawn a curtain over its own embarrassing operations. Over the last decade the *Times* has been a conspicuous crusader for the cleaning up of the environment, and it has scathingly exposed vested business interests that have refused to comply with government regulations, exhorting them to stop polluting the air and water with gases and chemicals. Yet several years ago, when government health officials found reason to believe that the chemical agents newspapers used in their pressrooms had a severe toxic effect on workers, the New York *Times*, along with the Chicago *Daily News*, the Chicago *Tribune*, the New York *Daily News* and the New York *Post* temporarily barred its pressroom to teams of medical investigators. These ·five major newspapers, in effect, challenged a federal agency of the U.S. government acting under the Occupational Safety Health Act passed in 1970 to investigate safety and health standards on their premises.

In recent years the paper has been subjected to an increasingly rough going-over for its errors of omission and commission. The drum-fire of criticism reached such a crescendo that at a meeting held by the Times Corporation for its shareholders, one stockholder asked Sulzberger why his newspaper did not strike back at the barrage of hostile articles. Sulzberger replied by referring to a favorable cover story on him that appeared in *Time* magazine in 1977. Sulzberger characterized the article as "excellent," but neglected to point out that the then chairman of Time, Inc., Andrew Heiskell, was married to his sister, Marian.

The struggling newspaper that Adolph Ochs took over in 1896 has expanded into a lusty conglomerate. In addition to the New York paper the corporation owns a dozen others in Florida and North Carolina. The Florida papers are operating with some of the most advanced computerized equipment in the industry. The Sulzberger family has also brought a network of magazines into its fold, headed by the immensely successful *Family Circle* and the popular *Tennis* and *Golf Digest*, the two leading magazines in their field. An Australian edition of *Family Circle* has been launched to become the number one magazine Down Under. An even more recent edition is *US*, a biweekly which began publication in April 1977. The New York Times Corporation also has broadcasting operations, including a television outlet in Memphis, Tennessee, and WQXR-AM and -FM in Manhattan. The *Times* has gone into book publishing, marketing trade books, educational publications, teaching films, audiovisual distribution equipment and multi-media learning kits. Moreover, the *Times* operates an Information Bank (a computerized information retrieval system) serving over three hundred corporations, libraries and government agencies here and abroad. It has a partnership interest together with the Washington Post Company and the Whitney Communications Corporation in the *International Herald Tribune,* Europe's only international daily newspaper. And the *Times* has an interest in two major companies in Canada.

This burgeoning newspaper, magazine and information retrieval complex that is reaching out to embrace every aspect of today's communications industry is an impressive testimonial to Adolph Ochs, the German immigrant boy who started out sweeping the offices of the Knoxville *Chronicle* for twenty-five cents a day. But, as the Romans and Napoleon learned, mortal man can reach too far. East is East and West is West. . . .

In 1962 "Punch" Sulzberger, in a euphoric mood, looked for new worlds to conquer. The *Times* was laden with honors, but one thing still eluded it. While it was America's newspaper of record, it was not a *national* daily newspaper like the *Wall Street Journal.* Sulzberger dreamed of making the *Times* America's first truly national daily in the general news field. As a step toward achieving this end, the publisher planned an edition of the *Times* to be printed and distributed on the West Coast.

In October 1962, D-Day arrived. The *Times* management dispatched ninety men to establish its outpost, installing elaborate electronic communications equipment for transmitting news from its editorial offices in Manhattan to its satellite three thousand miles across the continent.

However, the attempt to maintain a beachhead failed dismally, for Sulzberger and his staff had made a serious miscalculation. They had confidently expected West Coast readers to lap up the editorial formula that had been so eagerly accepted for generations by East Coast readers—an editorial mix that featured a heavy dose of national and international news and deemphasized local news coverage. Indeed, so certain was Sulzberger that California readers would embrace the outpourings of the *Times'* regular staff of reporters that he refused to provide a stable of western writers particularly attuned to the needs of native readership.

Westerners responded by boycotting the *Times'* clone of its own Eastern edition, remaining loyal to native newspapers which had the true "feel" of the local atmosphere in their editorial approach and which offered, among other things, fashion news that Pacific Coast women especially enjoyed, and that the New York *Times* played down.

During its sixteen months' losing effort, the *Times* not only suffered a continual hemorrhaging of money in its California investment, but also a bitter newspaper strike in New York, a strike that pitted newspaper management against the printers' union and placed a substantial additional burden on the *Times'* finances.

Sulzberger finally decided to call it quits and pull out of the West Coast. The retreat was a bitter pill for him to swallow. The U.S. government scarcely suffered more anguish in withdrawing its troops from Vietnam than the *Times'* management experienced in retreating from California.

But if this misadventure proved highly traumatic for Sulzberger's publication, it proved highly beneficial for another newspaper, the venerable Los Angeles *Times* in whose backyard Sulzberger's crew had so brazenly pitched its tents. The L.A. *Times*, run by the Chandler family, had played a historic role in the political and economic development of California for over a century. When the Chandlers found themselves under direct assault by America's most powerful newspaper, they reacted with fear and outrage. Feeling for the first time the hot breath of competition from a giant rival, the Los Angeles *Times*, which had dozed complacently for generations tolerating a second-rate editorial and newsgathering operation, began to run scared. The Chandlers launched a major housesweeping to improve their newspaper from cellar to attic. Traditionally skimpy in its national and international news coverage, the Los Angeles *Times* took steps to establish a stronger pipeline into Washington and sent correspondents abroad for the first time for on-the-spot coverage of news developments. While the *Times'* invasion of California proved disastrous for Sulzberger and his crew, it galvanized the Chandler family into turning *their Times* from a second-rate newspaper into a major force that is today a serious competitor of the New York *Times* itself.

The Los Angeles *Times* is only one of the Chandler family's numerous business ventures. Through the Times Mirror company, it owns a complex of newspapers, magazine enterprises, timber, ranchland and oil properties. For generations, however, the L.A. *Times* has been the family's most celebrated holding, serving as a bellwether of Pacific Coast conservatism and a lightning rod for the animosity of America's labor leaders and the liberal intelligentsia. It kept Los Angeles an anti-union center long after America's other major metropolitan areas had become unionized. The *Times* endorsed McCarthyism in the 1950s, and it made possible the launching of Richard Nixon's political career.

This publishing *imperium* was launched originally by Harrison Gray Otis, a retired Civil War army general who moved to California in 1882 and bought a quarter interest in the Los Angeles *Times,* a virtually bankrupt paper serving a sleepy little village of ten thousand inhabitants. Otis was a belligerent fellow with a booming voice and an aggressive walrus moustache. He carried himself like a warlord and thought of life in military terms. He called his residence the Bivouac and built a plant for the Los Angeles *Times* that resembled a medieval fortress bristling with battlements. On the roof stood the figure of an angry-looking American eagle with wings, hovering as if poised to attack the community. A violent paranoid, during labor troubles when his staff struck for higher wages, the *Times* publisher drove around the city with a small cannon mounted on the hood of his automobile. He dashed back and forth marshaling his forces against the strikers with the exuberance of a Mongol chieftain.

Before this tough old hombre passed on at eighty, he had amassed a legion of enemies. One political foe, Hiram Johnson, a senator from California and a champion of labor reform wrote, "In the city of San Francisco . . . we have nothing so vile and low, nothing so debased, nothing so infamous . . . as Harrison Gray Otis. He sits there in *senile dementia* with a gangrene heart and rotting brain grimacing at every reform, chattering impotently at all things that are decent; frothing, fuming, violently gibbering, going down to his grave in snarling infamy . . . disgraceful, depraved . . . and putrescent."

The Chandler clan descended on the paternal side from Harrison Gray Otis' son-in-law Harry Chandler, an opportunistic fellow who upon leaving Dartmouth College went west to cure himself of tuberculosis, settled in Los Angeles, married General Otis' daughter and joined the newspaper when it was

108

four years old. Otis and Chandler proved an irrepressible team. They not only boosted the *Times'* readership handsomely, but promoted a variety of real estate schemes to fatten their pocketbooks.

At the turn of the century Los Angeles was flooded with a tidal wave of immigration, and Harrison Otis and a clique of wealthy Los Angeles businessmen hit upon a smashing idea. One of the most fertile areas in southern California was the Owens Valley, which had been transformed from a desert into verdant farmland by the original homesteaders who had painstakingly developed a network of canals and irrigation ditches. In contrast to this blooming Eden, two hundred miles south and twenty miles northwest of Los Angeles lay the 140,000-acre San Fernando Valley, which was starved for water. Otis latched onto the notion of buying up the agriculturally worthless land in the San Fernando at cut-rate prices, then grabbing control of the Owens River and diverting its water supply into the San Fernando area to enrich it. The price of his own real estate would skyrocket, he figured, and he could unload it at a fancy killing.

To rechannel the water from the Owens into the San Fernando Valley required the building of a two hundred-mile aqueduct, the cost of which Otis and his colleagues could not meet out of their own pockets, so they conceived the scheme of enticing other people's money by running editorials in the Los Angeles *Times* calling for a public bond issue, presenting this to the citizens of Los Angeles as a project for the public welfare. The Otis clique planned to raise a scare that would stir up the deep-seated anxieties of Angelenos: the fear of a water shortage, something that had haunted Southern Californians ever since the earliest settlers. What Otis and his clique didn't intend to disclose was that the problem of supplying water for Los Angeles could have been solved by the expedient of building a storage reservoir above the Owens Valley to harness runoff from the High Sierras, augmenting the flow of the Owens River to the point where there would be enough water for *both* the people of Los Angeles and the Owens Valley. However, the Otis group was not interested in supplying the water needs of people, but in rechanneling water through the San Fernando Valley where they planned to buy acreage cheap and sell it dear.

109

Quietly, Harrison Otis, together with a clique of local bankers and businessmen, launched a syndicate that paid $50,000 for a three-year option on 16,500 acres of land in the San Fernando Valley. While negotiating to grab up land titles prior to launching their aqueduct, the group kept its movements a secret. During the three years needed to complete its purchases not a word leaked into the pages of the Los Angeles *Times.* The citizens were not told the happy news that a band of philanthropists was preparing to hand them an aqueduct to supply their water needs. Not until the last acre had been corralled and the deal was "in the bag" did the Los Angeles *Times* suddenly announce with journalistic fanfare the plans for the building of the 200-mile-long aqueduct and the need to raise $25 million through a bond issue to finance it. The *Times* frightened the taxpayers into approving the bond issue through a campaign of naked terror. Unless they voted for the bond, the newspaper warned, the area would dry up and people would be starving for water. The Angelenos promptly responded by voting for the issue.

There was one final hurdle to overcome. The real estate profiteers controlled all the necessary land rights in the Owens Valley from which the water was to be diverted. However, some of the Valley consisted of federally subsidized land, available by law to homesteaders. The problem faced by the speculators was, having snatched up land and water rights along the Owens River, how could they keep new homesteaders from moving in and acquiring at cheap, federally subsidized prices their own rights to land along the river, thereby thwarting the Otis plan to divert the Owens River into the San Fernando Valley?

There was one solution. The U.S. government had the legal right to withdraw from the market land previously set aside by homesteaders by declaring it to be part of the public domain. According to law, only timberland could be withdrawn in this manner. The Owens Valley happened to be as flat as a pancake, except for a few poplars and cottonwood trees, but the Washington panjandrums, if they so desire, can turn woodless acres into timberland and make the desert flow with milk and honey. Most conveniently for the Otis group the honorable Gifford Pinchot, President Theodore Roosevelt's chief of the United States Forest Service, suddenly decided that the Owens Valley was timberland after all, and he turned it by public proclamation into a federal forest district, which allowed him to withdraw over two hundred thousand acres from the homesteaders. The reason for the U.S. government's obsequious cooperation with the California land speculators has remained a mystery to historians. However, there were politicians in the Roosevelt administration who, if not bribed outright by the real estate clique, were obviously in sympathy with it. The Los Angeles *Times* was the major publicity organ of the Republican party on the West Coast and GOP politicos were beholden to the Otis group.

The stage was now set to build the aqueduct, though there was a slight alteration of plans that must have puzzled the more alert citizens of Los Angeles. The Otis interests had sold their bonds on the express promise that they would build the aqueduct all the way into Los Angeles proper. However, the moment the aqueduct reached the site of the property owned by the Otis gang, the constructors suddenly stopped building. There was no need to extend the aqueduct any further, since the land prices in the hitherto "agriculturally worthless" San Fernando Valley had gone through the roof, enabling the Otis people, who had grabbed up land at five to ten cents an acre, to subdivide their holdings and peddle it from five hundred dollars to one hundred dollars an acre, reaping one hundred million dollars from the venture.

However, the bond contract, as voted, had promised in print that the aqueduct would run into Los Angeles, so instead of bringing Mahomet to the mountain, the Otis group brought the mountain to Mahomet. They brought the City of Los Angeles up to the site of their aqueduct by persuading their political henchmen in the Los Angeles City Council to pass a bill annexing one hundred thousand acres of the San Fernando Valley to the city. This incorporation of the valley into Los Angeles forms the basis of today's metropolis.

Of course, there was a price to be paid for this deft manipulation. By diverting water from a valley already under cultivation and redistributing it to an uncultivated valley two hundred miles off, the land speculators left large numbers of farmers and ranchers in the Owens Valley with diminishing water supplies. The value of their farms and homesteads took a nose dive. In 1932 Will Rogers commented sadly in his newspaper column about the destruction of the Owens Valley: "Years ago this was a wonderful valley with a quarter of a million acres of fruit and alfalfa. But Los Angeles has to have more water for the Chamber of Commerce to drink, more toasts to its growth, more water with which to dilute its orange juice, and more water for its geraniums to delight the tourists . . . so now this is a valley of desolation."

The Chandler family has managed to live down the checkered past of its paternal ancester, Harrison Otis, thanks largely to the efforts of Dorothy "Buff" Chandler, the mother of the current publisher and a woman who has made her presence felt as imperiously as any dowager empress of old China.

Dorothy fought her own battle for women's liberation long before it became fashionable, developing from a self-effacing female into an emancipated and finally a domineering one. Today in her late seventies, she remains a highly controversial figure. As the wife of Norman Chandler, who is a descendant of Harry Chandler and was regarded by some of his associates as an amiable but weak publisher, Dorothy emerged as the power behind the *Times'* ruling echelon, becoming a vice-president, sitting on the board of directors and influencing profoundly the cultural life of Los Angeles.

Yet Dorothy started out a shy introvert, unfit for the role of matriarch. She met Norman Chandler, the *Times'* heir apparent, at Stanford where they were students, and married him in 1922. The Chandler family, boasting the bluest blood that could be mustered on the West Coast, were aghast that Norman should think of marrying the daughter of tradespeople.

Dorothy felt the Chandler disapproval keenly and was overwhelmed with feelings of inadequacy. After ten years of marriage marked by continual rebuffs from her in-laws, she collapsed emotionally and had herself committed to a psychiatric clinic in Pasadena where she stayed for six months. This, she claims, was the turning point in her life.

She emerged determined to become a force to be reckoned with by her snippity in-laws. She opened her own office at the *Times*, took over the women's page, and using her social connections and vast financial resources, spearheaded fund-raising campaigns to become the high priestess of Los Angeles' artistic life. Among other efforts, she raised money for the development of an arts complex, similar to New York's Lincoln Center. The Los Angeles Music Center today houses the Los Angeles Philharmonic, which Dorothy Chandler nourished into national prominence. Traditionally, Los Angeles society had been heavily WASP, tightly closed to Jews and other minority groups; "Buff" opened the Los Angeles beau monde to Jewish artists, bringing the Hollywood-Beverly Hills cosmopolites together with Pasadena's parochial bluebloods.

Moreover, Dorothy developed the confidence to play a vital role in changing the policy of the Los Angeles *Times*. Hobnobbing with the movers and shakers in cultural circles who were far more sophisticated than the philistine Chandlers, Buff was embarrassed by the simplistic right-wing philosophy the family newspaper had traditionally peddled. She had become an urbane cosmopolite, yet she was affiliated with a family whose mentality was akin to that of a feudal overlord.

When a public opinion poll called the Los Angeles *Times* the third worst newspaper in America, Dorothy Chandler decided the time had arrived to use her influence and persuade her husband, Norman, to change the newspaper from a rock-ribbed champion of the right to an exponent, at the very least, of middle-of-the-road respectability. Dorothy scored a signal victory when she induced her husband (she claims) to endorse Eisenhower over Taft for President in the 1952 Republican primary. Dorothy recalls that she pleaded with Norman, but when she failed to reach him with reason she resorted to her ultimate weapon: "I said to him, all right, you just stay in your bed and I'll stay in mine. Don't you dare come over until you change your mind." Norman insisted that this withdrawal of sex didn't have any effect on him. During the campaign he witnessed Senator Taft savagely insult a photographer who attempted to snap his picture. It was this rude act, he maintained, that decided him. "You didn't convince me, but Taft did," he told Dorothy. "Can I come back to bed tonight?"

The shift from a right-wing to a centrist policy was a major transformation. Norman Chandler's newspaper had, after all, been responsible for the political rise of Richard Nixon. The political editor of the *Times*, a power in the Republican party of the West Coast, had sought out Nixon in 1950 when Nixon was a political nobody and offered the *Times*' support, not only in editorials but for Nixon's fund-raising efforts if he ran for office. The endorsement of the *Times* persuaded other newspapers and Republican bigwigs to fall in line and this clinched Nixon's election to the 13th Congressional District.

Buff's in-laws became increasingly bitter at Norman's wife as she successfully persuaded her husband to move the paper more and more away from its right-wing stance and its support for politicians of Nixon's stripe. Indeed, the ultraconservative faction of the Chandler family so resented Buff that Norman's sister, Lady Crocker, refused to invite her to the gala dinner she gave each Christmas. Lady Crocker hoped that Philip Chandler, Norman's younger brother, would succeed Norman at the *Times* when the latter retired. Philip was highly conservative and would faithfully represent the interests of the right-wing faction.

Buff had other ideas. She determined to guarantee the ascension of her thirty-two-year-old son, Otis, whom she was convinced would carry on her own policies of keeping the *Times* in the mainstream of American ideology. Rather than wait for Norman to retire and face the uncertainties of an intra-family struggle, it would be safer, she felt, to persuade her husband to hand over his power now. Her idea was to convince the board of directors to establish, in addition to the post of publisher her husband held, a new position of chairman and chief executive officer, a job to be tailored especially for her son. Buff for months kept her scheme a secret, not only from the rest of the Chandler family but from her husband.

Then in 1960, she suddenly put it forward and succeeded in having it pushed through. Asked afterward by people critical of her behavior how she could refrain until the very last moment from confiding her intentions to her husband, Buff replied ingeniously, "I *knew* what Norman felt within himself even though he never said it." If you lived with a man as long as she had, she insisted, you could sense intuitively what was on his mind. Norman was as disappointed with the rest of the family as she was, Buff explained, but he wasn't entirely "up to doing anything about it."

In any event, on April 11, 1960, almost a thousand people gathered in the ballroom of a downtown hotel under the impression they were attending a birthday celebration for the *Times*. At the last moment Buff had disclosed her intentions to her husband. During the meeting in the hotel Norman stood up and brusquely announced he was resigninig as publisher and appointing his son, Otis, to succeed him.

The coup became the talk of the town. Buff Chandler's view of the proceedings was conspicuously different from those of other observers. Not only the right-wing faction of the Chandler family but many unbiased observers were aghast at what they considered to be the public castration of the publisher of the *Times*. Buff insists, however, that neither she nor her husband saw it that way. She claims that on the trip home from the meeting her husband said to her enthusiastically, "That was wonderful . . . making Otis publisher like that." But several close friends of Norman had other views. One source told a journalist that Norman had been devastated. After the meeting, he had seen the dethroned publisher break down and cry like a baby.

Otis Chandler was a quiet, soft-spoken, blond young man in his early thirties when he succeeded his father. He had been a star shot-putter at Stanford and was a rugged outdoorsman. He seemed interested in anything but settling down to the discipline of journalism.

The anti-Buff faction of the Chandler family was infuriated by the ascension of her son to the *Times* throne. And shortly it was to be humiliated even further. The Los Angeles *Times*, under the guidance of its new publisher, launched a series of articles lambasting the extremist right-wing John Birch Society. Two leading members of the Birch Society who had offered their mansion as a meeting place for Robert Welch, the society's founder, happened to be Philip Chandler, Norman's brother, and his wife. Philip had lost the chance to become the *Times'* publisher when Otis was named to the post. Now, this attack by the *Times* against the Birch Society which he fervently endorsed was the last straw. Philip quit the board of directors and severed his connection with the newspaper. Buff's takeover of power was complete. The right-wing faction of the clan was routed.

But Dorothy Chandler had triggered consequences she had apparently not foreseen. As one family observer notes, "Her role had been changed from a woman who slept with the boss to the woman who only talked to the boss over the telephone." In 1966, after her son and his business associates had made it increasingly clear that her participation in the affairs of the *Times* was not welcome, Dorothy Chandler "picked up her marbles" and retired.

Several years ago, in an interview with *Esquire,* the seventy-seven-year-old woman, who had become a recluse, admitted that it was extremely difficult to be shorn of power. "I haven't found the time to feel it's right to communicate with my Sagittarius son. . . . I can't just go into his office and say, 'Can I have an appointment?' That does not work." In any event, Otis Chandler has been strikingly successful in his stewardship. Not only has his newspaper's moderate stance served to dim the memories of its former right-wing extremism, but Chandler has turned the Los Angeles *Times* from a provincial journal into one with international horizons. Thanks to its proliferation of business interests the *imperium* built by the Chandler clan has come to dwarf the personality of the family itself. As recently as 1960, the Times Mirror Company was a privately held business with the Chandler tribe controlling over 60 percent of the capital stock. Since the enterprise needed money to expand and take on increasingly ambitious ventures, the Chandlers hired McKinsey, the management consulting firm, to advise them on how to turn an unwieldly family-run business into a modern communications juggernaut.

In 1964, the Times Mirror Company went public, becoming the first family-owned newspaper to do so, receiving a listing on the New York Stock Exchange. Four years later, the company underwent a restructuring of its top management when Dr. Franklin Murphy, a prominent educator and former Chancellor of UCLA, was named chairman of the board and Otis Chandler stepped up to become chairman of the executive committee.

Currently, the Times Mirror Company is one of America's most profitable publishing enterprises. It is running neck-and-neck with Time, Inc., in the race for the industry's leading spot in gross revenues. The Times Mirror colossus owns, in addition to the Los Angeles *Times,* Long Island's *Newsday,* the *Times Herald* in Dallas, Orange County's *Daily Pilot,* and the *Sporting News.* It operates four leading magazines, *Popular Science, Golf, Outdoor Life* and *Sky.* It runs a network of book publishing houses including New American Library, television stations (in Dallas-Fort Worth and Austin, Texas), and cable TV operations in New York and California. It has mills that turn out newsprint and wood products, and it owns over three hundred thousand acres of timberland. Otis Chandler personally oversees the newspapers, which generate 40 percent of revenues and profits. The Los Angeles *Times* enjoys the second-largest daily readership of all general newspapers in the nation, and the number one spot in advertising lineage.

This publishing conglomerate that was built on land grabs and a notorious water scandal has achieved a position of dazzling respectability. The robber barons have been apotheosized into sainted ancestors; the past with its matriarchal warfare and assortment of tribal feuds has been laid to rest.

Part Three

From *Godey's Lady's Book* to Guccione's *Penthouse:* The Adventures and Misadventures of America's Magazine Moguls

6

Henry Luce—Drumbeater for Conservative America

Henry Luce Achieves *Time* to Build a *Life* and *Fortune*

═══════════════

THERE ARE FEW more intriguing stories of dynastic decline than the tale of the celebrated Astor family. John Jacob the First founded a fortune that by the end of the nineteeth century had grown to over a hundred million dollars and was one of the largest in the nation. The early Astors had taken John Jacob's lead and plunged aggressively into New York real estate, snapping up bargains on Broadway and Fifth Avenue to make huge financial killings. But the latter-day descendants exhibited virtually none of the business acumen of their ancestors. They weren't shrewd enough to foresee that in the period following the First World War there would be a major shift in real estate values from the Times Square area, where the family had invested heavily, to Manhattan's Upper East Side, and they did not move quickly enough to cash in on the change. Urgently needing money, young Vincent Astor was compelled to unload some of the family's most celebrated holdings. He sold the Waldorf-Astoria Hotel plus parcels of land constituting the sites of the Paramount and Longacre buildings in Times Square. Also, since soaring taxes had made the upkeep of the family mansion at 840 Fifth Avenue—a palatial residence that had once been a Manhattan showplace—unfeasible, Vincent was forced to get rid of it and move into more modest quarters in the East Sixties.

Another Astor property that was in deep financial trouble was not a real estate holding but a magazine publication—*Newsweek.* Astor was the principal owner in a syndicate that controlled the magazine. Like the Astor real estate properties, *Newsweek* was in a moribund situation; its big competitor in the news magazine field, *Time,* was substantially ahead of it in readership and revenues. Henry Luce's publication was racy, irreverent, controversial and furiously irritating to large numbers of people. *Newsweek,* on the other hand, was dull. It was mildly liberal and while it should have appealed to an audience put off by *Time*'s cutesy mannerisms and right-wing bias, *Newsweek* was too uninspired to be adopted with any kind of enthusiasm by liberals or anyone else. The magazine became a white elephant for the Astor ownership group, and when Vincent Astor died prematurely, the property passed to the Astor Foundation, which began looking for a buyer for it.

Benjamin Bradlee, a limitlessly ambitious young editor who worked in *Newsweek*'s Washington bureau, got together with several fellow editors and decided to try to find the money to purchase the magazine for themselves, or failing that, to discover a buyer who would make the Bradlee group part of his management team. The asking price was eleven million dollars. To Bradlee and his associates this seemed a fantastic bargain. *Newsweek* had over three million dollars in cash on hand and a potentially profitable audience if the right publisher took it over and turned it into a more exciting magazine.

Bradlee's parents had been friendly with the Astor family and Bradlee knew Brooke Astor, Vincent's widow. The way seemed open for him to approach the sellers of the magazine, but the question was how to find the eleven million dollars to purchase it. Bradlee was convinced that the ideal source was at hand.

The young editor had worked at one time for Phil Graham, Katharine Meyer Graham's husband and publisher of the Washington *Post.* A shrewd evaluator of people, Bradlee was certain that the ambitious, volatile Graham would jump at the idea of acquiring *Newsweek* for his Washington Post Company when it became apparent to him that the magazine had a tremendous potential for a turnaround. And Bradlee was right. Obsessed with freeing himself from the shadow of Eugene Meyer, his father-in-law and owner of the *Post,* and anxious to make a move that would stamp his own imprint indelibly upon the company, Graham rose to the bait.

Learning that while the Astor group was the principal owner, almost a third of the stock was controlled by Averell Harriman, the multimillionaire heir to a railroad fortune, Graham sent an emissary to Rome where Harriman lived at the time to persuade him to release his holdings. Further, setting up headquarters in New York at the Hotel Carlyle, Graham embarked on an aggressive approach to the Astor Foundation representatives. He wrote out a check for two million dollars and waved it in front of the Astor people as an immediate down payment for the magazine. Thanks to his resourcefulness and his enormous charm, Phil Graham managed to wangle the deal for *Newsweek* out from under the nose of Doubleday, the book publishing company, which had also made an offer for it. And Ben Bradlee found a new employer.

The acquisition was consummated in March 1961 for $12.5 million. (The actual price was $15 million, but upon buying the magazine, Graham sold its interest in a television station for $2.5 million.)

With the purchase of *Newsweek,* the Washington *Post* not only extended its publishing empire but added enormously to its prestige. Graham plowed generous sums into his magazine, hiring a team of highly resourceful editors and reporters to turn *Newsweek* into a powerful rival of *Time.* With a stake in the news magazine field as well as in the newspaper arena, Graham's Washington Post Company was well on its way to becoming a major power in journalism.

The Graham family's purchase of America's second largest news magazine was more than an isolated episode. It was the most recent manifestation of a trend that had begun in earnest after the Second World War—the entrance of newspaper publishers into the magazine field to round out their publishing empires, adding to their on-the-spot newsgathering facilities the capability for in-depth articles, fiction pieces and the whole spectrum of editorial content that appears between the covers of a magazine.

Indeed, to serve the increasingly specialized demands of American audiences, the communications media has been evolving from companies operating in single fields into conglomerates that provide a wide variety of news information services ranging from the printed word to the electronic message.

In addition to the Washington Post Company, a number of newspaper publishers have sought to diversify their investment and enhance their profitability by snapping up money-making magazines. One individual who has been spectacularly successful in pursuing this diversification strategy is Samuel Newhouse who emerged after the Second World War as one of America's fast-growing newspaper publishers. In addition to his newspaper chain, Newhouse owns the Condé Nast empire, an operation that includes *Vogue, Mademoiselle, House & Garden* and *Glamour,* and the New York publisher Random House. The New York Times Corporation, for its part, has acquired the ownership of *Family Circle, Tennis* and *Golf Digest*. The Times Mirror Company, publisher of the Los Angeles *Times,* operates *Popular Science*. In Manhattan, Rupert Murdoch stirred up competitive waters shortly after buying the New York *Post* by acquiring *New York* magazine, along with its subsidiary the *Village Voice,* a pioneer of the counterculture. In 1978, Time, Inc., moved into the newspaper field and the Washington *Post's* backyard by buying the Washington *Star,* which for years had run a poor second to the *Post. Time* promptly announced it would plunge over five million dollars into refurbishing the *Star* in an all-out battle to win the patronage of Washington readers. In attempting this turnaround, the *Star* lost thirty million dollars during its first two years under new stewardship and *Time* eventually gave up the struggle.

Magazines, like newspapers, peddle the journalism of the written word but they play a different role. While newspapers have traditionally mirrored the journalism of the moment, the better quality magazines have sought to capture the literature of their times. Newspapers publish the raw material of true-life happenings, while magazines analyze these happenings in greater depth.

124

Like the newspaper moguls, America's magazine publishers have, from the earliest, been an audacious, irreverent crew. One of the earliest periodicals in America was put out by Joseph Dennie. His magazine the *Port Folio* which made its bow in 1801, was, in the words of its publisher, written for "Men of Affluence, Men of Liberality and Men of Letters." Dennie was anti-establishment with a vengeance. He had been against the American Revolution and campaigned editorially for a return of the colonies to Mother England. He charged that the Declaration of Independence was a document "filled with errors in grammar and misspellings," that the Constitution was "false, flatulent and foolish" and that democracy would lead to political anarchy. A close friend of John Quincy Adams, Dennie induced Adams to contribute to his irreverent magazine. The future President wrote most of the articles appearing in its initial issue and continued to contribute to it. Dennie's attacks became so outlandish that he was eventually arrested for "seditious libel" and put on trial. He was acquitted, but since he had become anathema to much of the community, Dennie continued to write his shocking polemics under the pseudonym of Oliver Oldschool, Esq.

Other early magazines were edited by men who became celebrated in American letters, although the magazines they edited on the way up have passed into obscurity. Edgar Allan Poe, a struggling young author from Baltimore, wrote his first successful story, "Berenice—A Tale," for the *Southern Literary Messenger;* he ended up as the editor in the 1830s. The *Knickerbocker,* published in New York, took its name from a book by Washington Irving, its most celebrated contributor, and Theodore Dreiser served as the editor of *Delineator,* a woman's magazine.

Magazines catering to women appeared relatively early in America. By the 1830's Sarah Josepha Hale, who later became famous as the author of "Mary Had a Little Lamb," edited *Godey's Lady's Book* which was enthusiastically received by the nation's distaff audience. Its ornately designed covers and art work were cut out and hung on the walls of many American homes. Mrs. Hale was an aggressive feminist. She campaigned tirelessly for improved female education and demanded that women should be admitted to medical schools and graduated as doctors. Besides battling for women's rights, she persuaded the government to designate Thanksgiving as a day of national celebration.

One of the biggest successes in the history of American magazines was the *Saturday Evening Post* which had a topsy-turvy career. The *Post* was launched in 1821 by two printers, Charles Alexander and Samuel Atkinson, and called itself "a family periodical." It developed a proud literary reputation during the nineteenth century, publishing the works of a star-studded cast of contributors: Edgar Allan Poe, William Cullen Bryant, Harriet Beecher Stowe, Ralph Waldo Emerson and Nathaniel Hawthorne, among others.

After the Civil War, its circulation began to dwindle as its editorial policy stagnated. Moreover, the magazine couldn't keep pace with the on-the-spot pictorial coverage of *Leslie's Weekly* and the aggressive promotion of *Godey's Lady's Book.* In the 1890s the magazine was forced into bankruptcy and, upon the death of its publisher A. H. Smythe, was put up for sale. Its fortunes had sunk so low that Cyrus H.K. Curtis, a newspaper publisher, was able to snap up the magazine for a mere one thousand dollars. When Curtis took over, the *Post*'s subscribers had dropped to a couple of thousand; its editor was a former newspaper reporter who was being paid ten dollars a week and who wrote for other publications on the side to fatten his income. Seeking a way to resuscitate the *Post,* Curtis decided to hire George Lorimer, a fledgling reporter from the Boston *Post,* on a temporary basis until he could find a more qualified editor. One powerful inducement for taking on the tyro, Lorimer, was the low salary he was willing to accept. Starting out on a pittance Lorimer stayed on to mastermind the magazine's comeback and launch one of the greatest success stories in the business.

A publisher who exerted an especially powerful influence on magazine journalism was Bernarr Macfadden, who also prac- tically single-handedly launched America's nudist industry through his advocacy of sunbathing and the exposure of the human body. Macfadden as a boy had been a physical weakling, but he zealously engaged in body-building exercises.

126

He became a weight-lifter, a professional wrestler, invented a muscle-strengthening machine and made the rounds of circuses and carnivals to peddle his contraption. A born showman, five feet six inches tall, with an enormous mane of hair, Macfadden developed a sales pitch that lured the crowds as he preached his doctrine. He sold his exercise machines by the carload and with the money he made from his increasingly health-conscious countrymen, he decided to launch a magazine that would further promote the virtues of his muscle-building exercises. This magazine, *Physical Culture,* was started in 1898 and carried on its cover two slogans: on the right of the page, "Postpone Your Own Funeral," and on the left, "Physical Weakness Is a Crime; Don't Be a Criminal."

Macfadden's timing was masterly. America, at the turn of the century, was exhibiting a rapidly growing interest in physical health. Macfadden peppered his magazine with pictures of young men posing in tights, proudly displaying their bulging muscles. Each issue was crammed with stories of happy young citizens who were leading the "Physical Culture" life.

Physical Culture caught on, not only because of its bodybuilding message, but because in promoting his program for health, Macfadden slyly drew the curtains aside from a subject previously taboo in American magazines—human sexuality. The body was holy, Macfadden insisted; none of its parts should be cause for shame. And this stance created a furor in a nation which in the early 1900s was steeped in Victorian prudery, a society in which millions of young women wore undergarments when they took a bath, ashamed to let the Almighty see them naked. Fathers were loath to discuss sex with their sons, and it was a rare mother who was bold enough even to hint about the secrets of physical love to her daughter before the eve of her wedding night. The other magazines of the period, the *Saturday Evening Post, Collier's, Harper's,* wrote primly of romances young men had with ladies who wore heavy corsets and yards of muslin. Macfadden exhorted Americans to strip themselves and expose their bodies not only to the rays of the sun but to the light of truth about man's physical functions.

Macfadden promoted himself as a reformer bent on enhancing, not destroying, the moral order. One of his concerns was the dangers of venereal disease, a subject around which American society had drawn a curtain of silence. In France, the dramatist Eugène Brieux wrote a play, *Damaged Goods,* which frankly discussed the problem of syphilis. Impressed with the play and the sensation it was causing on the Continent, Macfadden hired a writer to prepare a story entitled "Wild Oats" on the theme of venereal diseases. He published it in *Physical Culture* and stirred up a furor. The U.S. government arrested Macfadden on charges of peddling obscenity, sentencing him to a year in prison.

In retaliation, reform elements in America and England rose to the defense of the publisher. Upton Sinclair wrote an article and Bernard Shaw sent a letter supporting Macfadden, and President Taft was persuaded to rescind his jail sentence.

At sixty Macfadden enjoyed the body of a man of thirty with rippling muscles and not an ounce of spare flesh. And his sexual appetite continued to be enormous. At eighty he married for the second time, a beautiful woman forty years younger than he. Macfadden celebrated his eighty-first, eighty-second and eighty-third birthdays by limbering up his muscles parachuting from his private airplane and he continued to pilot the plane in solo flights around the nation.

It was in 1901, while on his honeymoon with his first wife that Macfadden hit upon an idea that was to revolutionize popular magazine journalism in America. When the publisher issued his story on venereal disease, the offices of *Physical Culture* were deluged with mail from men and women readers reciting their own experiences. Many told how they had suffered because of their ignorance about the facts of syphilis and gonorrhea. As Fulton Oursler, who later became editor-in-chief of Macfadden Publications, recalled, "Most of [these letters] . . . had the conscious ring of a public confession, such as is heard in a Salvation Army gathering, or in an old-fashioned testimonial meeting of Southern Camp religionists, namely, the folly of transgression, the terrible effects of ignorance. A whole series of tragedies, sprung from the American soil, were brought to the door of the editor."

The idea dawned on Macfadden of publishing a magazine devoted to true confessions, serving as a modern equivalent of the parables in the Gospels. The formula pioneered in *True*

Story magazine proved irresistible, and Macfadden's confession stories were to be widely imitated in the years to come. A woman confesses her sins, divulging all the racy details of her fall from grace in such a way as to titillate the reader. Then, after the dirty laundry is hung out piece by piece, it is washed in the lather of a moral lesson. The fallen woman repents and goes straight. All's right with the world and man is better for having bought a magazine from Bernarr Macfadden.

A publisher who was to play an even more influential role than Bernarr Macfadden, but in the field of serious news rather than sensational sex journalism, was Henry Robinson Luce. The son of a missionary, Luce was born in Tengchow, China, in 1898, and at the age of twenty-three began his journalistic career as a reporter on the Chicago *Daily News,* a year after graduating from Yale.

In 1923 with Briton Hadden, a schoolmate, he launched the weekly news magazine *Time*; he followed this up by starting *Fortune,* a financial magazine, in 1930, and six years later, *Life,* the pioneer of modern pictorial journalism.

Luce was the Savonarola of the journalistic world. Tall and thin, with severe features and piercing light-blue eyes, he constantly preached at people. A "good morning" from an employee would provoke from him not a mere "thank you," but a Sermon on the Mount. A sally from an associate about the weather would trigger a dissertation on the Creation. While Luce's staff of well-paid editors gloried in imbibing fine wines and eating at elegant restaurants, Luce, confronted with every hedonistic temptation, behaved like an English parson avoiding a house of ill repute. He had no lust for wealth. The money he made from his lucrative publishing empire embarrassed him. While Luce and his wife, Clare Booth, the dramatist, lived in a series of wealthy homes, their life-style was austere. The first of their domiciles, a several-thousand-acre plantation in South Carolina, was visited by Father Thomas Merton, the Trappist monk who had become their friend. Surveying the surroundings, Merton declared, "This would be a beautiful setting for a monastery." And the Luces donated their estate to the Trappist monks.

Although Luce was a dyed-in-the-wool conservative and an

unflinching fighter of Communism, he wasn't entirely inflexible in his politics. On a number of issues, notably in the area of civil rights, he took a boldly liberal stance. His instincts as a child of missionaries convinced him that segregating the black people was a violation of Christian doctrine. Moreover, although he was a Republican and a staunch spokesman for free enterprise, he displayed no resentment when a section of the *Time* magazine staff joined the New York Newspaper Guild. Indeed, he wished his "errant" journalists good luck. And despite his right-wing convictions, he was one of the first to disassociate himself from Senator Joseph McCarthy and his witch-hunts.

Time magazine, the first publication Luce founded, was the prototype of the "new journalism." Racy, irreverent, given to brisk, incisive language and construction of its stories around personalities, *Time* instituted what was then a unique approach to the news. Some critics deplored what they called the smug tone, the mannered terseness, and the self-conscious wit, but the magazine survived and prospered, changing America's vocabulary and its concepts of news presentation.

Life magazine, started by Luce in 1935, became America's dominant news-photo magazine. Indeed, Luce was the first magazine publisher to completely appreciate the possibility of using the camera to tell the news. Several of his fellow publishers had toyed with the notion, but they had been dissuaded by seemingly hopeless technological complications. They concluded it was impossible to produce such a magazine at a cost that would not be ruinous. Luce, however, sensing the drama inherent in news photography, was willing to take the necessary financial risk.

The Donnelley Company, a leading printer of magazines, began researching the feasibility of accelerating its printing runs using equipment to handle the glossy paper necessary for news pictures. It came up with a quick-drying ink, a thermal printing technology and a new type of paper that put Luce's magazine in business. This publication, which Luce initially wanted to call *Newsreel,* finally made its debut as *Life*. It received a tremendous reception from the public, greater even than *Time*'s, and it remained a leader in its field until television, with its on-the-spot moving pictures of news events, made still news photography old fashioned.

During the Great Depression, Luce conceived of his landmark publication *Fortune*, which was a highbrow magazine devoted to chronicling the adventures of the business world. In 1930 when he moved into the field of financial journalism, there was a daily financial newspaper in existence, the *Wall Street Journal*, and there were weekly business journals, *Forbes*, *Barron's* and *Business Week*, but there was no periodical committed to analyzing the business world as a sociological entity.

Luce summoned to his task the missionary zeal he brought to everything. It wasn't enough for him merely to record the doings of financiers and businessmen, he must expound a theology of American business. He took the unconventional step of recruiting not economists and financial analysts as his editors but poets, novelists and essayists. He envisaged *Fortune* not as a journal of economics, but as a literary periodical that happened to be devoted to business.

Luce's shrewdness was amply vindicated. Some of the best business journalists over the past twenty-five years have not been people trained in economics or finance, but generalists with backgrounds in the humanities who, because of their philosophical insights, have been able to analyze and place in the broadest possible context the significance of business and financial operations. One of the most distinguished mainstays of the *Wall Street Journal*, Vermont Royster, was a student of classical languages who could have been an Oxford don.

Moreover, Luce staffed *Fortune* with a number of writers opposed to his own conservative views. A smaller mind might have boggled at the idea of recruiting left-wing writers to head a magazine devoted to the business world. But Luce hired Dwight MacDonald, a radical essayist, Archibald MacLeish, a poet steeped in grass-roots socialism, John Galbraith, a New Deal economist and James Agee, a bohemian novelist. None but Galbraith had taken a course in economics.

Whether his choice of leftists was a stroke of genius or sheer luck, Luce's timing could not have been more fortunate. Nine days before the first issue of *Fortune* was scheduled to appear, in October 1929, the stock market crashed and America began a severe slide into the steepest depression in its history. The radicalism of Luce's writers meshed nicely with the drastically changed mood of the American public. Had Luce's fat, opulent-looking periodical, which in the words of one observer

131

"weighed as much as a good-sized flounder," been issued as an apologia for American capitalism, it would have died on the spot. But Luce successfully shaped *Fortune* to fit the times. Previously, most of the press had treated business as a sacred cow, operating on the premise that whatever was good for the captains of industry was great for the nation. Now that the capitalist system had broken down, *Fortune* was quick to present itself as a journal dedicated to finding out why.

The magazine launched a series of investigative articles questioning the operations of the steel and chemical industries, probing the wheeler-dealings of the armaments makers and the operations of monopoly enterprises like the United Fruit Company.

Then, as America climbed out of the Depression and moved onto the plateau of prosperity that followed the Second World War, Luce's magazine deftly adjusted its editorial policies, moving from the stance of an attacker of American business to a glamorizer of its achievements. It continued its role as prober of malfeasance and scandal, but its overall policy became one of emphasizing the romance of the nation's industrial leadership and its corporations. As America grew increasingly more prosperous, *Fortune* broadened its approach to other fields. It began publishing articles on the latest developments in psychology and the treatment of mental illness. It offered searching studies of the nation's affluent new life-style, reported on the new post-war breed of multimillionaires, the climb of blue-collar workers into the middle classes. The magazine became a sociological document of a nation in the grip of a rapidly developing technology.

With the emergence in the 1950s of television as the major source of on-the-spot news information, Luce's enterprises were forced to undergo a drastic adjustment and one of them, *Life*, the news-picture magazine, folded. *Fortune* also developed an identity crisis during the 1960s. It began to suffer severe problems in trying to cover an economy that had accelerated from a fast trot to a headlong gallop. Leisurely in-depth articles written for a magazine that came out once a month no longer could keep pace with fast-breaking developments that had a critical impact on the pocketbooks of Americans. Readers demanded more rapid notice of impending events. By the early 1970s, *Fortune*'s circulation was falling steadily while its advertising revenues failed to keep pace with its major competitors, *Forbes* and *Business Week*. Confronted with the need to thoroughly revamp its editorial operations or go under, *Fortune*, under the direction of Andrew Heiskell, the publisher, and Sidney Lubell, its editor, repackaged itself. Heiskell and Lubell streamlined *Fortune*'s format, went into biweekly circulation, shortened deadlines and published briefer, more crisply written articles with a feel for fast-breaking developments, rather than depending on sociological depth and encyclopedic detail.

7

A Grain Speculator Launches America's Top Snob Magazine

The Story of David Smart's *Esquire*

FROM THE BEGINNING there has existed in our society a small, hardy breed of citizens who stubbornly savored a journalism of the upturned nose and raised eyebrow. H. L. Mencken and George Jean Nathan became celebrated among the Smart Set for their *American Mercury,* as did Harold Ross for *The New Yorker.* But it is an irony of journalistic history that one of the prized artifacts of America's snob subculture has been a magazine that sprang from the rough-and-tumble world of New York's Seventh Avenue garment industry.

Esquire, the Man's Magazine, was founded during the Great Depression. It was launched by David A. Smart, a Midwesterner who grew up in Chicago, quit formal education after high school and went into the advertising business. Unable to grab a grubstake fast enough while huckstering merchandise, Smart became a speculative trader in the commodities market. He scraped together a little money and plunged it into sugar futures, whose price was skyrocketing because of shortages induced by the First World War. Smart ran his winnings up to seven hundred thousand dollars when suddenly the boom burst and prices nose-dived. Smart had not been clever enough to call the turn and he was caught short. He managed to get

134

out with fifty thousand dollars of his stake intact, but he was philosophical about his setback; he still had a lot of cash for a young fellow.

Sobered by the experience, Smart returned to advertising, setting up an agency with his younger brother, Alfred, who had specialized in writing copy for the men's clothing industry. They were joined by a crack salesman, William Weintraub, who helped them devise a series of razzle-dazzle promotions for the nation's haberdasher shops. One of their inspirations was to send out telephoto pictures of the latest styles in men's clothing. The idea was to snap pictures of fashionably dressed celebrities attending Broadway play openings and wire them to men's stores that subscribed to their service. They launched the scheme on the opening night of Florenz Ziegfeld's show *Smiles*, which had its debut on November 18, 1930, and they snapped pictures of Otto Kahn, New York's celebrated patron of the arts, and a cross-section of stage stars and Manhattan's high society. Dave Smart figured that budding Beau Brummels in the American hinterlands would be dazzled by the new styles of Café Society and would rush out to the nearest haberdashery to buy a suit, a coat and a top hat like Otto Kahn's. The campaign was a tremendous success and it irked Fairchild Publications, a trade publisher in the apparel industry, which behaved as though *it* were entitled to a monopoly on the business of ballyhooing fashions. Fairchild published an article claiming that the photos snapped by Smart were not pictures of the celebrities attending the Ziegfeld opening, but were fake photos posed for by models hours before the event. Smart was infuriated by these insinuations and decided to retaliate. He would enter the clothing apparel field with a trade publication of his own.

So the Smart brothers and Weintraub launched *Apparel Arts,* a lavish quarterly depicting the latest fashion in men's clothing together with actual samples of fabrics—the newest tweeds and linens—pasted onto its pages. The quarterly was distributed to America's haberdasher shops to be used as a sales tool by floor salesmen.

The editor of *Apparel Arts* was Arnold Gingrich, a Midwesterner and a descendant of Mennonites, who had received his education at the University of Michigan. He intended to become a writer, but discouraged from earning his living as a free-lancer, Gingrich entered the advertising business and developed a flair for writing colorful, bouncy copy for Kuppenheimer Clothes, a leading retailer. The Smart brothers were impressed with Gingrich's copy and invited him to join them.

Apparel Arts got off to a thumping start, but when the Depression engulfed America in the early 1930s, the men's clothing industry went into a tailspin. The customers trooping into haberdasher stores dwindled to a trickle and the demand for *Apparel Arts* vanished. The Smarts were convinced that to keep the financial roof from falling in they had to come up with a magazine that did not depend exclusively on men's fashions, but included stories and articles of general entertainment. David Smart installed Gingrich in a hotel room and walked off with the key after warning him that he wouldn't let him out until Gingrich had come up with a complete dummy for a magazine.

Gingrich and his associates experimented with various concepts, searching for the formula for a periodical that provided enticing entertainment as a "come on" for the men's fashions that would be featured in the book. They emerged with a dummy of a periodical and named it "Trend," which they considered an enticing title. However a lawyer searching through title files in Washington reported to Gingrich that "Trend" had already been used and was copyrighted. Gingrich suggested three alternatives: "Trim," "Beau" and "Stage." But the lawyer reported they were all copyrighted. Staring in frustration at a blank sheet of paper which was supposed to carry the title page for his dummy, Gingrich sat with his colleagues around the table one morning when a stenographer walked in with a letter from the attorney in Washington. The letter was addressed to "Arnold Gingrich, Esq.," a salutation that the attorney, an Anglophile of the old school, invariably used in writing to the editor. Gingrich glanced at the letter and straightened up. "That's our title—*Esquire!*"

The concept behind *Esquire* was thoroughly sound. It was to be a man's fashion quarterly selling for fifty cents, distributed to a thousand haberdasher shops across America. Each store was pledged to buy a hundred copies which would be sold to its customers. In short, advertisers were being offered a magazine guaranteed to reach a hundred thousand male customers at the lowest possible distribution cost.

However, by the first week in March 1933, when the Smart brothers finally produced the first rough dummy of *Esquire* to show to prospective advertisers, economic conditions in America had reached a crisis and President Roosevelt closed the nation's banks to prevent a run on them. When Gingrich and his associates first called on prospective advertisers with their dummy, they were received with a discouraging shrug. However, the financial crisis eased and Gingrich continued to press for acceptance of his periodical.

At this point *Esquire*'s total editorial resources amounted to a single author, a young man named Ernest Hemingway.

Gingrich had met the writer through a rare book dealer. The editor was an avid book collector and among the volumes he eagerly snapped up were first editions of the rising young novelist Hemingway. During that week in March when President Roosevelt had suddenly dried up the nation's money supply by ordering the closing of the banks, Gingrich showed up at the book collector's office and gave him seventy-five dollars for a first edition of Hemingway's short stories. To show his gratitude for being handed valuable coin of the realm at a time when money was so scarce, the book dealer offered to introduce Gingrich to Hemingway, a frequent visitor to his store. Hemingway, for his part grateful that Gingrich was collecting the first editions of his books, readily agreed to contribute articles to *Esquire*.

As part of his concept, Gingrich planned to have spicy, titillating cartoons served up alongside his sophisticated prose and he looked around for a clever cartoonist who was obscure enough to work for a minimum fee.

Gingrich contacted Russell Patterson, a top-notch cartoonist whose prices were too grandiose for him to afford, and asked him if he knew of any up-and-coming artist with the qualities he was looking for. Patterson reported there was a black youth living in Harlem who turned out wickedly witty cartoons that he couldn't sell to any magazines. To make a living, he submitted these cartoons along with assorted wisecracks and funny sayings for a few dollars apiece to Patterson for incorporation into Patterson's work.

Gingrich went to Harlem to visit the young black cartoonist, E. Simms Campbell, and found him sitting in a shabby unpainted room. Piles of unsold cartoons were heaped up against the walls and overflowing from shelves in the closets. The artist pointed to one pile and inquired, "How much will you give me for all of this down to here?" He ran his fingers down two-thirds of the way as if he were a wholesaler of grapefruit. Gingrich filled several cartons with the young man's artwork, lugged them to his office and E. Simms Campbell was in business for *Esquire*. Over the years he was to become celebrated and wealthy as an *Esquire* cartoonist. With his earnings he eventually was able to purchase a villa in Switzerland and he continued to send in cartoons for the next three decades.

During one of his early visits to the artist's Harlem study, Gingrich noticed a cartoon figure of a man with a Colonel Blimp moustache, clad in a boiled shirt with tie and tails. The editor was struck with the notion that the pompous little man would make a fascinating logo symbol for *Esquire*'s cover. He bought the rights to the figure, hired an artist to sculpt it and then photographed it for the cover of the magazine. And that's how the legendary "Esky" was born.

Having Ernest Hemingway in his stable proved to be a powerful weapon in Gingrich's campaign to enlist other "name" authors. The editor wanted the cream of America's literary crop, but he didn't have the money to buy it. He couldn't pay what the *Saturday Evening Post, Collier's, Ladies' Home Journal* or *Cosmopolitan* were offering. So he milked his association with Hemingway for all it was worth. Gingrich would approach a Mr. Big of the literary set, mention that Ernest Hemingway planned to contribute stories for *Esquire* and asked if he wished to send in stories too. In the middle of his sales pitch on Hemingway, Gingrich would take out his checkbook, whip out a pen and offer then and there to sign up the writer for a hundred dollars, which was all he was able to pay. Invariably, Mr. Big would look at Gingrich skeptically. "Hell, Hemingway isn't writing for only a hundred dollars, is he?" And Gingrich would confess, "To be honest, no. But Hemingway is our charter author. We have an understanding with him that no matter what we pay anyone else, we'll give him twice the amount."

"In other words, Hemingway's getting two hundred dollars a piece, right?" And Gingrich nodded. This was long before the day of runaway inflation, not only in American dollars, but in literary reputations. More often than not Mr. Big would be persuaded. A check waved in front of an author for a hundred dollars in immediate currency was better than the elusive thousand that might be lying in the bushes. So Gingrich was able to sign up name writers from the start.

When *Esquire*, The Magazine for Men, made its debut as a quarterly in October 1933, Gingrich published a manifesto explaining to his readers what his goals were. Although the magazine carried risqué cartoons and breezy stories larded with double entendres, Gingrich pointed out that "*Esquire* is not a 'stag' magazine devoted to the smoking-car type of entertainment. Its flavor is not that of 'we're all bad little boys behind the barn together.' On the other hand it . . . is not edited . . . for the sense and sensibility of the fourteen-year-old miss. . . ."

Esquire, with its spicy, eye-popping cartoons and sparkling prose, was a hit from the outset. Indeed, it was one of the few magazines in American publishing history to make money from the start. The first issue of 105,000 copies was sold out immediately although the magazine cost 50 cents a copy, a substantial price for the 1930s. Within four years its annual circulation soared from 100,000 copies to 700,000. Within twenty-four months after its debut, the magazine showed a profit of $160,000 which was virtually unheard of for the second year of a magazine. (Within a couple of years profits soared to over $1.1 million.) By 1936 advertising revenues had jumped threefold from $1 million to over $3 million. Exuberant over the success of their offspring, the Smart brothers launched a new magazine, *Coronet*, which like the immensely profitable *Reader's Digest*, was pocket-sized and carried no advertising.

In the early years, market researchers at *Esquire* worked up a profile of its customers that makes quaint reading today. Despite the early hopes for a "new" leisure class of working men and women, the magazine that sold for fifty cents a copy was bought by the more affluent members of society. The Smart brothers ended up boasting to their advertisers that *Esquire* catered to higher-income Americans. Ten percent of its readers, they reported, earned over five thousand dollars a year, and 80 percent made over two thousand. Five thousand a year was big money in the 1930s; indeed the American who earned five thousand in those pre-inflationary times had the resources to lead the hedonistic life of today's reader of *Playboy* with fifty thousand dollars and more to spend.

And for this fun-loving, money-spending reader, *Esquire* served up a mouth-watering menu of stories and articles. The first issue of *Esquire* carried a piece by Hemingway describing the delights of fishing for marlin. Charles Hanson Towne, a writer specializing in gourmet subjects, wrote "The Art of Ordering Food," telling readers how to obtain the house specialties in America's most elegant restaurants. And to complete its high-toned literary touch, *Esquire* carried a short story by John Dos Passos.

In subsequent issues, *Esquire* ran the best stories of Ernest Hemingway including the celebrated "The Snows of Kilimanjaro," and the finest short fiction of Thomas Mann.

Arnold Gingrich presided as editor until his death in 1976. As the prestige of *Esquire* grew, Gingrich came to express exquisitely the image of the aristocratic, tweedy patrician who acted for all the world as though he had been born of British landed gentry with a country estate in Sussex and a townhouse in Belgrave Square.

He developed from scratch what it took others generations to acquire—a totally aristocratic outlook and mode of living. He was as self-fabricated as his magazine which, conceived originally as a house organ for the garment trade, developed into a paradigm of urbane sophistication. To graduate from suit-and-cloaker into the pantheon of America's smart set was possible only in an upwardly mobile, classless America. It takes generations to breed a British snob. But Americans accept the instant snob as readily as they embrace instant coffee.

Gingrich sported a perky little moustache. He wore tweeds, and rakish hats plumed with feathers and brushes, adopting like Henry James the cultural characteristics of the upper class European. An expert in elegant antique cars and old wines, he kept a gold-plated espresso machine in his office, incessantly plying his guests with demitasses. Once when an editor had just joined the sanctum of *Esquire* and Gingrich casually mentioned the Henley Regatta, he was shocked that the newcomer, in his innocence, had never heard of it. He turned a cold eye on the younger editor and waved him from his presence.

Gingrich was a zealous fisherman and the author of a classic book on angling. He loved fishing so passionately he would get up at five or six in the morning to spend a couple of hours in a trout stream near his New Jersey home before arriving at his office precisely at seven-thirty. Another of his passions was playing the violin. He collected four of the world's finest violins—a Stradivarius, a Guarneri, a Steiner and an Amati, and although he was only an amateur, he played the instrument in his office for an hour or so every morning before his colleagues arrived. Sometimes one of his writers, Joseph Wechsberg, a passionate amateur musician himself, joined Gingrich for a session of duets. They would fiddle away in the dawn with only the cleaning woman listening tolerantly as she mopped the floors.

In 1945 after twenty-two years of building *Esquire* into a powerful house organ for the nation's intelligentsia, Gingrich retired, hoping to spend the rest of his years living off the wealth he had accumulated. He retreated to Switzerland, settling down in a villa above Lake Geneva, growing the wines he had become so expert in. However, his plan to subsist on the stock dividends generated from *Esquire* went awry. The magazine fell on hard times; Americans after World War II developed a new life-style. *Playboy,* in many ways an up-to-date version of *Esquire*, emerged to challenge the older magazine. And *Esquire* was forced to embark on a drastic editorial revamping.

During this period of transition, the price of Gingrich's stock began to tumble and the editor, to keep his life's savings from collapsing, heeded the call of management to come back and try to rescue *Esquire* from its doldrums. Like Cincinnatus abandoning his plow, Gingrich returned to lead the battle for survival. In this second stage of his career, a new troop of *Esquire* writers mushroomed up to take the place of the ones Gingrich had grown up with. Gore Vidal, Tom Wolfe, Norman Mailer, and Truman Capote began to appear in the pages of *Esquire,* supplanting Hemingway, Steinbeck and Fitzgerald. Gingrich had outlasted virtually all the celebrated writers he had recruited and published in the old *Esquire.* With the younger group and their new literary values he felt painfully out of phase. Yet he stayed on playing the role of elder statesman until he died in harness, from lung cancer, in 1976 at the age of seventy-two.

After Gingrich died, *Esquire* continued to experience declining fortunes. John Smart, the younger brother of David, the magazine's founder, grew weary of *Esquire*'s mounting losses—in 1977 the magazine plunged two million dollars in the red—and let it be known that he was looking for a buyer.

That year a team of Britishers showed up in pin-striped suits, declaring that they were out to buy into the American publishing scene "to avenge George III's defeat at Yorktown." The Britishers represented Associated Newspapers, Ltd, a powerhouse publishing empire owned by Vere Harmsworth (Lord Rothermere) whose flagship newspaper was the *Daily Mail*, a London tabloid that ran third in circulation to the *Daily Mirror* and the *Sun*.

Lord Rothermere felt he had just the man to operate the journalistic property he intended to acquire in Britain's former colony—Clay Felker, a former editor of *Esquire* and former publisher of *New York* magazine. And Felker, with his own money plus some financing from the Rothermere interests, bought *Esquire* and became its editor, its chief executive officer and finally its publisher.

Felker found his assignment exasperating. He had taken over the leadership of a magazine that was desperately in need of a new identity to stay alive. Once sui generis among American publications and serving as a prototype for *Fortune* and *Playboy, Esquire* was now struggling to rid itself of the image of a "me too" magazine. Felker was confronted with formidable odds. Between 1975 and 1977 *Esquire* had lost five million before taxes and there was no sign of a turnaround.

As a first move Felker changed *Esquire* from a monthly into a fortnightly publication. But he was unable to pick up enough advertising to justify doubling the number of issues. Moreover, in searching for readers, Felker converted *Esquire* into a version of *New York* magazine, aping the latter's obsession for trendy coverage of the Beautiful People. Readers and advertisers remained cool to Felker's efforts. *Esquire*, as one observer put it, operated in a journalistic no-man's land. "Readers have to need a magazine and they didn't need *Esquire*. You could start and finish your day without missing it." Felker, for his part, insists that a major obstacle he faced was the name of the publication he had inherited. People were comparing the current *Esquire* to the celebrated magazine of the past and they were disappointed. "If we had called the magazine anything else, people would have accepted it for what it was," Felker claimed.

In any event *Esquire* piled up losses of five million in 1978. To keep the magazine from collapsing, Felker sold his equity in it to Associated Newspapers in return for urgently needed cash. But the Associated Group, alarmed by the magazine's continuing losses and by the mounting red-ink operations of one of its newspapers in Britain, decided to stop pouring money into *Esquire*.

In 1979, Associated sold the venerable magazine to two young men from Knoxville, Tennessee—H. Christopher Whittle, thirty-one, and Phillip W. Moffitt, thirty-two, who had gotten their start in publishing when they issued *Knoxville in a Nutshell,* a guidebook for students at the University of Tennessee. This survey of desirable restaurants and entertainment spots became a big money-maker. By 1979, the One-Three-O Corporation, as their enterprise was called, was doing a $10-million business publishing guidebooks for 260 colleges. Needing more working cash to expand their operations, Whittle and Moffit went into partnership with the Bonnier Newspaper Group, a Swedish publisher, who paid them over $3 million for a 50 percent ownership in their One-Three-O Corp.

For some time the publishers had been casting an acquisitive eye at *Esquire,* convinced that the publication would fit nicely into their plans for reaching young adults as they grew older. After five months of bargaining One-Three-O succeeded in acquiring control of *Esquire* from Associated Newspapers for a purchase price that has not been publicly disclosed. The newcomers own over two-thirds of the stock and Associated Newspapers has retained less than a third.

Whittle and Moffitt pledged themselves to put five million dollars into *Esquire* over the next few years to overhaul it and make it a viable publication once more. They prepared to make changes in the editorial format, giving greater emphasis to men's fashions, a throwback to the years when Arnold Gingrich and David Smart promoted their periodical as a men's fashion showcase. *Esquire,* its new young owners pledged, would be geared to today's American male, a confused, harassed individual living in a society overwhelmed by militant female sexuality which, while it may have liberated America's ladyfolk, paralyzed large numbers of young men who could not deal with woman's new aggressiveness.

So the wheel has come full cycle. This celebrated magazine which was launched in far simpler times by a commodities hustler and a brilliant young advertising writer, and which became a leading organ for America's intelligentsia—the people who read H.L. Mencken and Dorothy Parker—has been purchased by two exemplars of today's youth culture. Moreover, *Esquire* which was founded originally to help demolish America's prudery is being shaped, according to its owners, to serve as an antidote for the sexual aggressiveness permeating contemporary society.

8

Clay Felker Unleashes *New York* Magazine, "House Organ of Modern Rome Before the Fall"

The *Village Voice* Hops Into Bed with Murdoch's New York *Post*

THE MAN WHO was forced to abandon *Esquire* in mid-passage is one of the most resilient individuals in modern American journalism, and it wasn't long before he obtained another command. He is a Missourian whose father, a crack newsman, served as the editor of *Sporting News*. Clay, who inherited his father's zest for the journalistic game, worked as a reporter for *Life* magazine before being hired by Arnold Gingrich during the 1950s to bring bounce into the editorial content of *Esquire*. Felker joined the fold along with two other ambitious young editors, Ralph Ginzburg and Harold Hayes. The trio jockeyed aggressively for power. Each had strong convictions as to what kind of magazine *Esquire* should become and they strove to win Gingrich's confidence. The editorial meetings were brawls. After each session, Gingrich dismissed his subordinates to contemplate, as he put it, "the blood on the gymnasium walls."

Cutting his eyeteeth on his rough-and-tumble fighting, Felker graduated *summa cum laude* in his mastery of a survival strategy. He left *Esquire*, joined the *Herald Tribune* for a stint, and when it collapsed after a brief period of merger with the

New York *World-Telegram,* he decided to become his own boss. Felker's father, Carl, although he had been editor of *Sporting News,* never received any stock options from the management and was at its mercy. Clay made up his mind he would not make the same mistake. He not only wanted to edit, but he also wanted to own a healthy, if not the controlling, interest in any enterprise he was associated with.

When the *World Journal Tribune* went under, Felker believed it had one asset which could be salvaged—the title of the paper's Sunday magazine section, "New York." He bought the name "New York" with the sixty-six hundred dollars he received as severance pay and he sought financial backing to launch a new magazine under this title.

Clay Felker had a powerful friend, Armand Erpf, a securities research analyst at Loeb Rhoades, the Wall Street broker. Erpf had made a name for himself on the Street as an advocate of newly emergent growth stocks that made his customers heaps of money during the bull market of the 1950s. Indeed Erpf became a cult hero among stock investors for his philosophy of plunging money into new young companies with strong earnings potential selling at bargain prices.

Erpf became intrigued with Felker's idea and he swung Loeb Rhoades' money behind it. Until he died of cancer in 1971, Erpf remained the chief financial power behind Felker's periodical.

New York magazine was conceived as an expression of the aspirations of sophisticated America. It became the quintessential "trend" magazine, read by people who have learned to keep their lips closed while reading print and who show up at smart bistros around the world. Focusing on the comings and goings of Celebrity Row and New York Café Society, the magazine describes the latest in gourmet foods, gourmet living, gourmet partying, gourmet sleeping around. *New York* magazine presents sex not in the buff, but in Gucci loafers. The magazine, as one commentator puts it, functions as "the house organ of modern Rome before the fall. . . . Leafing through dozens of copies one gets a kaleidoscopic impression of a city whose citizens worship at the shrine of power while staggering through their midlife crises and practicing bisexuality in their exercise salons as greedy divorce lawyers bisect their laissez-foutre marriages."

This journal of sophisticated consumption has launched the

careers of a covey of authors who, after earning their spurs at *New York* magazine, have zoomed into the literary stratosphere. These include Tom Wolfe, a philosopher of the New Journalism, Gloria Steinem and George Goodman, alias Adam Smith. When Norman Mailer, frustrated by the lack of understanding with which the public greeted his more recent novels, seemed to have arrived at a literary deadend, Felker rallied to his support and helped the novelist win a new lease on life as a nonfiction writer in the field of New Journalism. Richard Reeves honed his journalistic craft as *New York* magazine's political reporter and Nicholas Pileggi developed under Felker's aegis into a virtuoso reporter on the Mafia.

Having consolidated his position with one successful magazine, Felker eyed a publication headquartered only a few miles south of his own office—the *Village Voice*. This was the most prominent magazine of the counterculture, indeed a pioneer of American underground journalism. The magazine was the brainchild of Ed Fancher, a thirty-year-old psychologist, and his friend, Dan Wolf, a writer and student of philosophy who decided in 1955 that the time was propitious for launching a bohemian weekly in Greenwich Village. Fancher had been a ski trooper during the Second World War. He met Wolf while the two were studying at the New School for Social Research under the postwar GI bill of rights. Fancher ended up as the publisher, handling the business affairs of the *Voice* while Wolf took over the editorial chores.

Greenwich Village at the turn of the century had been the playground of a legendary avant-garde publication, the *Masses*, which preached such controversial left-wing politics that Max Eastman, its editor, narrowly missed going to jail under the sedition laws during the First World War.

In subsequent years, the *Masses* in the Village, and a host of bohemian magazines launched elsewhere, had tried to survive by hacking away at the Establishment but had folded for lack of support. The Fancher-Wolf team, however, started operations at a most opportune moment. Greenwich Village, which traditionally had sheltered struggling radical artists and a melting pot of ethnic groups at the bottom of the economic ladder, was being dramatically transformed in the aftermath of World War Two. Crumbling cold-water flats and heatless lofts had been demolished to make way for high-toned modern apartments as a flood of young new professionals who had recently graduated from college and were enjoying above-average incomes with which to satisfy their sophisticated tastes were moving into old Bohemia. These new Villagers differed from their prewar predecessors in that while they shared their leftist views, they had real money to jingle in the pockets of their prewashed jeans. Unlike their predecessors in the Village who were willing to shed their blood for the Revolution, the newcomers were anxious to toast it with sangria, and Wolf and Fancher were certain they would enthusiastically support their new magazine.

An especially avid proponent was Norman Mailer, whose sister was a long-time friend of Wolf's wife. Mailer not only supplied the name for the new weekly, the *Village Voice*, but handed over fifty thousand dollars to help launch it. Mailer's motives weren't entirely altruistic. He undoubtedly foresaw that the magazine could become an outlet for his own aesthetic and ideological pronouncements. Indeed he wrote over a dozen columns during the *Voice*'s early years but finally quit, cursing the typos that invariably cropped up to befoul his utterances. The mistakes of the poorly paid printer and the crudity of the newsprint that was being used infuriated him, he insisted. (More seriously, Mailer complained that Fancher and Wolf had adopted an editorial policy that was too square for him. He wanted the *Voice* to be more of a shocker to straitlaced sensibilities.)

The *Voice* made its debut in October 1955, but it took half a dozen years and losses of over $60,000 before it broke into the profit column. What finally put the periodical on its feet was a strike in 1962 by the New York Typographical Union local against the city's major newspapers. It turned out to be the longest strike in New York's newspaper history, lasting over three months, and it was manna from heaven for the *Village Voice*. Uninvolved with the uptown unions, the *Voice* continued to publish and it received unprecedented exposure on the newsstands. Shortly after the strike was settled, four newspapers folded under economic stress leaving only the New York *Times*, the *Daily News* and the *Post*. Meanwhile the *Village Voice*'s circulation had soared sevenfold, from just under 20,000 to over 130,000 readers.

The newspaper industry's labor unions had unwittingly

turned this radical sheet from a peripheral oddity into a highly successful publishing venture. By the mid-nineteen sixties the *Voice* was not only solidly entrenched in Manhattan but was acquiring a reputation elsewhere as an audacious, irreverent spokesman for the nation's burgeoning counterculture. The unpopular Vietnam War, marked by the eruption of campus demonstrations, the accelerating struggle of blacks for civil rights and the vigorous new life-style of American youth, provided head steam for the counterculture movement. Overnight this culture was "in" and the *Village Voice* rode the crest of the boom. To its pioneer contributors—cartoonist Jules Feiffer, and writers Gilbert Seldes, Michael Harrington and Nat Hentoff—the *Voice* added several talented writers who became spokesmen for the New Politics. Jack Newfield developed into a cult figure as an investigative journalist hammering away at the corruption of the Establishment and Andrew Sarris emerged as a hero of the nation's young cinema lovers with his incisive film reviews.

As the magazine acquired prestige, however, Fancher and Wolf found themselves compelled to handle such embarrassing matters as profit columns, bottom line earnings and surplus cash in the treasury.

To free themselves from the day-to-day drudgery of running their capitalist empire so they might lead a more leisurely life, Fancher and Wolf sold their company to Carter Burden, a rich young "limousine liberal" and the son-in-law of Bill Paley of CBS.

Learning that the *Village Voice* was for sale, Burden had gotten together with Bartley Bull, a long-time associate, to make an offer. Burden and Bull offered Wolf and Fancher three million dollars for four-fifths of the stock of the *Village Voice,* to be paid in installments over a period of five years. This arrangement, however, which also provided that Fancher and Wolf would remain connected with the magazine for this period, resulted in an uneasy situation. To scrape up the three million dollars for the deal, Burden and Bull had taken out a loan from the banks. Not only were they compelled to pay installments to Fancher and Wolf, but also to pay off the interest on the bank loan. As time passed, Burden in particular—he controlled 70 percent of the stock—began to feel an increasing need for ready cash. Among other things he had been divorced from his wife, Amanda, and was forced to make substantial alimony payments. Within five years after the purchase of the *Voice*, Burden was so strapped for cash, he began looking for a buyer to whom he could unload his stock in the magazine. The crisis was especially acute, because according to the agreement with Fancher and Wolf, Burden and Bull were due to wind up their five-year agreement with a one-shot seven-hundred-thousand-dollar lump sum payment and the date for this remittance was rapidly approaching.

A highly interested observer of these events was none other than Clay Felker. Having become the Pied Piper of America's smart set, Felker yearned to become a guru of America's art set as well.

And so, backed with money from the dutiful Loeb Rhoades, Felker made an offer for the *Village Voice*, and after a good deal of huddling, the *Voice* was sold to The New York Magazine Company—Loeb Rhoades group—for five million in an exchange of stock and money. With the proceeds Burden and Bull remained in the picture by buying 35 percent of the stock. Felker received 9 percent plus the editorship of the nation's most sprightly counterculture publication.

But trouble lay ahead. Felker, now in his early fifties, began to spend money on his magazine as though greenbacks were about to go out of fashion. This, coupled with financial reverses suffered by a new magazine he had launched on the West Coast, took a severe toll on corporate profits, and Burden and Bull, his partners, began complaining that they were dissatisfied with the bottom line results.

Indeed, Carter Burden had for some time lost his enthusiasm for his business marriage with Felker and wished to quit. He and Bull held the largest share of stock and there had always been the threat that if they sold out, Felker could find himself without a job. Now, uneasy at Burden's growing restlessness and in an effort to shore up his own position, Felker made a critical blunder; he approached the Australian publishing mogul Rupert Murdoch for help.

Felker and Murdoch were close personal friends; they partied together and socialized in the "Gatsby Set" of the East Hamptons. During one chat Felker confided to Murdoch that he was having trouble with Burden and Bull who were becoming increasingly restive over the corporation's declining

150

profits. In 1976, the business had suffered its first operating deficit in years, amounting to over six hundred thousand dollars. His major opposition, Felker reported, came from Burden who controlled 24 percent of the corporation's stock. Felker asked Murdoch whether he would be willing to come to his support by buying an interest in the corporation to offset Burden's influence.

Murdoch listened quietly to the proposal and had an inspiration. Why not enter into direct negotiations with Burden and his associates to buy their share of the stock and gain complete control of the corporation for himself? Without blinking an eye, he made his bid. Devastated, Felker huddled with his lawyers and instituted court action, trying to block the sale of the stock, claiming that he had been given the right of first refusal of the Burden holdings according to prior agreement. But this pitched battle on Publishers Row was as brief as it was furious. Felker was persuaded to agree to an out-of-court settlement, coming away reportedly with a million and a half dollars in return for his interest in the corporation.

Scarred, but hardly incapacitated, Felker seems to turn up time and again like a theme with infinite variations in the symphony of New York journalism. Most recently, and ironically, he surfaced at the *Daily News Tonight*, a direct competitor with Rupert Murdoch's own New York *Post*. Murdoch continues to play the role of Peck's Bad Boy, and his irreverent financial capers cause his competitors no end of bitter anguish. There is nothing that depresses well-heeled publishing moguls more than the emergence of a publisher with even more money to fling around than they have.

Murdoch has put together his communications empire with the loving devotion of a philatelist assembling the rare pieces of a great stamp collection. Beginning with an Australian newspaper he inherited from his father, Murdoch has built a fiefdom of 87 newspapers, eleven magazines and seven broadcasting enterprises in Australia, England and the United States. In England, where Murdoch operates the *Sun* and the *News of the World*, plus a string of 25 provincial newspapers reaching 27 million readers—politically anti-Labor—the *Sun* has been his most spectacular success. Murdoch purchased the *Sun* from the publisher of the *Daily Mirror* seven years ago, when the newspaper was floundering with a circulation of

151

around 650,000. He cut the paper to the size of a tabloid, saturated it with stories on sex and crime, and boosted its readership to almost four million.

Flush from his success in Britain, the publisher moved six years ago into America, buying the San Antonio *Express* and *Evening News.* Like the London *Sun,* these newspapers were barely eking out an existence, when Murdoch appeared on the scene and dramatically raised readership while stirring up civic leaders and scandalizing the citizenry. But the acquisition that brought the Australian publisher to the attention of most Americans was his purchase for $30 million, of the New York *Post,* the nation's oldest continuously published newspaper.

From a position where it enjoyed strong readership loyalty, the *Post* in the 1950's and 60's had steadily deteriorated. The quality of its hard news coverage declined (with the exception of the sports page where the standard remained high). Soaring labor costs combined with a series of crippling strikes at first redounded to the advantage of the *Post.* One by one, the afternoon newspapers in New York folded, leaving it the sole survivor. But the exodus of readers to the suburbs had an increasingly adverse effect and despite its monopoly position, the *Post*'s circulation slipped from a peak of 700,000 in 1967 to under 500,000 by the fall of 1976. Meanwhile, the tempestuous owner of the *Post,* Dorothy Schiff, engaged in an increasingly stormy relationship with editors who complained of her tight-fisted control over the budget, her demand that she personally approve every detail of the *Post*'s operations down to the out-of-town expenses of *Post* reporters. Finally, Clay Felker, the publisher of *New York* magazine and a close friend of Dorothy, brought her together with Murdoch and a deal was concluded in late 1976 to sell the *Post* to him.

When Murdoch moved into New York to peddle his brand of sex and grue, he found already entrenched a newspaper that had for years been enjoying a monopoly on those products, the *Daily News.* And the *News* was still capable of providing stiff competition for the allegiance of New York's masses. Captain Patterson had predicted that his newspaper wouldn't survive after his death. But the *News* continued to prosper under the leadership of his successors, editors and reporters of high professional skills.

Currently, the New York *Daily News* is locked in a vigorous struggle with the New York *Post* (and the Long Island journal *Newsday*) for control of the New York market. The *News* has been steadily losing ground. Over the last decade, circulation has tumbled from 2 million to a million and a half readers for its daily edition. Its profits have steadily eroded and in 1979 it lost its position as the nation's leading daily newspaper to the *Wall Street Journal*, while its profit margin slithered to a mere 1.7%.

In February 1980 the *News* brass came to an audacious decision, namely to plunge over $15 million into completely overhauling the *Daily News*, giving it a sleek, suave look and upgrading its content to attract the upwardly mobile American reader. As Nicholas Pileggi observed in an article in *New York* magazine, "The *Daily News* is going highhat. It's about to shift away from the blue-collar reader with his six-pack income to court the middle-income businessman and career woman with a taste for vermouth." Central to the improvement program were plans to put out an afternoon edition called *Daily News Tonight*, targeted squarely at the suburban commuter with a rising income who, on his way to the office in the morning, bought the New York *Times*. The *News* wanted him to be its reader on the way home. The afternoon edition was to feature financial news together with a "Manhattan Section" crammed with leisure and entertainment information like that run in the New York *Times'* Leisure and Entertainment Section. Most piquant of all was the announcement that Clay Felker, the editor who had earned his spurs with *Esquire* and launched *New York* magazine, would run *Daily News Tonight*.

With a typical display of zeal, Felker cleaned house, importing a crew of high-priced editors and writers at fancy salaries to take over the desks formerly held by hardworking, unglamorous scribes who had been with the *Daily News* through good times and bad. To accumulate his premium cargo, Felker searched high and low, even trying to see if he could wrest some prestigious people from Katharine Graham's Washington *Post* payroll. In its attempt to add class readership without alienating the masses upon which it had depended for six decades, the *Daily News* is taking a big gamble, in the opinion of seasoned observers. Declares the head of a publishing labor union, expressing obviously a partisan opinion, "I think the *News* is missing the boat. They're talking about upgrading the quality of the paper, but the biggest defect they now have is that they are no longer talking to their own readership. They seem absolutely antagonistic toward their black and Hispanic readers. They are also anti-union in a union town, and their editorials are written as though all of their readers were rich."

The *Daily News'* move into the "upscale" afternoon market was a direct response to the threat posed by Rupert Murdoch and his New York *Post*. But Murdoch was not complacent; in July of 1980, just before the *Daily News Tonight* was scheduled to appear, the *Post* instituted a morning edition and an end-of-the-day stock edition for good measure. The battle continues!

(After this book went to press, the *News* announced it was abandoning its afternoon edition because of mounting costs. Murdoch won.)

9

Crown Prince of the Youth Rebellion

Jann Wenner and *Rolling Stone*

━━━━━━━━━━━━

THE AMERICAN MEDIA have been profoundly influenced by the nation's changing lifestyle, its galloping technology and its increasing social instability. But no phenomenon has had a greater impact on it than the uprising of the nation's affluent young people—the contemporary *sans culottes*—an episode that has come to be referred to as the Youth Rebellion. Beginning in the 1960s an Underground Press mushroomed up on the college campuses at Berkeley and elsewhere, as youthful radical journalists launched a guerrilla attack in print against the Vietnam War, the U.S. Government and American capitalism.

These baby polemicists were hatched in an era of uninhibited sexuality and rampant narcissism, of Black Power and the Electric Circus. This was the Age of Aquarius and communal living, of peace demonstrators and the Flower Children, of "black is beautiful," the Weathermen, of the assassinations of John F. and Bobby Kennedy and Martin Luther King. It was an age given over to the drugs that killed a tragically high number of young men and women in their twenties.

But by the 1970s a number of these guerrilla journalists, incubated in the Underground Press, had been accepted with open arms by the Establishment. Their "outrageous" values had become the conventional wisdom of America. Working for *Ramparts, Rolling Stone* and *New Times,* the Young Turk journalists, through their subterranean contacts, scored major journalistic coups. They obtained the first story told by the participants themselves of the Patty Hearst kidnapping, provided firsthand accounts of the guerrilla operations of Che Guevara, and offered an exclusive on CIA infiltration of America's universities and student organizations. All these were scoops that turned those journalists toiling away on Establishment newspapers without the contacts enjoyed by the New Left journalists green with envy.

Yet this is nothing new. American journalism has always been heavily populated by reformed Marxists fattening on the profits of capitalist exploitation. At the turn of the century when the *Masses,* America's leading socialist magazine, was engaged in a financial struggle to survive, Max Eastman, its editor, learned that Mrs. August Belmont, the wife of the wealthy Rothschild House banker, was an easy touch for socialist causes; he presented himself to the dowager in her princely Fifth Avenue mansion and came away with a sizable check to keep his magazine alive. Another capitalist who gave money in the nick of time to keep the *Masses* from going under was Adolph Lewissohn, the multimillionaire copper magnate. He subsidized the magazine so that it could continue to crusade for the uprising of the working classes and the annihilation of the economic system from which Adolph Lewissohn had benefited so conspicuously. One left-wing journalist who ultimately became the High Priest of Establishment Journalism was Walter Lippmann.

At the turn of the century, Lippmann became a protégé of Mrs. Mabel Dodge, heiress to a vast fortune and one of America's leading society matrons. Mabel threw open the doors of her regal apartment on Fifth Avenue and 9th Street to unkempt anarchists, Wobblies, labor leaders from the Pennsylvania coal mines and nihilistic poets, all of whom gathered to discuss the latest theories of socialism and syndicalism. At a typical *soirée* in Mrs. Dodge's drawing room, Big Bill Haywood, a terrorist leader of the I.W.W. (International Workers of the World), charged by the police with a dozen bombings, rubbed shoulders with Alexander Berkman who had drawn a gun on Henry Frick, the steel magnate, and tried to assassinate him. Emma Goldman, Berkman's mistress, also appeared with the young Lippmann, who eschewed the terrorist philosophy of Berkman and advocated a socialist revolution accomplished at the polls by democratic means.

Subsequently, of course, Lippmann recanted his socialism and became an eloquent defender of enlightened capitalism. Finally, in his declining years, unable to endorse the Vietnam War, he broke with President Johnson, turned his back on the Washington Establishment and retired to New York where he continued to inveigh against Johnson's War with a final desperate burst of energy. It was as if the ghost of Mabel Dodge was standing over his shoulder egging him on.

So today's counterculture journalism has distinguished roots. It wasn't such a far cry from Max Eastman to Jann Wenner, from the *Masses* to the *Rolling Stone*. Jann Wenner started out in the best tradition of the guerrilla journalist who aims to succeed in modern America by first becoming a sticky thorn in its side. Like so many recruits to the counterculture, Wenner came from a solid middle-class background, in his case, a Jewish one. Short and stubby, with the big baby face of a capricious cherub, Wenner was not well educated; he was a college dropout and terribly insecure in his craving for power. He was especially sensitive on the subject of his small height. When he became successful and met celebrities who were as short as he was, he was exuberant. After being introduced to Norman Mailer, he boasted to a friend, "You know, he's just my height!"

Wenner grew up in a bourgeois environment. When he was a teenager, his family moved from New York to San Francisco. He entered Berkeley and was aggressively involved in campus demonstrations, *de rigueur* for the modern American rebel. He reported on the campus rebellion as a student journalist for NBC, then dropped out of Berkeley into the world of radical politics, drugs and rock and roll. He played guitar at topless bars, dabbled as a writer, and penned reports on rock music for an underground sheet. Ralph Gleason, a writer on jazz, suggested to him that he take over the music page on the Sunday edition of *Ramparts* and Wenner eagerly grabbed the assignment.

He became obsessed with rock music; it completely wiped

out the aching loneliness of existence. For Wenner, like multitudes of other kids in the 1960s, rock was not just another kind of music. Indeed, Wenner grasped the fundamental truth that music, far from being an insulated, esthetic experience, could be a politically potent weapon. Verdi's revolutionary marches and stirring choruses helped rally Italy's rebels under the banners of revolution to throw off the yoke of the Austrian government. Young Wenner felt that he and millions of American youths were committed to launching a revolt, "not of politics but of culture and life style to effect a total transformation of how one saw oneself, the world and young people's place in it." He decided to start a magazine that would report on the doings of the new rock groups that were mushrooming up around America, review their recordings and provide commentary on the behind-the-scenes world of rock.

Wenner persuaded relatives and associates to lend him seventy-five hundred dollars and induced a printer to give him credit and free office space in a converted warehouse in San Francisco. Significantly, he called his magazine *Rolling Stone:* no ties, completely detached, striking at random everything in its way.

In November 1967 the first edition of *Rolling Stone* rolled off the presses. Wenner had budgeted the issue for a readership of forty thousand, but even this modest figure had been set too high; only six thousand copies were sold and the rest came back from the newsstands. Entranced by Bob Dylan and the Beatles, exhilarated by a new group that had just been formed—Blood, Sweat and Tears—couched in an irreverent style that was peppered with four-letter words, the new publication struggled to survive.

In its early days, *Rolling Stone* was, in the opinion of some observers, a cross between a journalistic enterprise and a psychedelic nightmare. Editors of the magazine practiced what they preached: not only did they write about the drug scene, but some were lively participants in it. Some worked around the clock stoned, which added an extra dimension of uncertainty to the normally perilous job of putting out a magazine. Staffers constantly suffered from moods of euphoria followed by depressions. Any writer attempting to get a hearing for his work was faced with the problem Charlie Chaplin experienced in *City Lights*. Charlie, the tramp, meets a millionaire who, when drunk, embraces him as a soul buddy, but when sober, fails to recognize Charlie and throws him out of his mansion.

The atmosphere at the *Rolling Stone* was manic; there was time out for tequila, for inhaling laughing gas, for passing around joints, and for sunning oneself in the ecstatic awareness that life was indeed beautiful. Yet, the spirit was traumatic for outsiders, "square" people who weren't amused by the antics of the True Believers. When Wenner sent one early issue to the printer, a pressman, seeing the word "fuck" set up in type, ripped out the slug and walked out of the pressroom.

The magazine struggled for survival, but it had one invaluable asset. It had a fanatically loyal youth audience; the age of the average reader was nineteen, and in America of the 1960s this was no mean advantage. The average teenager from a middle- or upper-class family, pampered by his doting parents, had more discretionary dollars to spend on his whims than hard-working mom and pop had for theirs. When *Rolling Stone* got started, the typical middle class youth in America, according to market surveys, spent over a hundred dollars annually on rock and roll records and additional heady sums on stereo equipment. Record companies suddenly awoke to the fact that catering to youth was Very Big Business. Fifty percent of all record sales were going to rock and roll enthusiasts and *Rolling Stone* was the only paper that covered rock personalities exclusively, reviewing their latest discs, recommending to the nation's teenagers what records to buy. A favorable notice in the magazine of a new rock recording sent youngsters by the thousands into record stores. Before long rock performers were demanding from the record companies as a part of their contract a promise that the company would finance an ad campaign in *Rolling Stone*. And for their part, the record manufacturers queued up to give *Rolling Stone* loans to keep it going and followed these with lucrative advertising dollars. Wenner wangled a contract with Warner Communications, which numbered among its subsidiaries Warner Brothers Records, Atlantic and Elektra. Another Warner subsidiary, Independent News Service, took over the job of distributing *Rolling Stone* to the newsstands. When the magazine skirted financial ruin through lack of experience and the blunders of its neophyte crew, Independent News handed it a one-hundred-thousand dollar advance against future sales, a loan that was interest-free and unsecured by any collateral.

Actually, the first record company to rush in and devote itself to the care and feeding of Wenner's flock was Columbia Records. While Hindemith, Mozart and Mussorgsky had an academically honorable place in Columbia's catalogues, the big money was in the hot young grip of America's pop enthusiasts. Columbia provided critical loans to keep *Rolling Stone* going during its Valley Forge days. It placed a major advertising order with Wenner after the first half-dozen issues. Not only did Columbia advance money, but it offered to have its own salesmen distribute *Rolling Stone* through the nation's record stores. Soon these outlets were providing over 50 percent of Columbia's single record business, and when CBS realized that the inexperienced management running the magazine was helplessly lost in a maze of financial operations and the intricacies of accounting procedures, the record company recommended a management consultant who would set the magazine's books in order and lead it out of the wilderness. Moreover, it ordered its own art department to prepare a direct mail campaign for its new protégé.

The man who above all others held Wenner's hand and agonized with him during this period was Clive Davis, the reigning panjandrum of Columbia Records and the number one arbiter of corporate taste in the record industry. In 1965 Davis had vaulted from a position as attorney for Columbia Records to the top executive post, where he proceeded to ladle out money to *Rolling Stone* as a strategy for merchandising Columbia's records. Davis handed out money so frenetically that he became confused over its disposition. According to legal papers filed by CBS, large hunks of it found their way into his own pocket to support his hip life-style. Davis' gamesmanship was terminated in May 1973 when he was fired by CBS and served with a civil complaint alleging he had charged over fifty thousand dollars in personal expenses to his business account.

Meanwhile *Rolling Stone* became a critical, indispensable part of the youth culture and it scored major journalistic scoops, climaxing its efforts with an inside report on Patty Hearst's sojourn in the underground during her kidnapping.

And with Clive Davis' unceremonious exit from the scene, Wenner found a new multimillionaire to subsidize him. Max

Palevsky was a striking beneficiary of America's new technological age. He had hatched a fortune from the computer business. Formerly a poorly paid science instructor at UCLA, Palevsky scraped together twenty thousand dollars and started a computer softwares company, Scientific Data Systems. Within ten years, Palevsky was able to sell his firm to Xerox for close to a million dollars. Thanks to the terms of the purchase, Palevsky, who owned a healthy share of SDS stock, ended up as the single largest shareholder in Xerox and eventually reaped over fifty million dollars.

Palevsky was in his mid-forties, reportedly bored and seething with restlessness, and like many balding middle-agers, he had become inordinately fascinated with the youth scene. Looking for rejuvenation, he met Wenner and wrote a sizable check to *Rolling Stone* when the magazine was in one of its periods of financial stress.

However, the bond between Palevsky and Wenner was merely a mercenary business deal. Palevsky had relieved the *Rolling Stone*'s financial troubles with a check for two hundred thousand dollars, in return for which he demanded a percentage of the stock and an additional amount based upon the firm's earnings' performance. Under Palevsky's direction, the magazine made a vigorous financial rebound but Palevsky's tenure proved to be a brief one. The man had made a fortune in the computer business by using traditional capitalist methods of efficiency. His fascination with hallucinogenics and belly wiggling was not sufficient to erase his ingrained business sense and he fought with Wenner over the latter's alleged operational inefficiencies. Finally, he bowed out.

The exit of Palevsky was coupled with another crisis, one that threatened the magazine's very identity. The young people of the 1960s were struck with the ultimate fate of all human beings: they were forced to grow up. The Vietnam War came to an end. The Weathermen became corporation lawyers. The shock therapy of rock and roll had begun to wear off. It was no longer a music of revolution; it had become the music of the Establishment, consecrated by the huge profits pouring in from the citadels of capitalist enterprise. The innocence of rock had died. The Beatles were gone from the scene; new groups were playing Madison Square Garden for forty thousand dollars a night.

161

Actually, the euphoria of innocence had been shattered irretrievably during a nightmarish outburst of violence at a rock concert given in Altamont Raceway in the San Francisco suburbs in December 1969. Four young hippies were knifed to death by a member of Hell's Angels, a motorcycle band, as Mick Jagger and the Rolling Stones rocked and rolled on a platform above. Scores were left stunned with blood flowing from their mouths.

Altamont was the burial ground of the youth culture of innocence and it occurred appropriately as the decade was nearing its end. Reminisces one reporter who covered Altamont for *Rolling Stone,* "It was probably the worst day of my life—it was the ugliest, most depressing situation I'd ever been involved in. For the next three years there was not a single day when I did not think about Altamont. I stopped listening to music for a long time. I didn't want anything around me that reminded me of Altamont."

Wenner, who had an uncanny instinct for survival, came to the conclusion after Altamont that *Rolling Stone* would have to broaden its appeal beyond the rock scene in order to prosper. And as America entered the 1970s, the magazine turned to the greener pastures of the political arena, concentrating on left-wing politics.

In the same way that Wenner had impressed recording executives with his ability to stampede young music listeners into the record stores, he demonstrated to liberal candidates that he had enormous influence over the "youth vote." And with that link to the Establishment forged, *Rolling Stone* had arrived. The four-letter words were deleted and the magazine received its final consecration in the American pantheon: it was accepted for distribution in the nation's supermarkets. The Safeway chain began peddling copies to curious, susceptible housewives. *Rolling Stone* had successfully made the transition from mainlining to mainstreaming.

The Establishment press fell all over itself to shower Wenner with eulogies. *Time* magazine, which only a few years previously in a report on the youth culture had totally ignored him, now did a fulsome profile on Wenner. The chubby-faced publishing tycoon, all of thirty years old, became the darling of the media. One austere publication hailed him as "a young publishing genius." The *Columbia Journalism Review,* the bible

162

of the trade, eulogized Wenner for being the spokesman of "an entire generation of young Americans." The groves of academe were no less hasty in bestowing their accolades. Columbia University bestowed on *Rolling Stone* a National Magazine Award.

The old order had changed, giving way emphatically to the new. Gone were the obscene phrases, the irreverent thumb-on-the-nose attitude. Now that blue chip corporations like Colgate, Polaroid, Mobil and Toyota were besieging Wenner to advertise their merchandise in his pages, it behooved *Rolling Stone*, like Caesar's wife, to be above suspicion. When a picture of a girl, posed in a way that implied the possibility of fellatio, reached Wenner's desk, the editor struck the illustration from the issue.

In the fall of 1976 the publisher and the *Rolling Stone* moved from their headquarters in San Francisco into Clay Felker's backyard in Manhattan. The publication, which had been started on an investment of seventy-five hundred dollars, had reached a circulation base of six hundred thousand readers with billings exceeding eight million dollars annually.

Ensconced in Manhattan, Wenner made a flamboyant debut among the Beautiful People, giving a star-studded party to help raise money for Jimmy Carter's 1976 presidential campaign. Today the publisher socializes with Walter Cronkite and Ted Kennedy and shows up at the latest film screenings with the likes of Jackie Onassis. His magazine has become a barometer of trends, no longer counter-trends. It increasingly covers political celebrities and show-business personalities. It has run profiles of Princess Caroline of Monaco and Diana Vreeland, the high priestess of the fashion industry. Jack Ford, the son of the ex-President, was tapped by Wenner for an executive position with a new magazine the publisher launched in 1977 devoted to the outdoors and called *Outside*.

Despite its ascent to the mountaintop of trendy respectability, *Rolling Stone* continues to attract a startlingly young readership. The median age of its readers is under twenty-five. With its circulation of over six hundred thousand, *Rolling Stone* exerts an influence far greater than the number of its readers. For all its concessions to the Establishment, it remains a cult magazine.

In the spring of 1979 Wenner bobbed up wearing another

corporate hat. The previous fall, Daniel Filipacchi, a wealthy French publisher, resurrected *Look,* the celebrated picture magazine formerly owned by Gardner Cowles and the leading rival of Henry Luce's *Life.*

In May 1979, Filipacchi, who had lost seven million dollars in his *Look* venture, held talks with Wenner. The two agreed to go into partnership, merging the circulation, finance and service departments of *Rolling Stone* with *Look* while keeping the editorial and advertising operations of both magazines independent. While Filipacchi insisted he had not sold Wenner any significant equity in *Look,* he was so impressed with the publishing and managerial talents of the thirty-three-year-old founder of *Rolling Stone* that he asked him to become publisher and editor of *Look.* As a first step, Wenner declared he would convert the biweekly *Look* into a monthly journal.

The consolidation of the financial and service departments of the two magazines seemed to some observers like two families "hit with shrinking pocketbooks, deciding to move into one house to save expenses." In any event, Wenner continued to have his fling. *Look,* once the pride and joy of establishment publisher Gardner Cowles, came into the hands of a publisher who grew up in the American Underground.

10

The Massage Is the Medium

Pink Shots and Glossy Centerfolds—the
Eruption of the Sex Magazine Industry

═══════════════

TODAY THE MOST rapidly growing branch of the American
magazine industry is a new kind of pictorial journalism
undreamed of by the old-time editors of *Harper's* or *Leslie's
Weekly*—hard-core sexuality. Over the ages pornography has
had a venerable pedigree. *"Porne"* is the ancient Greek word
for "prostitute" and pornography means a "description of the
manners" of whores. Since the freedom to whore is currently
venerated as if it had been enshrined in the Bill of Rights, the
manners of harlots have become the manners of the masses.

For centuries the intelligentsia of the Western world has
battled for the right of erotic literature and art to be disseminated without government censorship. But there has never
been a consensus as to what eroticism is. Perhaps the most
lucid definition has been given by Blaise Cendrars, a French
writer who in speaking of Henry Miller's *Tropic of Cancer*
remarked, *"Il y a des passages qui m'avaient fait bander"*—"There
are passages which gave me an erection."

In the past pornography was entwined with theology. The
rapist was often pictured in the Middle Ages as the Devil, and
graphic paintings warned viewers of the rapacity of Beelzebub
if one allowed him to creep into human affairs. The pornogra-

pher appeared before the public without fear of reprisal since he paraded in the vestments of the preacher.

With time, erotic literature of secular origin became the privilege and pastime of an educated minority. The intellectual elite fought aggressively against government censorship of Joyce's *Ulysses* and Lawrence's *Lady Chatterely's Lover*. Today, eroticism has become democratized into pornography, and the literature of frank, open sex is aimed not at the highbrows, but at the fantasies of the blue-collar masses. When erotic literature was limited to high-priced, exotically bound editions available only to the few, the publishers of *Lady Chatterley's Lover* were hauled into court for daring to publish a paperback edition for the millions. The prosecutor asked the defendant, "Would you let your servant read this book?" Today the servant occupies his master's seat at the gourmet banquet of erotica.

Nowhere is today's pornography bigger business than in America's magazines. The publishers of sex periodicals are exuberantly raking in profits from over twenty million Americans who peruse them avidly each month. Indeed, "skin" magazines currently represent the biggest growth area in the entire magazine field.

The first magazine publisher to fully appreciate the profits to be made from stroking the human libido was Hugh Hefner, the founder of *Playboy*. Hefner started out modestly. He owned the rights to calendar photographs displaying the undraped charms of Marilyn Monroe and he hit upon the idea of starting a magazine exhibiting centerfolds of womankind in the buff. Hefner and several associates scraped together the seed money and put out their first issue of *Playboy* without even placing a date on it for fear there might not be a second issue. They were wrong. *Playboy* succeeded beyond their wildest hopes and in 1979 celebrated its twenty-fifth anniversary with a round of festivities broadcast on television during which Hefner announced that in addition to his magazine and book publishing company and string of Playboy Clubs in nine United States cities and three abroad, he planned to expand into pay TV, cassette and disc production. He now projects for cable TV an "electronic Playboy" which he feels "will accomplish in the 1980s on cable what we did in the magazine in the Nineteen-Fifties. There will be some nudity and it will be more adult than what is normally shown on TV." Hefner rides around in his $5-million personal plane, and he has a further consolation not to be sneezed at—the devotion of his twenty-eight-year-old daughter, Christie, who has joined *Playboy* and risen to become a company vice-president. This father-and-daughter relationship (Hefner has named Christie the heiress apparent to his $250-million empire) is unusual in an age marked by the alienation of youth from their parents and the dissolution of family relationships.

As for *Playboy*'s current readership, the message Hefner and his daughter are sending to advertisers is that its readers have grown up, they are no longer titillated simply by sex. The flower children and draft card burners of the 1960s, runs *Playboy*'s new pitch, are prosperous young businessmen today. "Those young men who wouldn't sell out in 1967," *Playboy* ads proclaim, "are buying in 1980 . . . 13 years later. They haven't lost one iota of their intensity; they have just totally redirected it. They've traded the SDS for IBM and ITT." If American business wishes to reach this market of mature young men, *Playboy* is their magazine.

In short, *Playboy*'s new readership, continue its promoters, are those erstwhile long-haired unshaven young men who have become the nation's rising new executives, its biggest consumers of material wealth. The new *Playboy* consumer drives a Corniche and lives in a fancy home because the erstwhile hippie "can afford most things now." The old guitar strummer and joints smoker at Woodstock has "matured" into a "mellow" man who "buys and buys and buys" to "really enjoy his experience." The *Playboy* reader has an insatiable lust for life. Declares a "typical Playboy reader" in a recent ad, "For years the important thing in my life was gloss; now it's texture." It is on this development that *Playboy* has hitched its strategy for survival.

And a struggle for survival is precisely the nature of the conflict in which the Hefners are now engaged. In 1969, Bob Guccione bowed with an American edition of *Penthouse* designed to outdo Hefner in the lavish display of sexuality. He presented pictures of young women showing their pubic hair, an item Hefner had modestly airbrushed or otherwise concealed. Guccione proudly lists as his publishing accomplishments the first photos of multiple sex—three and more couplings, his first display of complete frontal male nakedness and the sexual games of lesbians. He was also the first to show the male penis in an erected state, he boasts.

Robert Charles Joseph Edward Sabatini Guccione, born in Brooklyn in December 1930, was reared as a strict Roman Catholic and served as an altar boy. He prepared to enter the priesthood and went into a seminary, but several months there cooled him of his ardor for taking the vows.

He fell in love, married at eighteen and decided he would be a painter. "There is nothing closer to God's earth than an artist," he told one interviewer. Guccione went to Rome to study painting but found it was easier to make money doing caricatures, and so he worked as a free-lance cartoonist in addition to writing a humor column for college newspapers. He tried his hand at advertising copy, designed greeting cards and wrote direct-mail merchandising pieces. His marriage on the rocks, he turned up in Tangiers, then in London, drawing cartoons for British newspapers. Finally, he hit upon a bright commercial idea. He collected pin-up pictures of undraped females and peddled them through the mail, expanding his activities by merchandising the back issues of American girlie magazines imported from the States.

In 1965 Guccione took an even more ambitious step. He noticed that the British edition of *Playboy* was selling extremely well and that there was no periodical in the field to challenge its success. He figured the opportunity was ripe to launch such a publication. Having no money, he went knocking on doors soliciting funds. But nobody offered any. So he decided to try another device. An acquaintance taught him the basic elements of fashion photography in a single afternoon. The following day Guccione designed a brochure displaying a bevy of pulchritudinous ladies posed in various stages of undress. He induced a printer to produce his brochure on credit and mailed twenty thousand to people on a list compiled for him by a friend. It was a helter-skelter list, studded with the most unlikely prospects for a brochure of ladies in the nude— teenage schoolgirls, elderly retirees living on pensions, Anglican clergymen, the wives of members of Parliament.

Guccione's mailing triggered an uproar throughout Britain. Letters from infuriated citizens flooded the newspapers. Politicians rose in the House of Commons to demand the repeal of

Guccione's mailing privileges, and the Government filed charges against him under the Post Office Act which barred the mailing of obscene matter. Since this was not a criminal but a civil offense, the authorities couldn't forcibly enter Guccione's house to serve him with a writ. They had to lurk outside waiting to pounce on him the moment he emerged. The Government summoned him to answer the charges, but Guccione battled desperately for time. He barricaded himself in his residence for fourteen days while policemen patrolled in front of it, intent on nabbing him. During this period he used the phone to edit his forthcoming magazine which was being rushed out by a makeshift staff in a nearby office. Proofs were sneaked into his mailbox at night. Finally, when the magazine was ready for the presses, Guccione walked out of his house, accepted the writ and was fined £110.

The publicity generated by the mailing of the brochure, followed by the uproar in the House of Commons and the wide press coverage of his arrest, insured that the launching of *Penthouse* would be a huge success. The initial press run of over a hundred thousand copies was sold out in five days.

During the first few months while *Penthouse* was establishing its foothold, one reader wrote Guccione that he was in the practice of taking his teenage daughter across his knee and spanking her on the buttocks when she did something naughty. Guccione printed the letter and was astonished by the public response. Letters piled in praising and denouncing the father. Guccione realized he had stumbled on a bonanza. He launched a column soliciting letters on the sexual experiences of his readers and he was deluged with mail from people describing their hangups, dalliances and fantasies for the edification of other voyeurs. This became the hit feature of the magazine.

Encouraged by his London success, Guccione decided to try an American edition of *Penthouse* challenging *Playboy* on its home territory. He did this on a shoestring of $150,000, consisting mostly of borrowed money. The magazine was launched in the fall of 1969. Guccione took lethal aim at Hefner's "rabbit" and after suffering initial losses began relentlessly closing the circulation gap. By 1973 *Penthouse* had climbed to over 3 million in readership, 95 percent of which was derived through newsstand sales, compared with 75 percent for *Playboy,* sparing Guccione the heavy expense of mail promotion to lure subscribers. By 1975 *Penthouse* threatened to reach and overtake *Playboy* as the number one magazine in its field.

Nevertheless, Hefner seemed entrenched. He had been on the scene for sixteen years and *Playboy* enjoyed a readership of over five million. For three years after *Penthouse* was launched in America, Hefner maintained a stony silence, presumably fantasizing that *Penthouse* would die if he refused to recognize its existence. However, as the *Penthouse* circulation continued to climb, Hefner made a countermove, launching *Oui,* which exuded a raunchier atmosphere than *Playboy,* one closer to the spirit of *Penthouse.*

The battle heated up. Guccione hired Xaviera Hollander, the "Happy Hooker," to give sex advice to the *Penthouse* lovelorn, and Hefner retaliated by recruiting Linda Lovelace, the star of *Deep Throat,* to offer advice to the *Playboy* faithful.

In 1974 *Playboy* was outselling *Penthouse* by six to one. By 1977, its lead had been cut to a nose. (*Playboy*'s circulation had fallen to below the 5.5-million mark and Guccione's readership had risen to almost 5 million.) Moreover, *Hustler* and *High Society,* two other skin sheets, were moving up rapidly on the track. Despite Hefner's feverish ministrations, Guccione continued to close the gap. While *Playboy*'s circulation had been steadily eroding from a level of over 7 million in 1972, *Penthouse*'s circulation continued skyrocketing. At the end of 1977, the two magazines were running neck and neck with a guaranteed circulation of 4.5 million apiece.

The publishers have engaged in acrimonious recriminations over each other's tactics. In 1974 *Penthouse* filed a forty-million-dollar suit against Playboy Enterprises charging that the latter, to boost its advertising, informed potential space buyers that *Penthouse* had inflated its guaranteed circulation figures. "When a guy resorts to those sorts of tactics," exploded Guccione, "it can only mean he's panicking." Hefner responded by claiming that *Penthouse* had infringed upon its trademark in taking out ads mocking the *Playboy* rabbit.

Guccione today is one of the Beautiful People. He lives on Manhattan's Upper East Side in an apartment once owned by Judy Garland. Many of his French and Italian furnishings also belonged to her. He has plunged heavy sums into backing movies such as *Chinatown* and *The Longest Yard*. And he pursued a hunch to make a film on the Roman emperor Caligula, fabled for his insanity and his marathon sex orgies. Envisaging the movie as a Cecil B. De Mille epic replete with explicit sex, Guccione persuaded writer Gore Vidal to prepare a script to be entitled *Gore Vidal's Caligula*. Guccione put fifteen million dollars into producing the film, building sets that lavishly re-created ancient Rome. He selected as director a man whose only previous film had been work on a spy thriller set in a Nazi whorehouse. Vidal balked at changes he was asked to make in his script, walked out, and the most massive sexual debauches ever promised for moviegoers seemed on the brink of abortion. But Guccione pressed on with his project, hired another director and completed what has turned out to be the most expensive porno movie yet made, at a cost of over seventeen million dollars.

Meanwhile, other publishers have rushed in with even more explicitness than that displayed by *Penthouse*. Larry Flynt's *Hustler* became the third largest seller after *Playboy* and *Penthouse*. Flynt exuberantly reveled in the sex he tossed around, boasting that his was "a magazine that nobody quotes." Bowing in 1974 with a sale of 160,000 copies, *Hustler* within two years was selling 2 million copies a month and earning $20 million in annual revenues.

Meanwhile the business kept proliferating. A rash of sex magazines has hit the newsstands, vying to outdo one another in sensationalism. Each publisher peddles his product claiming nuances that make his magazine distinct from its competitors. One publisher boasts, "Think of the largest breasts imaginable—our girls have larger ones." Another publisher runs pictures of a "contortionist with no pubic hair." The pressure on editorial ingenuity is becoming acute as the demand for novel journalistic aphrodisiacs is inexhaustible.

One fascinating aspect of the sex publishing industry is that key editorial positions are held by women who don't at all mind making a living out of publicly displaying female genitalia. This may be an Age of Feminism and Gloria Steinem may grumble against the practice of women being used as sex objects to gratify the lust of the chauvinist male. But a surprising number of females don't hesitate to make a buck in glossy photoprint. Bob Guccione, the publisher of *Penthouse*, hired a female managing editor, and his closest companion and associate publisher is a woman. At least one cartoon editor for *Playboy* and its affiliate *Oui* has been a woman, as was *Playboy*'s photography editor on the west coast.

Some of these women insist that the publications they work for present a "less degrading" picture of the American female than the more genteel women's magazines do. Avers a female executive of *Penthouse*, "I don't think we present an offensive view of women. There's something much more obnoxious about the articles in women's magazines telling you ten ways to snare a man, although they're much more subtle." And Christie Hefner herself argues, "A damaging perspective of women is much more likely in a women's magazine which tells you the way to happiness is a clean kitchen sink, a white laundry or the right man." In short, imply these feminist editors, there's much more dignity in a woman spreading her legs before a national audience than doing the laundry for her husband and children.

In one striking instance a woman rose to become the head of one of the raciest magazines in the business—Sue Richards, who was the publisher of *High Society*, until July 1977 when another female succeeded her. Ms. Richards, a comely lass, started out as just another female "drudge," one of the millions of unemancipated women slaving at dull jobs; then she suddenly found her métier. She met Harry Reems, the superstar stud of pornographic movies and her mission in life became clear in a way as startling as the conversion of the prophet Paul on the road to Damascus. Reems persuaded Ms. Richards to try her hand at making porno movies. She did ten of them. "They were the most positive sexual awakening of my life," she recalls. "They were good money and now I know the difference between good sex and bad sex."

Ms. Richards, together with financial backers, entered the glossy sex sweepstakes with a magazine that, unlike its competitors, appeals to a substantial percentage of women readers. Fully 20 percent of its voyeuristic following is female. Observes Ms. Richards, "I think women can be turned on by female nudity, at least I can be." Believing in practicing what she preaches, the attractive young publisher featured herself in titillating poses in her magazine. Ms. Richards has received ecstatic letters from male readers raving over the size and quality of her most intimate endowments. Reporters have flocked around her, entranced at the opportunity of interviewing the stunning young publisher who posed for her own pages. "I was a little worried about dealing with [advertising] clients after I first posed, but it's been okay . . . about 50 percent of them came on back to me."

Ms. Richards insists that the majority of the magazine's readers are not sex fanatics or perverts, but ordinary people who "are interested in fantasy rather than an active sex life." Asked by a reporter what her mother thought of her success she answers, "She's mildly receptive to the magazine; at least her daughter was doing something on her own."

One sex publisher who has built a cult following by spicing his raunchy offerings with political and social satire is Al Goldstein, a former insurance salesman who in 1968 got together with a friend named Jim Buckley (no relation to the conservative politician) and launched *Screw* magazine. Just as Hugh Hefner built an image of himself as an urbane swinger, Goldstein promoted himself as a fumbling *schlemiel* who was constantly failing with women and needed to pay hookers for sexual gratification. The formula tapped an amazing response from lonely, sexually starved men who, Goldstein observes, "have a right to their pleasures just like the rest of humanity."

On one occasion Goldstein declared that *Screw* is aimed "at college professors at Harvard who secretly masturbate." And he added, "seriously, a demographic survey showed that our readership is just behind that of *The New Yorker*, which either means we have a brilliant readership or that the people interviewed are psychopathic liars."

Goldstein has given sexuality a sociological cutting edge, coupling pornography with irreverent politics to stimulate the intelligentsia in their upper as well as nether regions. The publisher of *Screw* has taken on America's system of justice, the Catholic Church, the Nixon Administration, the FBI and "capitalist imperialism." The U.S. Government indicted him for a piece he published, written by a female contributor, who indulged in a fantasy of what sexual intercourse would be like with John Lindsay and Norman Mailer, when both were running for mayor of New York. (The author decided that if the phone rang in the middle of copulation, Lindsay would stop to answer it, but Mailer would continue humping.) The police confiscated the issue for being "unduly offensive." Goldstein has been arrested numerous times, has spent almost a quarter of a million dollars on lawyers and court expenses, and as this book is being written, was fighting to have his latest conviction overturned.

The irreverent publisher has been close to feminist circles and he has been mercilessly needled by them. One friend taunted him, "If you make all that sex available to men through the ads run in *Screw,* why don't you do the same for women?" Goldstein replied that it would be futile, since women aren't willing to pay for sex. To prove his thesis, he prepared an ad for a massage parlor for women, a pure invention of his, which he ran in an issue of *Screw.* The ad announced that now sex was available for women at "The Golden Tongue Salon." The address he inserted was the location of a police station on Fifty-first Street. The cops who received calls from venturesome females took it as a huge joke and invited them over. But the station captain was furious and had Goldstein arrested.

Recently the publisher's imagination took a heady new turn. He ran pictures in *Screw* showing "Poppin' Fresh," a doughy character created by Pillsbury, the food products company, for its advertising campaign, having sexual intercourse with a girl friend, "Poppie Fresh," in a skillet over the Pillsbury advertising slogan, "Nothing says lovin' like something from the oven . . . and Pillsbury says it best." The Pillsbury people weren't amused with Goldstein's wit. They slapped a $1.5-million suit against the publisher for copyright and trademark infringement, charging that "'Poppin' Fresh' is a corporate spokesman" who always is presented so as to "project an image of wholesomeness and decency." Goldstein argues that the Pillsbury suit infringes on his rights of free speech and that by bringing him into court the baking firm has become "a national laughing stock."

When Goldstein began to prosper he bought out Buckley, his partner, for half a million dollars and launched a cable TV program show called *Midnight Blue* which peddled "soft core" porn entertainment. Ironically *Midnight Blue* was carried in New York City by Manhattan Cable TV, a subsidiary of Time, Inc., the publisher of the venerable establishment magazine. *Time* roundly blasted the pornographic industry in a cover story but confessed in a footnote to its polemic that its own

174

subsidiary carried Goldstein's *Midnight Blue* program. It apologized for this, explaining that "as a condition of their franchises" cable TV companies must turn over time on their channels for public access by individuals and community groups. Manhattan Cable, *Time* claimed, was unhappy about *Midnight Blue*.

While Al Goldstein's aim is to provoke satirical laughter as well as sexual titillation, Larry Flynt, the publisher of *Hustler*, is considerably less pretentious. Although for centuries pornography under the label "eroticism" has been a hobby of the intellectual elite, Larry Flynt, a man with no formal education, launched a magazine designed frankly to appeal to the fantasies of America's steelworkers and truck drivers. Flynt, who has conceded that his chief aim was to "become a millionaire whether by robbing a bank or publishing a magazine," was indicted for peddling obscenity and convicted by a jury in Ohio. While his case was under appeal the publisher showed up on a platform to address an audience in Waterloo, Iowa, on the "Power of Positive Thinking." Sharing the platform with Flynt was another positive thinker, Bert Lance, a Georgia banker who at the time was serving as President Carter's budget director. Flynt told the audience he had developed a tremendously positive attitude towards life because he had recently been converted into a "Christian patriarch" who was "willing to die for his God." It turned out that Flynt had received the Word of God from none other than President Carter's sister, Ruth Carter Stapleton, an indefatigable saver of lost souls. Shortly after his conversion newspaper reporters were surprised to see Larry Flynt at a nightclub in Newport, Kentucky, celebrated for its striptease shows. The publisher assured the press that his visits to nightclubs did not in the least conflict with his new Christian beliefs. "There are more integrated bordellos than churches," he pointed out. "If all my critics who worry about me would work as hard at Christianity, we would make it a safer world for Christ to return to. We can't wait 2,000 more years."

This "born again" Christian, who has discovered that the purest form of democracy exists in whorehouses, narrowly missed suffering a martyr's end. In March 1978, after spending the morning testifying at his obscenity trial, he was shot down and seriously wounded in the street by two men who jumped out of a Chevrolet. President Carter's sister rushed to the hospital to pray for his recovery.

Paralyzed by his wounds, Flynt underwent physical therapy in the hospital. According to Paul Krassner, one of Flynt's colleagues who took over as editor of *Hustler* while the publisher was convalescing, Flynt had planned before being shot to show his gratitude to Ruth Stapleton for converting him to God in the finest way he knew how, by inviting her to pose dressed in pink for a centerfold in *Hustler* and running a headline on the cover page informing his readers "Ruth Carter Stapleton Shows Pink For *Hustler:* What Will Jimmy Think?"

At the conclusion of his obscenity trial Larry Flynt was convicted on eleven counts and given eleven consecutive but suspended one-year jail terms, in addition to being fined $27,500.

The publisher of *Hustler* has amassed a fortune of over $10 million but has spent much of it. He spent thousands of dollars running down leads on the assassination of President Kennedy. He bought a half-million-dollar home in Colorado and a $4.5-million private airplane which he subsequently replaced with a smaller, more modest one. He started a money-losing magazine called *Ohio,* which at this writing he has been trying to sell. He purchased the Los Angeles *Free Press* and then folded it. And he gave over $250,000 to Ruth Stapleton to help her carry on her missionary activities.

All things considered, in studying the output of Hefner, Guccione and company, future historians of our contemporary mores could scarcely be blamed if they concluded that Americans live for and think about nothing but sex.

Yet this conclusion could be erroneous, if the result of a Lou Harris poll conducted in conjunction with ABC News in the spring of 1980 has any validity. The pollsters who asked men and women of all age groups across the nation to rank the importance of their fifteen top leisure activities came up with fascinating results. For the men interviewed, having sex ranked only in the eighth position of importance. For women, it ranked ninth. Given priority ahead of sex by the males were eating, watching television, fixing things around the house, listening to the radio or music, reading books, engaging in outdoor activities. For women, eating, reading books, listening

176

to music, watching television, participating in social activities were deemed more important than having sex.

If this poll is any indication of the true state of affairs, then the profitability of the skin game may well lie in its being a shell game. Perhaps people are buying all those flesh magazines and flocking to those blue movies because sexual fantasizing is taking the place of active sex. Or perhaps the Harris-ABC pollsters asked their questions of the wrong people, the handful who have miraculously managed to keep their heads together in these febrile times.

11

The Triumph of Optimism

Hard Knocks for *Harper's* and the Incredible
Success of DeWitt Wallace's *Reader's Digest*

SINCE THE SECOND World War, the growing egalitarianism of
American society has swept everything before it. There are no
contemporary H. L. Menckens dedicated to pulverizing the
pretensions of the Booboisie. Writers with Mencken's critical
gifts and lethal vocabulary have been co-opted by the Establishment to receive its heady emoluments. Elitism has become a
dirty word in the lexicon of today's society.

A striking symptom of the decline of elitist values is the
plight of the highbrow magazines which once took pride in
writing for the educated elite. Prominent among them is
Harper's, founded in the middle of the nineteenth century by
the Harper family, which also launched a book publishing
enterprise. For over a hundred years *Harper's* played an
influential role in America's social, political and literary life. It
published the works of America's and England's leading
novelists, was the first, for example, to serialize the books of
Dickens, Thackeray, Trollope, and the writings of Mark
Twain, Stephen Crane and Bret Harte. *Harper's* first editor,
Henry J. Raymond, who subsequently became the manager of
Abraham Lincoln's campaign in 1864, turned the magazine
into an internationally prestigious journal of sociology and

economics. *Harper's* also scored heavily in political journalism, highlighting its achievements with a series of brilliant articles and Thomas Nast cartoons that exposed the corrupt activities of New York's notorious Tweed gang near the close of the last century.

For a century *Harper's* survived the ups and downs of the American economy, but within the last decade the pressures of social change have been close to overwhelming. Thanks to the emergence of television and its overpowering influence, and the general decline of elitist values, *Harper's* had to struggle along, suffering from a drastic drop in circulation and revenues until it was picked up by a communications empire run by the Minneapolis Star and Tribune Company in 1965. But its losses continued. In the secure old world into which it had been born, *Harper's* had been able to survive without carrying any advertising except on behalf of its affiliated book publishing company, but by the summer of 1980 the social and economic milieu had changed beyond recognition. The owner of *Harper's*, fed up with the mounting losses from its cultural tribune, was ready to throw in the sponge.

However, executives of two nonprofit foundations, operating outside the arena of money-making and able to indulge in the luxury of preserving a cultural heirloom, came to the rescue of the dying magazine. Jay Roderick MacArthur, the fifty-eight-year-old son of John D. MacArthur, who had made a fortune in the insurance business and who had created the John D. and Catherine MacArthur Foundation in Chicago, launched negotiations to try to save *Harper's*. Jay MacArthur had a background in journalism which made him especially sympathetic to its plight. He had cut his teeth as a newspaperman in Paris on the staff of the *International Herald Tribune* and had also put money into publishing a magazine of theater arts. (MacArthur's uncle, Charles MacArthur, along with Ben Hecht, wrote *The Front Page*, a memorable play about the newspaper business.) Adding to MacArthur's financial clout was the willingness of the Atlantic Richfield Foundation—an organization established seventeen years previously by the big oil company—to join with him in the purchase of *Harper's*. Robert O. Anderson, the chief executive officer of the Atlantic Richfield Company, is a man of cultural background, a lover of the arts and the chairman of the Aspen Institute for Humanistic Studies, an organization devoted to maintaining a liaison between the business community and the world of scholarship.

At the eleventh hour, *Harper's* magazine was bought by the MacArthur and the Atlantic Richfield foundations. While it has been rescued by the proverbial knights galloping in on their white chargers, in the view of many hard-bitten observers the future remains dismal for *Harper's* and similar publications. The notion of an elitist leadership establishing trends of thought and values for other Americans is anathema to businessmen, Madison Avenue advertisers and all others who have a vested interest in a homogenized society where sheeplike behavior is essential to the consumption of the mass-produced goods and services spewed forth by American industry. As Lee Lescaze, writing on the demise of elitism in today's culture, observes, "The highbrow magazines are dying as a result of judgments made on Madison Avenue where they have little support. In a world in which magazines are discussed in terms of 'revenue streams' and 'revenue per reader' . . . [cultural] magazines [like *Harper's*] are seen as too old and too stodgy."

"The trouble," says a leading Madison Avenue magnate, is that *Harper's* readership "has shown no vitality. When advertisers look at this magazine, they see old, gray people. They don't see young, vibrant audiences." "In 1980-speak," comments Lescaze, "young and vibrant people do not read long magazine articles. It is deemed impossible to be simultaneously vibrant and possessed of a long attention span." One's attention span need be only great enough to cope with *TV Guide* or the latest nude centerfold in *Penthouse*. Lengthy "thought" articles are indigestible to an audience whose ability to concentrate has been deflowered by years of television watching. Of the almost eight billion copies of magazines being bought annually, the top seller is *TV Guide* (Over one in every eight Americans buys a copy of *TV Guide*.) Ranked 120 in readership is the *Saturday Review*. The *Atlantic* is ranked 214, and *Harper's* is in the 245th spot.

If intellectualism has fallen on hard times—the *Saturday Review* and the *Atlantic* along with *Harper's* have undergone severe economic tribulation—the grassroots optimism of the *Reader's Digest* has triumphed beyond even its founders' expectations. The *Digest* isn't a magazine; it's a national monument, invulnerable, sacrosanct. It enjoys a worldwide readership greater than that of any other magazine (although in America it occupies the number two position, having been overtaken in recent years by *TV Guide*.) And it was founded by DeWitt and Lila Acheson Wallace, neither of whom had any previous experience in journalism. In launching the *Digest* in 1921, this husband-and-wife team staked their money on the belief that readers will respond to an optimistic view of the human race. Unlike the "put-down" magazines of the 1920s permeated with the sophisticated cynicism of H.L. Mencken and George Jean Nathan, the Wallaces pitched their appeal not to the nation's highbrows but to the grass-roots American.

The 1920s was an age of rampant skepticism. Smarty-pants pundits made a career of taking potshots at American Babbitry and the bourgeois values of the Bible Belt. But the Wallaces believed in the inherent decency of life, and their credo of uncompromising optimism which seemed to fly in the face of the prevalent mood proved to be resoundingly right. Group sex, narcissism and ego-massaging psychotherapy may be "in" today, but the huge readership of the *Reader's Digest* demonstrates that other values are also being deeply felt in America.

Over the years sophisticated critics have continued to ridicule the magazine. John Bainbridge, a writer on *The New Yorker*—that editorial haven for literary snobs—wrote of the *Digest* back in the 1930s: "The quality of optimism . . . is not strained. It drips from every issue as sweetly as syrup from the maple tree. It is a brave and tender philosophy that has been well stated in the optimist's creed displayed in the Mayflower Donut Shops, which adjures all wayfarers throughout life whatever may be their goal, to keep their eye upon the donut and not upon the hole." The *Digest* in its optimism, complained Bainbridge, preaches that misfortune, ill luck and evil must be endured since they result from the higher wisdom of the Almighty. It is the philosophy of Dr. Pangloss in Voltaire's *Candide*. This is the best of all possible worlds and our misfortunes are blessings in disguise.

Is death a tragedy? Not at all. It need not even be distressing. Confides the *Digest*, "Someday you are going to die and if you are like most of us you are probably afraid to die; you believe

181

that death will be unpleasant. In that you are wrong. It is not unpleasant to die."

Is it a tragedy for a mother to give birth to a mongoloid child? Not at all. One such mother wrote a piece for the *Digest* observing, "Agony can be made to account for something."

Is it a curse to be poor? Not necessarily, according to the *Digest*. For physical poverty may be the soil that nourishes a strong spiritual life. This the *Digest* preached during America's worst depression—in the 1930s when millions of Americans were out of work and thousands of former doctors, lawyers and bankers sold apples on street corners in order to survive. "I look back on my adventures in life," observed one *Digest* writer, "and think of the happiest people I ever met. They were mostly poverty-stricken." Material possessions, observed the *Digest*, can be an obstacle to spiritual fulfillment.

This spirit of unquenchable optimism has, as noted, brought down upon the heads of *Digest* editors the scorn of cynical jesters and abrasive wits. America's intelligentsia has had great fun at the expense of this homespun, foursquare philosophy. Nobody seems to like it except the magazine's sixteen million readers.

Moreover, the Deep Thinkers of America—those pundits who flourish in the groves of academe—have derided the *Digest*'s practice of condensing the wisdom of the ages for its readers. One writer, again in *The New Yorker*, observed: "If literature can be condensed like milk . . . the *Digest* has the most expert technical facility for doing it."

On the other hand, even condensed literature can have startling effects. When reporter John Hersey's 1944 story of John F. Kennedy's wartime exploits aboard PT-109 was published in *The New Yorker*, a magazine of relatively small circulation, the senior Kennedy saw a golden opportunity. Joseph P. Kennedy approached the editors of the *Reader's Digest*, where his conservative stance as Ambassador to England's Court of St. James's had won him friends, and suggested that they condense Hersey's article in the *Digest*. They readily agreed. The one hitch—*New Yorker* editor Harold Ross's refusal to allow a *New Yorker* piece to be reprinted in the plebeian *Reader's Digest*—was overcome when Kennedy shrewdly suggested that the *Digest*, instead of paying *The New Yorker* and the Kennedys, should donate all proceeds from the reprint to the wives and children of naval officers and seamen killed in the War.

The *Digest* condensation when it finally appeared focused the reader's attention almost exclusively on the courage of Jack Kennedy when the PT boat under his command was sunk by Japanese in the Solomon Islands.

Old Joe Kennedy was elated by this journalistic coup and he was justified in his enthusiasm. The impression was conveyed to millions of Americans that Jack Kennedy was an authentic war hero, and it proved to be an immensely powerful instrument for building young Jack's image, facilitating his entrance into politics and his rise to the Presidency.

In 1946, two years after the appearance of the War Hero story, Joe Kennedy entered his son in his first political contest, the Massachusetts primary which was being held to choose a Democratic candidate for Congress. The war was over. The electorate had been swelled by thousands of returning veterans and there was great uncertainty about how they would vote. To capitalize on the legend of Kennedy's heroism, the candidate's brain trust decided to order thousands of reprints of the PT-109 article and distribute them to every registered Democrat in the district. This *Digest* mailing to Boston voters, in the view of seasoned political observers, provided the impetus that led to Jack Kennedy's overwhelming victory.

Proponents of the *Digest*'s journalistic approach point out that Wallace and his editors have been the largest single force responsible for getting the American public to read nonfiction. Until the advent of the *Digest*, American books and magazines were heavily fiction-oriented. It was axiomatic that the public had no interest in serious news topics. However, thanks to the tremendous impact of the *Digest*, magazine and book publishers have swung over to presenting serious subjects for discussion.

The image that the *Digest*, as the world's most widely-read magazine, has promoted of America abroad has also had enormous influence. The homespun, upbeat spirit of the *Digest*, presenting Americans as inherently decent, spiritual people, has been in sharp contrast to the usual image exported by Hollywood films, *Playboy* and *Penthouse*, which so often portray America as a grasping, acquisitive and cynical society.

183

"Articles published over the years in the *Digest* extolling the triumphs of George Carver and Helen Keller," observes one social commentator, "have probably done more than all the U.S. Government's propaganda combined to allay the fears, prejudices and misconceptions of the U.S. in other lands."

At the same time, critics of the *Digest* have charged that there is another side to the magazine's homespun optimism—a political slant that has been heavily conservative. Its preaching of restraint and discipline rather than self-indulgence, its concept of a universe that distributes rewards and punishments as the results of individual efforts and transgressions and its campaign against permissiveness are all facets of its conservative (some would say reactionary) credo.

During the Second World War and in the early postwar years the *Digest* lured into its editorial sanctum a number of flamboyant, eccentric editors. But the single most powerful voice on the *Digest* (after Wallace) for a period of eight years before he died in 1952 was Fulton Oursler, who moved from Bernarr Macfadden's publications to join the *Digest* staff. Oursler had promoted Macfadden's revivalist journalism with extraordinary success. A Protestant by birth, he had become an agnostic in his early adulthood and at the same time a skilled amateur magician. Having gone through a period of financial and emotional setbacks, however, including the agony of watching his wife turn into a self-destructive alcoholic, Oursler underwent a spiritual crisis and converted to Catholicism as a result of pilgrimages he made to the Holy Land. He also wrote a book as a result of his travels called *The Greatest Story Ever Told*, which became one of the biggest sellers of all time. Oursler dramatized his story of Jesus for radio presentation and it became one of the most successful programs on the networks. His feel for the pulse of America coupled with his own spiritual redemption proved irresistible to DeWitt Wallace. Oursler became a senior editor of the *Digest* and went around the country making speeches to educators and business groups, serving as a missionary for Wallace. Over seventy of Oursler's articles eventually appeared between the covers of the *Digest,* far more than any other contributor.

William Roy DeWitt Wallace was the son of a minister and classical scholar, the grandson of a clergyman, the son-in-law of a minister and the brother-in-law of two other members of the cloth.

He quit college in his sophomore year and moved around restlessly, landing a series of jobs and getting sacked from them. He ended up in the army, served during the First World War in the Argonne campaign as an infantryman with the 35th Division, and was severely wounded by shrapnel. While lying on his back in the hospital, he had plenty of time to turn over an idea for a magazine that had taken root in his mind. Most magazine articles, he was convinced, were too long and took too much time for busy people to read. Indeed, readers who wished to be kept well informed usually found that the kernel of really worthwhile information lay buried beneath reams of unnecessary verbiage. Few people had the leisure or the money to dig through all the magazines published each month and extract the vital information they needed to keep abreast of developments. Wallace was fascinated with the possibility of doing this job for the reader—that is, leafing through and extracting the most valuable articles presented in the American press and condensing them between the covers of a magazine small enough for a man to carry around in his pocket or a woman in her pocketbook. Moreover, this magazine wouldn't carry a line of advertising.

Wallace returned home after the Armistice and took a job with the publicity department of the Westinghouse Electric Company. When he was fired because the management decided to cut its payroll, he vowed he would never again depend on anybody else's paycheck. Wallace drew up a prospectus for his new magazine and asked his brother Benjamin and their father to lend him three hundred dollars apiece to help prepare copies of his prospectus and a dummy of the publication. And he went around to other friends scraping together a grubstake of five thousand dollars.

He put together thirty-one articles culled and condensed from a spectrum of the nation's magazines, worked up two hundred copies of his pocket-sized model, and mailed them to a dozen leading magazine publishers in Manhattan plus a number of wealthy backers from whom he hoped to raise more funds. The response was nil. All the magazine publishers turned thumbs down on the project.

Despite the chilling reception he met with, Wallace clung to his idea and he encountered someone who shared his enthusiasm. She was Lila Bell Acheson, the daughter of a Presbyterian minister, whom Wallace had met some years previously in college. After graduating Lila had traveled around the country doing social service work. She visited the Middle East on a relief mission, and returning home in 1921 she met Wallace again. They fell in love, became engaged, and while planning for their marriage they worked together promoting the pocket-sized magazine. The couple proved to be a matchless duo. DeWitt—his friends called him Wally—was tall and bony, over six feet tall; Lila was small and dainty, five feet three inches. Wallace was shy, retiring; Lila was gregarious, extroverted. DeWitt was a chronic worrier who suffered from spells of deep melancholy, tortured by feelings of insecurity and self-doubt. Lila radiated self-assurance, an optimist to the core. As one close friend put it, "Wally is the genius but Lila unwrapped him."

In the fall of 1921 the Wallaces organized the Reader's Digest Association in a rented basement apartment under a speakeasy at One Minetta Lane in Manhattan's Greenwich Village. On October 15 they got married. They mailed a prospectus to a list they had compiled of prospective subscribers and then they left for a two-week honeymoon in the Poconos. Upon returning home, they found to their astonishment and delight that fifteen hundred people had mailed in subscriptions for a year of the *Reader's Digest* along with checks and money orders at three dollars apiece. (Single copies were to be priced at twenty-five cents.) With forty-five hundred dollars thus collected, the co-editors embarked on making up the first issue. They placed an order of five thousand copies with a printer in Pittsburgh and when the shipment reached their Greenwich Village apartment in February 1922, they asked several neighborhood shopkeepers they had become friendly with to help them wrap up the copies. Then the exuberant newlyweds lugged the mailsacks into the street, hailed a cab, climbed in and drove to the post office. On the way home they dropped off at a corner bistro and toasted the health of their venture.

Their hopes were extremely modest. The *Reader's Digest* described itself on the masthead of its initial issue as "The Little Magazine." And the Wallaces figured that if they were lucky and it really took hold, it would sell ten thousand copies at its peak bringing them an income of about five thousand dollars a year. This was a respectable sum in those days and the couple would have been more than satisfied with it. But it was a wild miscalculation. Within ten years the Wallaces were to become millionaires. (The five thousand copies of the first edition have long since become collector's items.)

The opening issue carried the message of spiritual uplift and pervasive optimism interspersed with quotes and homely anecdotes that would become the magazine's trademark. The lead article was a condensation of an interview with Alexander Graham Bell, entitled "How To Keep Young Mentally," that had originally appeared in the *American* magazine. The inventor of the telephone told how he had succeeded in keeping mentally young throughout his seventy-four years, younger than the majority of men half his age. Explained the *Reader's Digest* in a paragraph accompanying the interview, "Mentally he seems to have discovered a Fountain of Youth which keeps him perenially alert and vigorous."

Another article entitled "Don't Growl—Kick" insisted that anybody upset by a manufacturer from whom he had bought something defective shouldn't waste any anger or frustration. All one had to do was to write a note to the company president. "Corporations really have souls. The system is much better than the average fellow knows, and somebody is waiting to attend to this very matter."

Along with this cheery note were cracker-barrel quotations from America's captains of industry. There was also a line from Billy Sunday, the evangelist: "Try praising your wife, even if it *does* frighten her at first." And a remark from John Wanamaker, the department store mogul: "A real good smile and a hearty handshake cost but a minute."

There was also an article that was to herald the *Digest*'s long crusade against cigarette smoking. It quoted a famous trumpet player warning against the evils of tobacco: "One cigarette will kill a cat."

At the end of the first year of publication—with seven thousand subscribers in the fold—the Wallaces decided to move their home and office from Manhattan to more quiet surroundings. Chancing upon a real estate ad extolling the virtues of Pleasantville, a town forty miles north of New York, they found new lodgings on an estate owned by Pendleton Dudley, a wealthy Manhattan publicity man, who was fascinated with the Wallaces' little magazine and became a staunch friend and a valuable counselor. For twenty-five dollars a month the Wallaces rented a room over Pendleton's garage which they used as a combined office, sitting room and bedroom. They cooked their meals on a gas stove crammed into a corner and washed in a stall shower in the garage below. They hired three girls to handle the subscription lists and other clerical chores, and as the need for space grew they rented an empty shed adjoining the garage for an additional ten dollars a month, converting it into the magazine's office.

For three years the Wallaces lived, worked and struggled in these cramped quarters. When the circulation had reached twenty thousand readers, bringing in gross revenues of over fifty thousand dollars, they purchased property next to Pendleton Dudley's and built a dwelling to serve as a house and home combined. Steadily, the *Digest* circulation grew. By the end of the nineteen-twenties, circulation had soared to 290,000 copies. By the mid-thirties subscribers' mail to the *Digest*'s office had reached such proportions that the town of Pleasantville (population 5,000) was forced to build a larger post office just to handle the magazine's correspondence.

Initially, the Wallaces' stock in trade was reprinting articles from the nation's leading magazines and for the first few years DeWitt pounded the pavements of Manhattan going from one editorial office to another to plead for articles. Wallace would request an appointment, compliment an editor upon an article he had read and ask for the right to reprint it in his little magazine. He was not often refused. Most of the magazine editors weren't quite certain of the exact nature of Wallace's business but they were only too happy to let this shy, retiring fellow who spoke so diffidently about his work reprint their material since he was giving them free publicity. Reminisces one top editor, "I figured Wallace was just another crackpot with a crazy idea. But I couldn't see how I could lose by humoring him. I was too busy to deal with him directly so I turned the chore over to my secretary." In return for receiving articles free of charge, Wallace promised editors that he would carry no advertising in his magazine, for if he appeared to be cashing in on advertising with the articles they gave him gratis, the editors might well decline his request for material.

Indeed, during the first few years Wallace was obsessively secretive about his operations. Since he was getting free handouts from editors, he was afraid to let it be known how well he was doing financially. Wallace kept as low a profile as possible, presenting the appearance of genteel poverty, and other editors for some time had no inkling of how magnificently the *Digest* was getting on. But by 1929, readership had soared to 290,000. When the Depression erupted sending thousands of businesses into bankruptcy, Wallace continued to buck the trend and the circulation of the *Digest* kept snowballing. At the very depth of the Depression, its readership had zoomed to over 850,000. The following year it catapulted to 1.5 million and twelve months later to 1.8 million.

Under these circumstances it was obviously impossible to keep the burgeoning success of the *Digest* a secret indefinitely. As early as 1929, when the realization that Wallace had struck a journalistic gold mine finally sank into the consciousnes of the publishing world, *Scribner's* magazine announced that it would have no further part in abetting the *Reader's Digest's* forays into its own circulation. It withdrew from Wallace the right to reprint its articles. The *Forum* and the *Atlantic Monthly* hinted they would follow suit. Meanwhile, the *Saturday Evening Post* and the *American* magazine, which from the start had refused to give Wallace their articles, publicly reaffirmed their position.

Threatened by a general boycott of magazines whose articles had been the lifeblood of the *Digest,* Wallace faced a serious crisis. In this extremity, Kenneth W. Payne, the influential editor of the *North American Review* and a personal friend of Wallace, took up the cudgels for him. He buttonholed the publishers and editors of top publications, arguing that far from being a threat to them, Wallace, by reprinting their articles in his magazine, was giving them widespread publicity. Moreover, Payne contended, Wallace was increasing readership for the whole magazine industry by developing a growing interest among Americans in reading non-fiction.

Kenneth Payne did a yeoman job luring his fellow editors back into the Wallace fold. The rebellion against *Reader's Digest* was nipped in the bud, and Wallace's flow of editorial content continued. Shortly after his stellar missionary performance, Payne formally joined the Wallace family, becoming a *Digest* editor. Within a couple of years he was earning over one hundred thousand dollars annually.

Nevertheless, Wallace continued to be haunted by the nightmare of being suddenly cut off from his editorial supply. Not only was he entirely dependent upon the goodwill of other editors for his articles, but imitators of the *Reader's Digest*—pocket-sized magazines reprinting popular articles and gunning directly for Wallace's readers—began mushrooming on the newsstands. Up to now *Reader's Digest* was sold exclusively through the mail, but as a defensive move Wallace entered into an arrangement with distributors to put *Reader's Digest* on the newsstands.

To further lessen his vulnerability and protect his sources of articles, Wallace proposed to magazine publishers that they enter into long-term contracts with him giving him the exclusive rights to reprint their articles in return for substantial sums for this privilege. The majority of publishers agreed.

Despite these measures, Wallace was not entirely relieved. To cement his position and make himself completely invulnerable, he began originating his own ideas for articles and hiring editors and writers to carry them out. Since his magazine had skyrocketed to success on a reprint formula, however, Wallace determined to maintain this approach by quietly offering original ideas for articles to other magazine publishers who would print them in their entirety, giving him the right to reprint in a condensed version. This concept of "planting" articles in other magazines was a milestone in the development of *Reader's Digest,* and was undoubtedly the major reason for its long-term growth. Wallace realized that America's leading magazines were spending the bulk of their money on fiction, not serious non-fiction. The *Digest* now had the cash and the talent to create its own expert articles in the non-fiction field. Moreover, as Wallace explained, "We just weren't able to find in other publications enough articles of lasting interest and scope to fill up the needs of our own magazine."

Accordingly, Wallace and his crew of experts went into the business of conceiving ideas for original articles and hiring leading free-lance writers to execute them. One of Wallace's pioneering efforts was an article, "Sudden Death," about the rising rate of automobile accidents. Written by J.C. Furnas, it presented in graphic detail the facts of auto fatalities on

America's highways. The article became a sensation. Four million reprints were sent out by the *Digest*. Police departments, accident prevention groups, civic service groups all over the nation ordered reprints of "Sudden Death." It was dramatized over the radio. Judges read excerpts from it to traffic offenders brought before them. And one jurist punished offenders by making them copy the article line by line.

Before long, Wallace was publishing more original articles than reprints in his *Digest*. The strategy of quietly planting articles by name writers in leading magazines catapulted Wallace and his magazine into a position of tremendous influence. Yet the publisher himself remained compulsively secretive about his business. When *Fortune* magazine sent a writer and a photographer to Pleasantville to interview and take pictures of Wallace for a story about the *Digest,* they discovered upon getting off the train that there wasn't a single sign in Pleasantville to indicate where the *Reader's Digest* offices were located. Questioning a passerby on Main Street, they were told to walk up Wheeler Avenue past the stationery store, the firehouse and a luncheonette and at the corner of Bedford Road ask the cop who directed traffic for further directions. The writer and photographer approached the policeman who steered them to the Mount Pleasant Bank Trust Company.

Upon entering the lobby of the bank, they found a directory on the wall with the names of three tenants, but there was no mention of the *Reader's Digest.* They mounted a narrow flight of wooden stairs creaking with age and one flight up, hidden away in the rear, they came on a sign reading "Please keep this door closed." It was the one door that did not bear the name of the tenants listed on the directory below, and so by a process of elimination the *Fortune* team decided to go through it. They pushed open the door and stumbled into the cramped quarters of the *Reader's Digest* editorial offices.

The reporter wrote of the owner of this furtive enterprise that boasted a circulation of two million readers, "He is tall, lean, slightly stooped and he is dressed in the tweedy elegance of the English professor with a private income." The writer found him painfully bashful, thoroughly uncomfortable with newcomers, inclined to speak in a halting, indecisive manner.

Wallace appeared to the writer of *Fortune* and to his own colleagues to bristle with contradictory character traits. A

191

persistent crusader in print against the harmful impact of cigarette smoking, Wallace at the peak of his working career smoked two packs a day. A retiring introspective man, not normally accessible to his staff, he displayed bursts of exuberant conviviality. He was a poker addict, frequently playing all-night games with members of his staff.

Another surprising trait of the publisher was his passion for flying. During the 1930s Wallace became disenchanted with the commercial airlines, complaining they flew at too high an altitude for him to get a good look at the countryside. He bought a Fairchild four-passenger plane, got a pilot's license and hopped around at an altitude of 1,500 to 2,500 feet, taking in scenery to his heart's content. Whenever he grew restless, he would walk suddenly from his office, drive to the airport, hop into his plane and open up the throttle, frequently without letting his colleagues know that he had taken off or where he could be contacted.

Once a celebrated author meeting a *Digest* editor for a story conference reported that he had just received a letter from Wallace complimenting him on an article he had submitted. The editor went to his boss's office to ask him to join the conference, but Wallace was nowhere to be found. It turned out that the publisher had left without notice and flown his plane to a resort in the Pocono Mountains to study a bundle of manuscripts in privacy. On another occasion he slipped away from his desk and was not heard from for a week. Afterwards, his staff learned he had bobbed up in Hawaii with a trunkful of articles he wanted to consider in solitude. From Hawaii he flew to India, sending telegrams back to his office detailing decisions he had made about certain articles he wanted published. Wallace took a fiendish delight in flying; several times he terrified his wife by flying his plane low and buzzing the roof of their home. Moreover, he drove his auto so recklessly his colleagues used every stratagem to avoid riding with him.

Lila Wallace, the publisher's wife and co-publisher, gave up active editing during the early years of the magazine's existence. But her presence has remained palpable. When the *Digest* finally emerged from its hideout to admit it was the world's top-selling magazine (its influence had become so notorious it had to abandon its shabby old offices at the rear of the bank and move into a building of its own in Pleasantville),

Lila decorated its new offices with draperies, Georgian tables, walls in light pastel colors and leather-finished desks. She also conceived the idea of putting four winged horses, painted in green, on a white cupola adorning the top of the new *Digest* building. These winged horses became the magazine's emblem. "According to the Greek myth," Mrs. Wallace pointed out, "when Pegasus dances on his little feet, writers get their inspiration."

Having survived the Depression unscathed, the *Digest* in the 1940s began the first stages of an expansion around the world. During the Second World War millions of American soldiers abroad eagerly read copies of the pocket-sized magazine mailed them from home. Convenient to carry around, the *Digest* became a prized bit of Americana. These GIs acted as missionaries acquainting people around the world with the magazine. Before the war was over, the circulation of Wallace's magazine had skyrocketed to over nine million readers. The first edition actually to be published overseas predated World War II by several years. It was an edition published in Great Britain in 1938. (A Spanish-language edition was introduced in 1940.) The British *Reader's Digest* quickly attained the biggest circulation of any monthly published in the British Isles. The *Digest* spread to Latin America and to over twenty other countries. To cut the price of the overseas magazine to fit the pocketbooks of its readers, Wallace rescinded his traditional policy of refusing to accept advertising. In its foreign editions, *Reader's Digest* began taking ads. By the early 1950s the *Digest* had been launched successfully in Sweden, Italy and Finland, was appearing in Spanish and Portuguese in editions all over Latin America and had become the fastest selling magazine in Japan. It was being read in fifty-eight nations.

Shortly before the war, the *Digest* began condensing best-selling books, and this became one of its most popular features. In addition to its regular edition, the magazine commenced putting out a number of school editions featuring reading and vocabulary aids for students in colleges and high schools. Editions are published in Braille and on records for the blind. The *Digest* also went into book publishing and movie-making.

Over the years the *Digest* has attracted a collection of brilliant, idiosyncratic "roving editors" largely from America's conservative camp who, because of the prestige of their journalistic pulpit, have influenced millions for good or for evil depending upon one's political viewpoint. Among the roving editors were Eugene Lyons, editor of the right-wing *American Mercury*, an apostate from socialism; Stanley High, editor of the *Christian Herald;* William L. White of the *Emporia Gazette* and Fulton Oursler, a defector from agnosticism. They were a formidable array of eloquent spokesmen ranging from moderates to extreme right-wing zealots.

One of the most fascinatingly perverse conservatives to become associated with the *Reader's Digest* was Max Eastman who, as noted elsewhere, began his journalistic career as the socialist editor of the *Masses,* and when the Bolshevik Revolution broke out in 1917, became an ardent Communist and close friend of Leon Trotsky. Eastman translated Trotsky's history of the Revolution into English and continued to serve as Trotsky's translator during his years of exile after Stalin expelled him from Russia. In later years Eastman became not only a fanatical anti-Communist, but a zealous witch-hunter of American liberals, branding any kind of thinking which deviated from arch conservatism as crypto-Communist.

In the course of his unorthodox intellectual pilgrimage, Eastman became friendly with a number of world celebrities and he wrote about them amusingly. On one occasion he recalled an interesting encounter with Sigmund Freud, whose concept of psychoanalysis was just beginning to fascinate Americans.

Freud, impressed with part of a book Eastman had written comparing him to Karl Marx, invited the author to meet him in Vienna. Eastman knocked on the door of the house at Bergasse 19 and was ushered into a big roomy study crammed with books and carpeted with richly tufted rugs.

Eastman found Freud to be smaller, more slender-limbed than he had expected, with a curious aura of femininity about him. (This femininity, Eastman observed, was characteristic of most of the great men he had encountered.) Eastman was shocked by Freud's virulent anti-Americanism. Referring to the recent war (the 1914–1918 conflict with Germany), Freud remarked that the United States had made a mistake in going in to help England and France. "Your Woodrow Wilson was the silliest fool of the century, if not of all centuries." Before Eastman could put in a word for his country, Freud concluded,

194

"And Wilson was also probably one of the greatest criminals—unconsciously, I am quite sure."

"What makes you hate America so?" Eastman finally asked.

"Hate America?" Freud retorted. "I don't hate America, I regret it . . . I regret that Columbus ever discovered it!"

Today the *Digest* is less virulently anti-Communist than it was in the days of Eastman and his associates, less prone to look for the Russian bear under every American bed. It has lost some of its appetite for preparing an auto-da-fé for dissenting liberals. Moreover, it has softened its hard-shell moralistic approach to life. It runs informative articles on sex and accepts advertisements from the whiskey industry.

In 1973 DeWitt Wallace, who with the help of his wife, transmuted a five-thousand-dollar investment into a billion-dollar business, retired at the age of eighty-three. His influence, however, continued to be visible in key policy-making issues for several years thereafter. And until his death at ninety-one Wallace, together with his wife, Lila, continued to control 100 percent of the Reader's Digest Association stock. The *Reader's Digest* is today what it has been for the more than half-century of its existence, a privately held business, which, because it has no need to raise capital from the public, has been able to ignore the SEC, keep the public from peeping at its finances or make any accounting of how it is being run. (All statistics, including the figure of a billion dollars in annual revenues, are the result of informed guesses by outsiders, not certain knowledge.) Furthermore, this behemoth of the publishing industry remains a bastion of undiluted free private enterprise that has not been breached by the labor union movement. While *Digest* employees receive generous wages, they do so solely at the discretion of their employer, not because of the pressure of organized labor. The benevolent despotism displayed by the *Reader's Digest* management is a corruscating memorial to the times of Frederick the Great.

Meanwhile, Wallace's successor, John O'Hara, a hard-nosed, no-nonense Irishman who spews out orders between bites on a cigar, is running an empire whose center has been steadily shifting away from the magazine field into such diversified activities as book publishing, book clubs, distribution of musical records and hi-fidelity equipment. While the *Digest* remains the world's most widely read magazine, issued in thirty-nine

195

foreign editions, it has as noted lost first place in America to *TV Guide,* and currently the magazine contributes to only about half of the corporation's total revenues. The remaining income is generated by the non-magazine operations which have been spun off into autonomous ventures controlled by the parent firm.

In the process of distributing its wares, the *Digest* has become one of the world's largest mail order businesses with customer lists so valuable that management keeps one of the two copies that exist, in addition to the master list, in a vault and the other copy buried at an undisclosed spot to prevent their being stolen by competitors.

But if the Reader's Digest Association is changing its character under the direction of President O'Hara and Editor in Chief Edward Thompson, it has lost very little of its buoyant optimism. And is it any wonder? The Wallaces' business, hatched amidst the saloons of Greenwich Village, outstripped their most sanguine expectations, and is today a principality unto itself.

Part Four

On the Seventh Day the Lord Sayeth, "Let There Be Television"

12

Soap Opera at NBC—The Rise and Fall of the Sarnoff Dynasty and Other Fun and Games

Wheeler-Dealings at "Black Rock," Bill Paley's Legendary Lair

================

IN AN EFFORT to exploit a rapidly developing new technology and the shifting tastes of a society that is growing increasingly more unpredictable, the media moguls no longer confine themselves to a single area such as newspapers, magazines or television. They are engaged in ambitious acquisitions to provide media coverage in all its aspects from the printed word to electronic communication.

Indeed, a most dramatic trend is the merger of publishing with electronic journalism. Magazine publishers with painful memories of how television pushed a number of periodicals to the wall have within the last decade been retaliating by moving aggressively into the television field. Indeed, Time, Inc., in an effort to establish a foothold in television, launched several years ago what has turned out to be the nation's largest cable-television operation: Home Box Office. Cable-television, the wiring of home subscribers to broadcasters, is providing the single biggest competitive threat to the Big Three television networks and it has become the most promising area of growth in the entire industry. (Recently, Home Box Office moved into motion picture production to provide movies for its own TV outlets.) In making a substantial capital investment, Home Box Office has become the pioneering force in cable-television, developing a satellite distribution system which is on the verge of revolutionizing the operations of commercial television. In addition to Time, Inc., a number of newspaper publishers, including The New York Times Company and the Times Mirror Company, have moved into the television industry, acquiring cable-television systems of their own.

For their part, the Big Three TV networks have tried to counter the incursions of magazine publishers by acquiring their own print outlets. Currently, CBS owns twenty-five magazines, including such breadwinners as *Field & Stream, World Tennis,* and *Woman's Day.* ABC's forays into magazine (and newspaper) publishing have been especially far-reaching. It operates under its corporate umbrella a string of farm, trade and leisure activities magazines, including *High Fidelity, Musical America* and *Modern Photography,* and it owns a communications company involved in the publishing of religious books and recorded music. ABC also owns *Los Angeles* magazine, formerly a member of Clay Felker's *New York* magazine family, and it has acquired a substantial interest in the Chilton Company, a publisher of magazines and books. The Washington *Post* for its part has moved into the acquisition of television stations and so has the New York *Times,* with a string of radio and TV outlets.

The desire of magazine and newspaper publishers to move into the television business is understandable. Television has become the nerve system of America's age of communications. Indeed, it is no longer simply a communications medium. It has been raised to the status of an environment. Thanks to television, an increasing number of Americans are coming to look upon existence as a performance to be witnessed on a small rectangular screen. And the figures on that screen, whether they are politicians, junk peddlers, pimps, blues singers or Arab terrorists, have become superstars in the drama of life.

"Television," observes historian Daniel Boorstin, "regulates our opinions on almost everything—how, when and what we eat; when we sleep; how we raise our children; what our children think of us; what we buy or don't buy; what we think of lawyers, doctors, policemen and law-breakers; how we act in

200

matters of sex and race; how we debate our national issues; indeed, what we believe or imagine to *be* our national issues."

Psychiatrists and sociologists may be expressing concern about growing alcoholism and heroin addiction, but the most widespread addiction in America is television watching and the withdrawal process is agonizingly painful. In 1977 the Detroit *Free Press* decided to do a survey on how families who are habitual television watchers change their behavior patterns upon temporarily withdrawing from the habit. The *Free Press* offered 120 families $500 apiece if they would permit the newspaper to withdraw their television sets for thirty days and interview them on how they spent their leisure hours. Ninety-three of the 120 families approached turned the $500 down because they were unwilling to part with their TV set on any terms. One of the housewives who rejected the cash explained, "My husband would never permit it. He comes home from work, sits down in front of the TV. He gets up twice, once to eat and once to go to bed."

However, 27 hardy families agreed to give up TV for a month, and 5 of the 27 were selected for the test. Their withdrawal behavior was bizarre indeed. One couple stopped speaking to one another under the strain. Six days after the set was removed the husband "buried himself behind a newspaper and never came out." Two people started chain smoking. Two resorted to more sex. Virtually all were plunged into deep depression, manifested by highly nervous behavior. "Adults and children found trouble participating in discussions that revolved around last night's football game and the latest *Charlie's Angels* caper." When it was over the editor of the *Free Press* who had conceived the experiment admitted he was flabbergasted by "how much trouble we had giving $500 to give up the TV."

Clearly, the impact of the video screen has sobering implications. Not only has television emerged as the unrivaled source of fast-breaking, on-the-spot news, but the graphics revolution that has been threatening to diminish if not obliterate a culture founded on the written word is reaching its zenith. Newspapers, magazines and books communicate through the written word. To be a member of the receiving audience one must have at least elementary reading skills, some inkling of spelling and sentence structure. One must possess literacy, which has historically been the litmus test for civilized man. However, for millions of Americans, thanks to the influence of television, the ability to understand the printed word has become, in the words of journalist Tom Wolfe, virtually "a mandarin skill. It's a special elitist talent like weaving medieval tapestries, illuminating old ecclesiastical manuscripts or playing the Elizabethan lute."

It is a stroke of irony that David Sarnoff, the individual who more than any other presided over the birth of America's radio and television broadcasting industry, was himself a cultural elitist, a lover of literature, a lifelong worshiper of intellectual and educational uplift. The stand-up comedians, the narcissistic talk show panelists, the brassy sitcoms launched by the video revolution were temperamentally a world away from Sarnoff's private, introverted self. He was everything the bulk of his television audiences were not. He was at home in the world of ideas; he found it difficult to indulge in small talk. He didn't enjoy football, golf or any of the other sports his corporation made huge profits on. He confessed in the final years of his life that one of his regrets as a father was that he hadn't been able to relate sufficiently well to his three sons as they were growing up; unlike them, he was incapable of getting a kick out of a baseball game. While millions of Americans raved over Charlie McCarthy, the ventriloquist's dummy, Sarnoff became intimate friends with Samuel Chotzinoff, the music critic, whose wife was the sister of Jascha Heifetz. Sarnoff lured Arturo Toscanini to America, and provided him with an orchestra and carte-blanche authority to present classical music over the airwaves.

In an industry notorious for its greed, the accumulation of wealth was relatively unimportant to Sarnoff, who received modest pay for his contributions. The father of the Radio Corporation of America, and in the early 1940s the unchallenged leader of the industry, accumulated only a tiny fraction of RCA stock. Sarnoff's greed was to acquire more and more knowledge of electronics technology, not dollars.

A Jewish immigrant from Russia, brought up in poverty on the Lower East Side of New York, Sarnoff never became a big business tycoon in the ordinary sense. He left that to the little men who followed him. Today the people running this industry are fanatical followers of popular consensus. They live by the ratings and the popularity polls. Originality, dissent, defiance of popular taste and opinion, adherence to personal principle and conviction are unknown to the current administrators of America's most powerful communications medium. But Sarnoff's entire life was a battle against the prevailing opinion of his times. In his early years he struggled against a widely prevailing skepticism that short-wave radio could ever take over the job of transoceanic and transcontinental telegraphy, or that people would live to see coast-to-coast broadcasting over radio networks. He prophesied that radio would one day enter the living rooms of millions of people, predicting this at a time when the means for making this "miracle" possible had not even been invented. Named president of the Radio Corporation of America on the eve of the Depression of the 1930s, Sarnoff, despite the skepticism of the radio industry and the opposition of his associates at RCA, made the decision to plunge millions of dollars into the research and development of commercial television. The technological problems were formidable and there was grave doubt that there would ever be a profitable market for it; nevertheless, Sarnoff gambled fifty million dollars on black and white television, and then he plunged another one hundred and thirty million dollars into developing color television before RCA made a penny in profits.

Sarnoff himself had a reverence for learning. From his earliest days as a kid on the Lower East Side, he determined that he would never be one of the uneducated masses. To him as to most other Jewish immigrants—the People of the Book—ignorance was a scandal. As a child in Russia he had studied the Talmud under an uncle who was a rabbi, and while he never went beyond high school because of his need to earn money for his family, he became well-educated by reading voraciously, developing into an eloquent lecturer.

Sarnoff was born in the province of Minsk on the Russian steppes in February 1891. His father was a trader, going from door to door, selling shoes and clothing in exchange for livestock and groceries. (The region was so primitive that money was virtually unknown and people subsisted on a bartering system.) When Sarnoff was three, his father sold out his inventory and left for the United States, promising to send for his family. It took him six years before he could earn enough money to buy tickets for their voyage to America. Shattering his health in the struggle to accumulate money, he became an invalid and died when Sarnoff was a teenager.

Sarnoff's mother and her children made the crossing as steerage passengers. Landing first in Montreal in July 1900, the family went on to New York and moved into a crowded tenement house on the Lower East Side, paying ten dollars a month for rent. Their father was sick and unable to work full time so David, the oldest of the three children, was compelled to find a job at the age of ten. For two years he peddled newspapers on Broome and H Streets but the competition among newsboys was ruthless. David was skinny and under-sized and he continually had to fight with older, tougher neighborhood kids for whom he was no match.

The solution, he decided, was to buy his own newsstand in another neighborhood where he might have a better chance to survive. He learned that a newsstand was for sale on the West Side, in Hell's Kitchen, a region heavily populated by Irish immigrants.

The price of the newsstand was two hundred dollars, an impossible sum for young Sarnoff to come up with. He spoke to neighbors about his problem, and one day he returned after work to his tenement flat where a stranger, a woman in her middle years, greeted him. "I hear you are working to support your parents and that you would like to buy a newsstand. I'm going to help you do this." The lady opened her pocketbook and handed the boy two hundred dollars. He was so astonished he failed to ask his benefactress who she was.

This occurred in 1904. Twenty years later, when Sarnoff was already a top executive in the radio industry and one of the most powerful men in the world, he attended a meeting at the home of a wealthy philanthropist, convened to arrange a fund-raising drive for European Jews. Sarnoff, upon entering the living room, noticed a white-haired lady whom he was certain he had seen somewhere. He couldn't take his eyes off her and finally he walked up to her.

"I'm sure we have met somewhere. Do you recognize me?"

"No," replied the woman.

"I'm going to test your memory. Can you go back to the early 1900s to an old tenement on Monroe Street on the East Side?

A kid of thirteen came home to find you waiting for him and you gave him two hundred dollars to buy a newsstand?"

The lady looked puzzled; then she remembered. And she explained the riddle that had puzzled Sarnoff since 1904. "I was a secretary to a wealthy philanthropist interested in charities for the poor. My job was to interview and select immigrant youth who I believed would be worthy recipients of his money. I had heard reports about you from your neighbors telling me how hard-working and resourceful you were and how you wanted to own a newsstand to support your family. And now, here you are!"

Sarnoff entered the field of wireless telegraphy that was to catapult him into worldwide fame and launch America's broadcasting industry entirely by accident. Once he had achieved his newsstand in Hell's Kitchen, Sarnoff dreamed of one day becoming a reporter, since a newsman's life seemed crammed with glamour. One Saturday afternoon when he was fifteen he dressed himself in his best and summoned up the nerve to visit the offices of the newspaper located nearest his newsstand, James Gordon Bennett's *Herald* at Broadway and Thirty-fifth Street. He went up to a man sitting in a cage that looked like a bank teller's post.

"I'd like a job," began Sarnoff. "Can you tell me whom to apply to?"

The man scrutinized him. Skinny, undersized, Sarnoff looked younger than his years. "I could use a new messenger boy. If you are willing to work for $5 a week and ten cents an hour overtime, I'll take you on."

Sarnoff accepted eagerly. He put on a uniform and discovered to his astonishment he had been hired not by the New York *Herald* but by the Postal Telegraph and Commercial Cable Company. He had walked by mistake onto the premises of the Cable Company, which among other things handled the telegraph and wire dispatch messages for the *Herald*.

Although he was only a messenger boy who delivered dispatches by bicycle, he became mesmerized by the world of telegraphy and wireless. The idea of messages being sent across the ocean and continents fueled his imagination and stirred his desire to be a participant in the burgeoning new technology. He went without lunches to save up money to buy model telegraph equipment and a book of instructions and codes. He studied the book every spare moment, kept the instrument in his bedroom at home and practiced on it every night before he fell asleep.

The manager of the Cable Company, appreciating his enthusiasm, permitted him to work on the equipment in the office when no dispatches were coming over the wires. Within a few months Sarnoff had learned the Morse Code and was able to operate the equipment skillfully.

Suddenly he lost his job as a messenger boy. One of his teachers in school discovered that he had a splendid singing voice and he encouraged Sarnoff to join the choir of a synagogue in his neighborhood. Sarnoff sang for the High Holidays, earning a dollar and a half a week to add to his income from the Cable office. However, when he informed his boss at the Cable Company that he would be out on Rosh Hashanah singing in the synagogue, the boss replied that messages had to be delivered, Jewish holidays or not, and he wouldn't let him be absent. When Sarnoff insisted on his right to sing, he was dismissed from his job.

A friend he had made at the Cable Company told him about a new wireless office, however, the first to be opened in Manhattan by the American subsidiary of the Marconi Wireless Company.

"Why don't you try the Marconi Office? I hear they have been advertising for a man."

On September 30, 1906, Sarnoff walked into the Marconi Company at 26 William Street and asked the chief engineer for a job as assistant operator. The engineer looked at him quizzically. "We don't need an operator but if you don't mind being an office boy we can use one and we can pay you $5.50 a week." Sarnoff accepted and kept his eyes peeled for a chance to advance.

An opportunity turned up dramatically. He had become an ardent admirer, through his studies, of Guglielmo Marconi, the inventor of the wireless, and when the Italian came to New York to carry out further research, Sarnoff summoned up the courage to approach him and ask if he could help him in his work. Marconi was impressed with Sarnoff's enthusiasm so in the hours following Sarnoff's duties as a messenger boy, he worked as an assistant to Marconi, carrying papers, lugging supplies, making deliveries and telephone calls, exulting at his chance to share in the life of the father of the wireless industry.

Sarnoff's apprenticeship to Marconi paid off. He became an assistant wireless operator for the Marconi Company, and when he discovered the job was open for an assistant operator at the company's station on Nantucket Island, the seventeen-year-old Sarnoff asked to be sent there. It was a dreary job in a remote island outpost and few operators were willing to go, but Sarnoff spent two years there, acquiring further experience in the job.

Wireless was still in its infancy in those years and only a handful of operators were skilled in it. Sarnoff, thanks to his Nantucket experience and his appetite for hard work, became the fastest wireless operator on the East Coast.

When John Wanamaker, the department store magnate, decided to install radio stations in his New York and Philadelphia stores that would be the most powerful ever equipped in the commercial wireless field, Sarnoff applied for the job in the New York store and got it.

Again, luck intervened. On April 14, 1912, while Sarnoff was operating his wireless equipment at the Wanamaker station, an event took place that turned him overnight from an obscure wireless operator into a household name around the world and, at the same time, revolutionized the prospects of radio. Sarnoff was already known among his professional associates as the speediest wireless operator on the American continent, but his name meant nothing except to the handful of initiates in the field. This April evening on which the young operator sat by his wireless was a slack one; virtually no news was coming across. Sarnoff was on the verge of dozing off when suddenly his muscles tensed. A message from fifteen hundred miles out at sea had begun coming in. The passenger ship *Titanic*, on its maiden voyage from Southampton to New York, had struck a submerged iceberg and was sinking rapidly. A vessel fifteen hundred miles away was flashing warnings of disaster, feverishly asking for help.

When the news broke, a number of operating stations and wireless posts began transmitting the messages across America. President Taft, realizing that they were jamming the airways and preventing the latest messages from coming through clearly, ordered that all stations except the one at Wanamaker's be closed. The Wanamaker station, which was the most

207

powerful commercial station on the American continent, remained open and the job of keeping the nation informed devolved on the twenty-one-year-old Sarnoff.

For seventy-two hours Sarnoff remained transfixed, the earphones wrapped around his head, receiving and decoding messages, hardly eating or sleeping. The anxiety-stricken relatives of the passengers were awaiting names of the survivors who were being picked up by the *Carpathia*, a ship that had steamed to the scene. Sarnoff, as soon as the names came in, contacted the newspapers, who rushed editions onto the streets, headlining the news. The next of kin pressed hysterically into the Wanamaker radio office and the police had to be called out to prevent riots. Other patrolmen guarded Sarnoff so that he could perform his duties unharassed.

Recalling his ordeal and the burden of responsibility placed upon him for three frightening days, Sarnoff observed, "I passed the information on to a sorrowing world and when messages ceased to come in, fell down like a log at my place and slept the clock around."

The catastrophe of the *Titanic*, in which over fifteen hundred passengers met their death, brought to the attention of the American public the overwhelming importance of radio wireless. A number of ships had been within range of the sinking *Titanic;* had they been equipped with wireless they could have saved scores of additional passengers.

As a result of this catastrophe, Congress passed a law requiring all vessels carrying over fifty passengers to install radio equipment and maintain constant communication while at sea. Educated to the importance of radio wireless communications for safeguarding lives at sea, Americans inevitably came to appreciate the potential of radio for other uses.

By the end of the First World War, David Sarnoff had become one of the most knowledgeable men in the radio business and, inevitably, the ranking executive when the Radio Corporation of America was started, in December 1919, to produce and merchandise radio equipment. RCA was in effect a reorganized version of the old American Marconi Company. General Electric emerged as the owner with the majority control of stock, and in subsequent years GE was joined by Westinghouse in a partnership ownership of RCA. When it became obvious that radio was ready for coast-to-coast broadcasting, RCA launched the nation's first network, NBC, in January 1927. A few months later the Columbia Broadcasting System was organized and by 1928 William Paley had taken over its leadership to become Sarnoff's big rival.

William Samuel Paley had been born in Chicago in 1901. Upon graduating from the University of Pennsylvania, he went into his father's cigar business. But the industry eventually went sour. During the First World War men in the trenches started smoking cigarettes and they brought the practice home with them. As cigarette smoking swept the country, cigar sales, which had soared during the 1890s and 1900s, dropped off drastically. By 1927 the daily production of La Palinas, Paley's brand of cigars, had tumbled from six hundred thousand to four hundred thousand. At this point the Paleys were approached by the representatives of a small chain of radio stations, the Independent Broadcasters Inc., who talked them into advertising La Palinas over their network. Commercial radio was only five years old and big business had not yet been attracted to it as an advertising medium. No one really knew how large an audience was out there, or whether radio advertising really paid. However, with sales drastically off, and clutching at any straw, the Paleys signed a contract to pay fifty thousand dollars for thirteen weeks of radio ads. "This could be the biggest blunder we ever made!" declared Bill Paley's uncle as he affixed his signature.

The Paleys were astonished by the results. Not only did the sales of La Palinas rise, they skyrocketed by 150 percent. The contract was quickly renewed. Within six months the Paleys' production increased from four hundred thousand to a million cigars a day.

Young Bill Paley took a long hard look at radio broadcasting and decided to enter the business. Independent Broadcasters was owned by a friend of his father's, Jerome Louchheim. Other interests were occupying Louchheim's attention and he was happy to sell out. Paley obtained a twenty-four-hour option for control of the radio chain and on September 25, 1928, three days before his twenty-seventh birthday, he bought it. Independent Broadcasters was more like a spider web than a network; it consisted of a few small stations east of Mississippi and south of the Mason-Dixon Line. Paley renamed the chain the Columbia Broadcasting System. He bought control of it for four hundred thousand dollars. Today Paley's share of stock in CBS is worth over eighty million.

Sarnoff and Paley plunged into a rivalry to achieve domination of the blossoming industry. Sarnoff, despite his early and spectacular successes, began to take his lumps. Primarily interested in the long-range technological possibilities of radio rather than in immediate dollars-and-cents profits, Sarnoff insisted on plunging RCA's money into heavy research and development. Again and again he stirred up bitter opposition among RCA shareholders and his own business associates.

One serious setback involved RCA Victor Records, the corporation's most profitable subsidiary after its broadcasting operations. When the record industry was on the verge of moving from the old 78 rpm record to long-playing discs, Sarnoff bet RCA's money on the development of a 45 rpm version. But CBS technologists weighed in with a 33 ⅓ rpm disc that took the industry by storm, forcing RCA to cancel its entry at a heavy loss.

Even worse, in the late 1940s CBS, which had remained a perpetual second to NBC in radio ratings, suddenly overtook NBC and became the number one entertainment network. NBC had spent years and vast sums of money nursing such stars as Edgar Bergen, Red Skelton, Burns and Allen, Amos 'n' Andy and Jack Benny. And one after another they were grabbed by CBS who lured them with a tempting capital gains package arrangement, enabling them to lower taxes and emerge with heftier profits. Although NBC could have held its stars with the same offer, Sarnoff stubbornly refused to do so. NBC, he argued, had built these personalities into what they had become by gambling on them when they were nobodies. If he were to plunge into competitive bidding with CBS to keep them in the fold, he felt, he would be giving in to a Frankenstein monster—the star system—which would ultimately ruin the broadcasting business.

After the Second World War, when the phenomenon of television erupted on the scene, the rivalry between Sarnoff and Paley escalated even more dramatically. A whole new market for exploitation opened up and the financial stakes soared higher.

The basic scientific principle of television had occurred to scientists as early as 1873, when a telegraph operator in

Ireland reported that his instrument was reacting differently in sunny and cloudy weather. Scientists were quick to deduce from this that light and shadow could be transmitted electrically.

John Logie Baird's experiments with various light-sensitive photoelectric cells in the early 1920s produced primitive but significant results. By 1925, the British Broadcasting Corporation had cautiously initiated a half hour of experimental television broadcasts. Meanwhile, the United States had plunged into research of its own to make television a commercial reality. In 1928, General Electric sponsored America's first televised news event, Al Smith's acceptance of the Democratic nomination for the presidency. The picture was transmitted to two receiving sets in a laboratory.

Sarnoff's corporation beat the Columbia Broadcasting System to the punch, becoming the first to transmit television commercially in America. The initial telecast took place at the opening of the New York World's Fair in 1939.

However, the pace of development, interrupted by the outbreak of World War II, remained slow. By 1946 only a few thousand television sets were in the hands of the public. Major advertisers had not yet been enticed into sponsoring programs, and the industry was operating on an exceedingly tight budget. "Actors who don't eat are popular in television," joked one insider. Whenever feasible the studios used puppets instead of flesh-and-blood actors who demanded wages. Animals in the zoo became featured performers; snakes and ducks developed into stars.

With the uncanny knack he had displayed in making radio and subsequently black and white television a reality for Americans, Sarnoff pioneered the commercial introduction and acceptance of color television, and once again he stirred up bitter opposition. CBS engineers had developed a mechanical scanning system for changing black and white into color television. But since this system was incompatible with black and white sets then in use, millions of viewers would have had to convert their sets to color at significant expense. Sarnoff, on the other hand, invested RCA's money in developing an all-electronic system of color television. The system was not yet ready for commercial use and CBS beat RCA to the market with a mechanical rotating disc system. Despite the howls of irritated RCA stockholders and the skepticism of virtually everyone connected with the industry who were convinced that an all-electronic color system could not be perfected, Sarnoff held back until RCA was ready with such a system and then launched it with great success.

Sarnoff triggered another controversy when it became clear that his oldest son, Robert, was to succeed him at RCA. Originally Sarnoff had wanted his son to be a lawyer. But Bob, upon leaving Harvard and spending time at the Columbia Law School before going into the war as a naval communications officer, decided to give up law and enter advertising. He worked on one of the Cowles publications, moved over to *Look* magazine, and decided eventually that he was not enthusiastic about the publishing business and wanted to get in on the ground floor of television. He joined NBC as a time salesman, went into network programming, then program production, and rose to become vice-president of NBC's film operations, subsequently emerging as executive vice president of NBC itself. In 1955, Bob, then thirty-seven, became president of NBC and finally was appointed chairman of the board of RCA. Sarnoff insisted that his son's thorough grounding in every phase of the NBC operation made him eminently qualified for his high post.

In fact, Sarnoff's ability to choose his son as the crown prince of a two-billion-dollar, publicly-owned enterprise in an age when major public corporations were staffed with managerial outsiders was virtually unprecedented, and not without repercussions. Bob Sarnoff was unable to free himself from his father's shadow. During his tenure as chief of RCA upon his father's retirement, he continued to be called "Bobby" by his associates who also referred to him as "the General's boy." During board meetings Bobby sat at the head of the table beneath an oil portrait of his father who looked down upon the conclave magisterially as if to remind everyone present to whom they owed their positions of power.

Yet young Sarnoff managed to stamp his own personality upon the operations of RCA. He expanded corporate assets by authorizing the acquisition of the Hertz Corporation, the number one auto rental firm, and of Random House, the book publisher, leading RCA into two highly promising new areas of business.

However, Sarnoff also made major miscalculations. In the early fifties RCA had moved tentatively into the burgeoning field of computer manufacturing. But when Bobby Sarnoff took over, wishing to put his personal imprint on a major achievement he decided that computer technology was the area in which to launch the company's major expansion program. At the time, RCA had been unable to make an appreciable dent in a market dominated by IBM; it was limping along with only 3 percent of the business. Beginning in 1968, Sarnoff plunged heavy sums into an all-out crash program to try to close the gap with IBM. Thanks to this offensive, RCA computers more than doubled their share of the market to just under 8 percent. But then in 1970 a sharp depression hit the business and RCA's computer operations began rolling up heavy losses. The board of directors put pressure on Sarnoff to give up the struggle against IBM and stop the hemorrhaging losses. Sarnoff was compelled to take RCA out of the field. In doing so, the corporation had to write off a whopping investment of $490,000,000, one of the largest losses in the history of American business. The write-off, which reduced RCA's entire net worth by 25 percent, sent shock waves through Wall Street, and RCA's stock went into a nose dive.

Other unfortunate matters popped up. Associates grumbled that Sarnoff was allowing his private life to influence his business decisions. In 1974 he had married diva Anna Moffo, who had been a star at the Met and internationally for over a decade. Miss Moffo happened to be under contract to record for RCA Victor, and after her marriage to Bobby Sarnoff her husband began to heavily promote her discs. The soprano recorded the title role of Massenet's opera *Thaïs*, and Victor pulled out all its promotional stops to peddle the album. Unfortunately, some critics claimed, Miss Moffo's voice had suffered of late. Andrew Porter, a leading music authority, writing in *High Fidelity* magazine, went out of his way to be cruel. "Poor Miss Moffo: Anyone whose eye has been caught by the recent advertisements 'A Voice For All Seasons,' 'The Incomparable Anna Moffo' . . . and then hears the new recording of *Thaïs* may well conclude that she has been made the victim of a cruel and quite unamusing joke . . . she appears to have lost any secure control of her voice; sustained notes

213

either sag or collapse in a breathy wobble. The freshness and easy charm have gone and nothing takes their place. The soprano seems to find it so difficult to sing Massenet's notes (or an approximation of them) that all questions of interpretation, of inflecting the phrases and creating the character, scarcely arise . . . all in all, it would have been kinder—to Miss Moffo, to Massenet, to everyone concerned—to wipe the tapes and bury the recording in decent oblivion rather than trumpet it as something that deserves to be heard."

This ungallant review and others in a similar vein were profoundly embarrassing to RCA and they didn't help Bob Sarnoff's case with the corporation's board of directors, where his support eroded. A number of RCA directors who had been personal friends of David Sarnoff and whom he had relied on to help elect his son chairman of the board had quit their positions. Their seats were taken by outsiders who felt no loyalty toward the senior Sarnoff. The majority of the directors who ended up serving with Bobby Sarnoff grew increasingly dissatisfied with him, and they swung behind Anthony Conrad, the RCA president and number two official of the corporation. Conrad had already assumed many of the duties normally held by the chairman, because Bob Sarnoff took frequent trips abroad and was away for long periods from the home office. In the spirit of insurgent officers preparing a coup d'état against their generalissimo, the dissenting board of directors quietly groomed Conrad as the man to take over.

Sarnoff himself seemed blithely unconcerned over the turmoil that was brewing. Psychologically entrenched in his dynastic role, he took no steps to ward off the threatened uprising. In the fall of 1975, in the eighth year of his regime, Sarnoff departed from Manhattan for a speech-making trip in Europe, followed by a visit to RCA business installations in Asia, and then a flight to Australia where his wife was singing. It was "highly injudicious" as one associate put it for Sarnoff to leave his disenchanted troops behind him. He unwittingly prepared his own noose, knotted it and pulled the trapdoor from under himself.

The insurgent directors and officers industriously rounded up enough votes from disgruntled members to oust the RCA chairman. A board meeting was scheduled for noon, November 5, at RCA's executive offices; Bob Sarnoff's contract with

RCA was due to expire at the end of the year and the officially announced reason for the meeting was to vote on its renewal.

In fact, the night before the scheduled board meeting, a compensation committee assigned to determine executive salaries and pensions met secretly at New York's exclusive Union League Club. Besides RCA's seven outside board members, the committee consisted of the dean of the Harvard Business School, Lawrence Fouraker, and Thornton Bradshaw, a top official of Atlantic Richfield. The members debated the matter over dinner and then remained at table for several hours continuing their discussion. They weighed Sarnoff's accomplishments, took a hard look at the $490,000,000 write-off caused by the ill-fated computer venture and arrived at a consensus before they disbanded. They decided Sarnoff's time was up.

The board members had hatched their plot with such secrecy that Sarnoff now returned to New York, had not the slightest inkling of how explosive the meeting scheduled for the next day would be. He came to work on the morning of November 5 under the impression that the meeting had been called merely to discuss routine business matters. He took the elevator to his office on the fifty-third floor of the RCA building, and sat down to attend to his mail. A little after 11 A.M. Arnold Smiley, the chairman of R. H. Macy and Company and head of RCA's Compensation Committee, walked in and informed Sarnoff that a major item of discussion had been added to the agenda of the meeting to be held within one hour—Sarnoff's resignation as chairman of RCA.

According to Smiley, Sarnoff "handled himself with great dignity and courage." After a pause, Smiley asked him whether in view of the circumstances Sarnoff would prefer not to attend the board of directors meeting. Sarnoff shook his head. He would attend and preside over the meeting as he had done for the past eight years. He didn't want to dodge anything.

At twelve-thirty the seven-man board of RCA directors filed into the conference room and Sarnoff entered from his own office, taking his seat at the head of the table just below the portrait of David Sarnoff, who had taken a struggling electronics firm and turned it into a leader of the world's communications industry.

The recommendation of the Compensation Committee was

215

introduced. A vote was taken. A show of hands was requested. Every director raised his hand for Sarnoff's resignation with the exception of RCA's general counsel who abstained from voting. However, when the vote carried, he concurred to make the action unanimous.

The toppling of the Sarnoff dynasty took just thirty minutes. Sarnoff, however, had one prerogative remaining to him. He could adjourn the meeting for lunch. He did so, quietly ate a meal in the office of his public relations advisor and composed a letter of resignation. The board of directors reassembled at three in the afternoon and elected Anthony L. Conrad to be the new chief executive.

Although the Sarnoff regime had been uprooted, the beneficiary of the palace revolution didn't last very long. In September 1976, less than a year after he had achieved power, Conrad was compelled to submit his own resignation. The Internal Revenue Service had found that he had failed to file personal income tax returns for five successive years. The RCA board, with the blood of the Sarnoff execution still dripping from their hands, met hastily to confront this new embarrassment. The corporation had been in the process of making a public offering of five million shares on Wall Street. Now it notified the Securities and Exchange Commission that it was withdrawing the issue. And the board chose Edgar H. Griffiths, executive vice-president of RCA and president of its Electronics and Diversified Business Division, to succeed Conrad.

The Sarnoff regency had crumbled at a most appropriate time. There was no longer any pretense that television's mission was one of educating the public. In the helter-skelter sweepstakes to win the ratings war, RCA had fallen into third place behind CBS and ABC, a brash newcomer organized in the early 1950s. Griffiths, in an attempt to move RCA up on its rivals, offered a million dollars in salary and bonuses to a new wunderkind of entertainment programming Fred Silverman. Silverman had masterminded CBS's programming in prime-time hours and had kept the network in the number one spot for five years before being lured away by ABC which, under his ministrations, promptly jumped from the number three spot into first place in prime-time program ratings. There were some purists who looked upon Silverman's road to the top—

Soap, Three's Company, Laverne and Shirley—with a jaundiced eye. Other champions of the people's democracy stoutly defended Silverman's vision of America. In any case, Fred Silverman emerged as America's virtuoso of popular entertainment, playing with genius upon the pipes of mass susceptibility.

Today the industry Sarnoff and Paley pioneered has become, in the phrase of producer Norman Lear, "a captive of a total winner mentality." The ratings race is its prime concern. Let a network drop a few points in the popularity contest and executive heads roll. The life of a television executive is as as expendable as a commissar's in Stalinist Russia. In recent years, RCA has fallen behind in the sweepstakes. Not only has CBS overtaken it in its network entertainment programming, but ABC, the industry's upstart, has leapfrogged to the top.

ABC came into being in 1953 and was put on a substantial financial footing when Leonard H. Goldenson, head of United Paramount Theaters, merged it with the then struggling American Broadcasting Corporation. Goldenson effected the consolidation despite the skepticism of his business associates who insisted there was no room for a third network in America. NBC and CBS at the time had a hammerlock on the advertising market and network ownership of local stations. Moreover, they had under contract all of TV's entertainment stars. "To survive against these odds we had to be innovators," reminisces Goldenson. He couldn't just follow in the footsteps of the giants and be a "me too" operation; he had to break eggs to make a revolutionary new omelet.

Goldenson started out with only a handful of stations covering a little more than 30 percent of the nation and it seemed impossible for him to lure advertising away from the giants, which he had to do to survive. But ABC, unable to buck the line against its heavier rivals, pulled trick plays out of its bag. The practice of the industry had been for advertisers to sponsor and actually control entire programs and arbitrarily move them from one network to another in the search for higher profits; Goldenson innovated the practice of selling individual minutes instead of whole programs to the advertisers. In this way Goldenson and his network kept control of its programs. His appeal to advertisers was that in spending fewer dollars to share in the backing of a single program the advertiser had more dollars to spread around to hedge its bets. They responded to Goldenson's concept and flocked to sign up with him. Subsequently, CBS and NBC followed Goldenson's practice, dropping their original policy of package selling.

ABC first forged into the lead in sports telecasting, and by the fall of 1975 had surged into first place in prime-time network programs on the strength of such popular hits as *Happy Days*, unseating CBS which had held that position for the previous twenty years. Then ABC unveiled Alex Haley's *Roots*, capturing the largest audience ever to that point and further entrenching its hold on the number one position. In its rush to the top ABC raided the local stations of its rivals right and left, taking away over twenty affiliates, half from NBC and half from CBS. ABC's stock on Wall Street soared as its earnings expanded fourfold.

Meanwhile, hedging against future uncertainties in a fast-changing market, Goldenson's firm has been aggressively diversifying into other businesses. American Broadcasting Company, the parent of the TV network, publishes magazines, owns entertainment parks, operates a highly profitable record company and runs a string of movie theaters along with the ABC Entertainment Center which is a community of offices, theaters, shops and restaurants in the Century City district of Los Angeles. One of the biggest money-making properties among ABC's recent acquisitions is *Los Angeles* magazine. Goldenson's firm also operates two profit-making entertainment parks in Florida and one near Atlantic City. Nevertheless, despite its aggressive diversification, 80 percent of ABC's profits is derived from its broadcasting and affiliate operations.

Now eighty, William S. Paley has headed CBS for fifty years, outlasting the administrations of eleven Presidents of the United States, spanning the years from the invention of the Model T Ford to the Concorde, from the silent movies to flights to the moon.

Sitting in his office on the thirty-sixth floor of CBS's forty-million-dollar headquarters, dubbed "Black Rock," working at an antique desk that once served as a gambling table in a Paris casino, surrounded by Picassos, Klines and a silver-framed picture of his late wife Barbara, Paley has much to reminisce about. He discovered Bing Crosby, Kate Smith, Frank Sinatra and the Boswell Sisters and developed them into radio stars. In the early years, believing that radio should be used to educate the masses, he gambled on a program, *Invitation to Learning*, that discussed the great books of the past. Despite the skepticism of his colleagues, the program attracted a devoted listening audience of several million people, many of them lacking formal education, who would never have been exposed to the great achievements in literature had it not been for Paley's adventurousness. In those early years he also sponsored Admiral Byrd on an expedition to the South Pole and had a radio transmitter set up in the Antarctic from which Byrd sent a weekly report to the American people.

Paley's greatest accomplishment, however, was in the field of radio journalism. In the early 1930s, to cover the aggressions of Hitler and Mussolini, Paley assembled a news staff that made journalistic history. Under Paley's stewardship some of the foremost talents in broadcasting journalism were developed: Edward R. Murrow, William L. Shirer, Quentin Reynolds, Eric Sevareid and Elmer Davis. Paley introduced Pope Pius XI, Mahatma Gandhi, Albert Einstein and Bernard Shaw over the American airways. He broadcast Adolf Hitler's historic address to the Reichstag after he took power, and the dramatic abdication speech of King Edward VIII.

Over the years Paley has hired several lieutenants whom he appeared to be grooming as his replacements. One able candidate was Dr. Frank Stanton, who served after the Second World War as president of the CBS network under Paley and who finally retired without being given the chance to take over the reins from his boss. Paley then hired Arthur Taylor, a man in his thirties with a background in the humanities, who had been an officer of International Paper and the chief official of First Boston Corporation. He assumed the presidency of CBS in 1972, but in 1976, with CBS losing its number one position in prime-time entertainment programming, Taylor was abruptly dismissed and John D. Backe was chosen as the heir apparent. Before becoming chief operating executive Backe had headed CBS' publishing division consisting of Holt, Rinehart and Winston; Popular Library; and a string of twenty-five magazines including *Field & Stream,* and *World Tennis.* Backe also played a major role in engineering the acquisition of Fawcett Publications and its profitable book publishing operation. But Backe in 1980 went the way of Stanton and Taylor, leaving Paley in control. Paley owns 1.7 million shares of CBS stock worth over $80 million and refuses to abdicate his powers, defying the ambitions of his talented underlings. Reports one financial writer: "There is paranoia in the ranks [of CBS]. Morale is low . . . a sense of frustration is developing . . . that the ship is being led by an aging man with a failing memory who [remains] the chief and often sole decision-maker." Indeed, no one has yet been able to certify Paley for the scrap heap. His memory, fading or not, is certainly longer than that of any of his entourage. He emerged in an age when one could have a genuine love affair with the broadcasting business. Today all that remains is a whore's embrace. The video tube surrenders itself not to the lover but to the highest bidder.

While relinquishing the titles of chairman of the board and chief executive officer, Paley remains the actual presiding head of an enterprise consisting of a television network earning just under a billion dollars a year, a radio network generating a quarter of a billion dollars, a phenomenally successful record company providing over five hundred million dollars a year in sales, a direct mail company, a publishing complex, a string of retail enterprises and a musical instrument business. Paley continues to hold the corporation in his eerie grip. "No one in television has ever had the will to win like Paley," observes an associate. "It's not enough to be ahead in daytime and news— he has to win all the marbles." The two-billion-dollar empire continues to be run, as one CBS executive officer puts it, "as Mr. Paley's Candy Store."

In recent years Paley has made some serious blunders, particularly through his impulsive attempts to diversify. CBS bought the New York Yankee baseball team which proceeded to plummet in the American League standings. The broadcaster plunged into the movie industry, buying Cinema Center Films, a producer of three-dimensional movies which excited no enthusiasm among the public and lost twenty million dollars. CBS went into an electronic videotape recording venture that was committed to the wrong technology, and Paley's company had to write off a heavy investment. On the other hand, Paley struck gold in the 1930s buying for a mere half million dollars what later became known as Columbia

Records, the company's second largest profit center after network broadcasting operations. Yet Paley continues to minimize his own role. Recently he told the press, "I mean to be here as . . . a person to whom people can come to for advice and guidance, and I might kibbitz once in a while, but I'll never give an order and anything I do by way of trying to persuade will be done through the chief executive officer."

Over at NBC, the roulette wheel is also spinning. Jane Cahill Pfeiffer, the first woman ever to be named chairman of NBC, left precipitously in 1980 as NBC's ratings continued to tumble. Meanwhile, Maurice Valente, President of RCA, was shown the door after only six months on the job. This former executive vice-president of International Telephone and Telegraph Corporation, according to an RCA spokesman, "did not meet our expectations." At the same time that Valente was eased out of his post, the board eliminated the position of president and created the office of chairman, consisting of five executive vice-presidents headed by Edgar H. Griffiths, who subsequently resigned, yielding his position to Thornton Bradshaw who came over from Atlantic Richfield. In June 1981, Silverman quit as NBC's chief executive officer.

As the television networks persist in strenghtening their grip over America's collective psyche, they are going to have to confront many problems of behavioral responsibility, technological controls and business ethics. Undoubtedly one of the most bothersome questions of all is how to deal with the minority racial groups who have been barred traditionally from employment in the television industry.

In the late 1960s, as a result of an epidemic of riots that broke out in the black ghettos, several commissions were hastily established by concerned white liberals to explore ways of opening up the media as an outlet for black anger and frustration. Television was the most powerful branch of the media, influencing the daily lives of the American masses. Yet, when blacks turned on the tube, all they saw were white people living out a white life style.

The Ford Foundation decided to fund a public affairs network show entirely devoted to the black community—its problems, its anxieties, its pride. Ford invested $500,000 to develop *Black Journal*, the first network show to be controlled by blacks from the top down. Introduced in June 1968 and headed by William Greaves, who has won over forty international awards as a producer of documentary films and was elected to the Black Hall of Fame, *Black Journal* became a landmark in the history of television.

Greaves was the first to bring to the video screen before millions of white Americans a host of black people America knew nothing about. And he made their opinions instantly known on the national scene, provocative and disturbing though many of these were. Greaves reminisces with a wry chuckle, "There's no question about it. Some of the statements of the blacks who appeared on our shows were challenging. Some were frightening. Some disparaging. Some insightful. And, oddly the show attracted more white than black viewers. The response of the white audience fell into two categories. One group was supportive of the show, curious, questioning and interested, considering it a badly needed education in black attitudes and grievances. But there was a vindictive, belligerent faction of the audience which was infuriated that 'those crazy white liberals had let those blacks get on the air and curse us out. We ought to hang those rascals!'" Under Greaves' stewardship the entire spectrum of black life and black participation in the American community was explored and commented on from a uniquely black perspective. *Black Journal* won an Emmy for its contributions, and regional black shows mushroomed up all around America modeled after Greaves' prototype. *Black Journal* became a training ground for a host of black producers, directors and technicians who subsequently made careers for themselves in the television industry.

Today Greaves concedes that the situation in television has changed somewhat for the better. An increasing number of black artists have gained a foothold in the business. Black reporters have surfaced on the leading news shows. Nevertheless those black producers and directors who persist in being more socially aware than their fellows are faced with frequent frustration. "Social awareness has a very poor track record on Madison Avenue," Greaves concludes.

In any event the crystal ball of television's future is extremely clouded. As the Big Three network conglomerates continue to strengthen their hold over America's habits of thought, the implications become increasingly ominous. Two sociologists,

Grubbner and Gross, have made an extensive survey of how differently Americans who are heavy watchers of the video screen perceive life and the world compared with others who watch television infrequently or not at all. The sociologists used as a standard of heavy TV viewing people who spend more than four hours a day in front of their sets. Light viewers were classified as those who spend two hours or less before the screen. The researchers took a nationwide sample of all ages and educational levels and found that 65 percent of TV's heavy watchers were substantially more paranoiac than the lighter watchers. Asked the question whether the majority of people could be trusted, 65 percent of the heavy watchers answered that "one can't be too careful of other people." Only 48 percent of light viewers gave a similar response. Over 50 percent of heavy viewers felt that they could become the victim of a crime on any given day. Less than 40 percent of the light viewers felt this way. Continuing heavy exposure to television, concluded Grubbner and Gross, is creating a growing climate of hysteria and paranoia.

There are other equally tragic behavioral patterns in our television society. Professor Neil Postman of New York University points out that the video screen has turned America into a nation without children. "Adults and children tend to watch the same programs," he observes. "They even watch at the same time." At one time the printed word separated children from adults, "those who were learning to read from those who know how." Television has obliterated this distinction "because it requires no instruction to grasp its form and because it does not segregate its audience. It communicates the same information to everyone, simulateneously, regardless of age, sex or level of education."

TV has destroyed the traditional concept that certain areas of life are reserved only for adults and are not considered suitable for children. "Television forces the entire culture to come out of the closet. In its quest for new and sensational information to hold its audience, TV must tap every existing taboo in the culture: homosexuality, incest, divorce, promiscuity, corruption, adultery, sadism. . . ." Even in commercials, the young share adult secrets from "vaginal sprays to life insurance to the causes of marital conflict."

While the television age has killed the innocence of child-

223

hood, it is difficult to determine, concludes Professor Postman, whether it's childhood that has been destroyed or adulthood. For television promotes a mentality that is childish whatever one's chronological age. It has instilled "an obsessive need for immediate gratification, a lack of concern for consequences, an almost promiscuous preoccupation with consumption." The result is that the distinction between children and grown-ups has been erased. Postman concludes that this obliteration of childhood is catastrophic. "I believe that adults first need to be children before they can be grown-ups. For otherwise they remain like TV's adult-child all their lives, with no sense of place, no capacity for lasting relationships, no respect for limits, and no grasp of the future."

Conclusion

HOWARD BRAY, EXECUTIVE director of the Fund for Investigative Journalism, has pointed out in an article in *Washington Journalism Review* that more than a century ago Karl Marx defined power in a society as control of the means of production. That power in America today, however, as the historian Arthur Schlesinger, Jr., observes, is control of the means of communication. And the nature of this control is currently undergoing a profound transformation.

The newspaper business is embarked on a far-reaching technological revolution that is changing the very nature of its existence. The highly individualistic, free-wheeling newsman typified by Hildy Johnson, the managing editor in Ben Hecht's *The Front Page*, has become obsolete as the soaring costs of putting out a newspaper have thrust the industry into an era of automation. Most of America's larger daily papers have automated their entire editing and composing processes. In the newsroom reporters are punching out their stories on a keyboard hooked up to a video display terminal. Using similar VDTs, editors are calling up stories they want revised and edited. Automatic typesetting machines have been added to complete the system.

Virtually every phase of production has yielded to the new technology. For instance, thanks to a breakthrough in electronic photography, achieved by the National Aeronautics and Space Administration, in the course of developing photographic techniques for planetary exploration, methods for computerizing news-photo libraries have been established. News pictures can now be stored in computer data banks and retrieved by the user as easily as written data can be summoned up.

For their part, publishers are becoming increasingly aware that they are moving from the newspaper into the data information business. "Today we operate with ink on paper," declares one publisher. "Tomorrow, our operation may well consist of telephone wires that connect our newsroom with a computer terminal in the home of our subscribers." Already more and more Americans are getting their news entirely from television, and eventually they could be reading the news on television as well as watching it. Indeed, prototype models of a completely televised newspaper are currently being tested around the country.

Publishers are facing the advent of these developments with ambivalent feelings. On the one hand they are intrigued by the opportunities that are opening up for them if they take full advantage of the situation. On the other, they are alarmed at the possibility that merchandisers of electronic data banks and telecommunication systems will move in to seize control of the market as newspaper journalism is transformed into an electronics information industry.

A nagging question arises: who will ultimately provide the electronic data bases for American readers? Data bank producers are already ideally suited to offer much of the information that has traditionally been peddled by the newspapers.

Papers are read for more than just the news they provide. They are read for advertisements, information on sports, cultural events, TV and radio programming and movie schedules. Giant electronic distribution producers like American Telephone and Telegraph and International Business Machines, who have had no experience whatsoever with printed newspapers, are equipped to provide information systems for advertising a multiplicity of products and services. To cite one instance, department stores could run sales information on home video screens and interested buyers, operating computerized home terminals, could log their credit card numbers into the system and automatically be charged for transactions. Already AT&T has moved aggressively into the data information field through its ubiquitous wire services in an attempt to snatch markets from the publishers of the printed page.

To avoid being eliminated, some of the larger, more resourceful newspaper publishers—the New York *Times,* Times Mirror Company, Dow Jones, for instance—have hurriedly been acquiring data bank facilities and television outlets. Indeed the Times Mirror, publisher of the Los Angeles *Times,* has become the nation's sixth largest operator of cable-television stations due to its acquisition of Communications Properties, Inc., an aggressive CATV concern. Currently the Times Mirror Company owns twenty-six stations that are in the process of being linked together by satellite transmission. The Knight-Ridder newspaper chain has plunged aggressively into electronic information systems featuring home computers and TV screens. Its computers connect up with a phone line to a Knight-Ridder data base. By pushing a button a family can have flashed onto its TV screen information on news events, sports, weather, consumer advertising, movie and entertainment happenings.

The coming of the fully electronic newspaper, delivered on home television screens, could trigger a radical transformation in the pattern of news processing operations with tomorrow's smaller, local newspapers serving as little more than news-gathering outposts while the leading chains gather up more and more of the business. In the approaching new age of Big Brother, prophesies one industry leader, "news stories will be keyed into a central computer location where they can be edited, abstracted and indexed. Local editors will make up their papers from the data banks of central computers. News will be delivered to the home television screen via phone lines, cables or ordinary broadcast signals. As their traditional role diminishes in importance," this observer concludes, "newspapers will be controlled by a relatively few people."

This concentration of the means of communicating news and editorial content into the hands of a powerful few could have ominous implications for the future of American democracy. As one publisher puts it, "Traditionally newspapers have played the role of presenting information to the public, ascribing significance to it and interpreting it. The best of them have served as a watchdog in our society." Given a future in which electronic newspapers gain wide acceptance, the usurpation of the duties of the press by owners of computerized information systems, operating outside the traditional framework of a newspaper industry that is safeguarded by the First Amendment of the Constitution, could have far-reaching consequences. As one top publisher puts it, "AT&T, which with its vast capital assets and nationwide communications network is in the strongest possible position to merchandise tomorrow's electronic newspaper, is hardly an ideal trustee for nourishing the free discussion that is the lifeblood of democracy." At the same time, the handful of traditional news publishers and editors who might survive the assault on the printed word by adapting their operations to the exigencies of the new technological era will hardly be in a position to uphold the historic freedom of the press. It would not be at all reassuring, observes one commentator, for the New York *Times* to carry on its front page, in place of "All the news that's fit to print," the inscription "All the news that's fit to compute."

Just as the possibility exists that the printed newspaper may become extinct, the technological revolution in communications is threatening to change the face of the television industry which has played an overwhelming role in sabotaging the printed word. Ironically, the Big Three networks, whose competitiveness caused a shake-out in the magazine business, are being confronted with newly emerging rivals who threaten to push *them* to the wall. The domination of the networks that control the traditionally licensed airwaves may be drawing to an end, thanks to developments in satellite communication systems through which television journalism as well as entertainment can be launched from virtually any spot on earth immediately and cheaply.

One of the major competitive threats is cable-television. Starting inauspiciously, with many people insisting that it was a violation of their rights to be forced to *pay* for TV shows, cable-television is making serious inroads into the broadcasting market because of the growing disgust of audiences with the product of the traditional networks. Abetted by a series of advantageous court decisions and a friendly U.S. government which has regarded CATV as a welcome relief from the monopoly the Big Three networks have exercised on TV news and entertainment, the cable-television industry is exploding. By 1980 almost fifteen million households, or one fifth of all American homes equipped with television sets, had become tied into cable systems.

A fundamental ingredient in the expanding technology of cable-television is the stationary orbit satellite which makes possible the distribution of programs nationally rather than on a local or regional basis, providing cable-TV producers with the potential to compete across the board with the major television networks.

One socially beneficial result of the rapidly growing cable industry is the increasing fragmentation of TV audiences. Traditionally, a huge American audience has been delivered up passively to the Big Three networks. Cable-television is threatening to break up this mass audience by catering to special groups. Points out one CATV executive, "In the past, lowest common denominator thinking was the glue-all of network broadcasting; the larger the audience, the greater the profits. Now cable stations are thriving by using precisely the opposite approach—'Narrowcasting.' Just as special interest magazines have arisen to replace the old general appeal periodical, so cable programming promises to offer a video supermarket catering to the tastes of specific, well-defined audiences."

One free-wheeling multimillionaire, Ted Turner, the owner of the Atlanta Braves baseball team and the proprietor of a cable-TV operation that serves audiences around the country, has turned his TV station in Atlanta into the nation's first satellite "superstation" (as he calls it), launching an around-the-clock cable-television news service that presents the first serious threat the news departments of the Big Three networks have ever faced. A variety of programs targeted for specific interests and a further fragmentation of audiences is being readied over cable TV, including a black entertainment television network that follows in the footsteps of *Black Journal* will offer socially conscious movies and other events of particular interest to the black community.

The giant strides cable-television has taken have the commercial networks running scared. They are sending up a howl to the regulatory services in Washington. Jack Valenti, president of the Motion Picture Association of America, has allied himself with the networks in their jeremiads. Bewailing the social harm that cable-television will inflict on America if allowed to expand unchecked, Valenti declared in a recent article in the *Washington Journalism Review,* "We're heading for catastrophe in the free television business in my judgment. In the next four to seven years free television is going to be a barren wasteland and this country is going to be two nations—one divided into those who can afford pay-cable and those who can't. I think the political implications of that are dire and gloomy. . . . By parliamentary fiat, basic cable television is granted a special privilege that I am not aware is proffered to any other business enterprise in this country. That is, it's allowed to buy the product that it perforce must have—programming—at an outrageous, comically low price."

Whichever vested interests prevail and whatever the merit of their arguments, the impact that telecommunications as a whole has upon society not only in America but around the world is immense and growing. "The advent of communications satellite, cable television, and the emerging new technology of fiber optics has served to tremendously increase the number of information channels that can flow to and from a home or office," points out a leading communications engineer. "The marriage of satellite and cable is going to make it ultimately possible for almost any programmer or distributor to create his own special purpose TV network, beam it up to a satellite and let earth-station-equipped cable TV systems offer the programs to their subscribers." Once programmed, a computer is an intensely personal device. It reacts to human input and can randomly create new responses to human actions. "As our programming becomes more sophisticated, our personal relationships with the computer will become enhanced."

The difference between broadcasting as we know it and computing, say the technological experts, is the difference between watching and participating. The computer has already evolved into a gaming medium in a manner that TV has never been. The most radical developments in telecommunications will put active program control and creation into the hands of the audience itself.

Observes one engineer, "We are entering a technological revolution [in which] satellite-microwave-cable systems are about to change the face of broadcasting forever as mankind becomes increasingly huddled into a wired global village. Technologists are positively aglow with a cornucopia of visions for tomorrow. In the neo-video age to come, they say, people will be able to select a restaurant to eat in or a home to purchase by punching several buttons on a hand-held keyboard. In the years ahead television sets will be converted into home computer terminals, enabling viewers to read pages from books and newspapers on their TV screens and obtain a multiplicity of information from the availability of antique lamp shades to diet recipes."

In this tomorrow, an increasingly televised society, apart from its technological impact, could have profound political and social consequences. Television is already the nerve center of our civilization, the Leviathan of our culture. It has fundamentally changed the American political process, thanks to its compulsive habit of arbitrarily handpicking national celebrities. As Tod Gitlin, writing in the *Columbia Journalism Review,* points out, America's political leaders have traditionally had followers. "They have looked back toward their constituents in order to lead them forward toward goals. Celebrities, however, have [only] fans. Democratic leadership is accountable to the political base; celebrities are accountable to no one but the media. For the media are, among other things, in the business of entertainment; they need to create, reinforce and circulate celebrity, and they have their own criteria for generating it . . . news is what is made by people who have been certified as newsworthy."

Americans are becoming increasingly confused over the difference between political leadership and celebrity status, Gitlin argues. We are increasingly a society in which an appearance on the Johnny Carson show is regarded as an exercise in political power. Concludes Gitlin, "Against its own convictions . . . our journalism may have helped engender a political culture which is more hospitable to the single visions of authoritarians than to the complexities . . . of democrats."

The culture that television fosters is indeed only a few steps short of authoritarianism. It is not at all far-fetched to suppose that the video hucksters who so exuberantly peddle de-

231

odorants will be prepared to sell dictatorship to American consumers whenever a sufficiently persuasive Big Brother commands them to do so. The coming of the first American dictator may well be the last and most spectacular event to be broadcast by an American communications industry still in control of its own destiny. Thereafter, events created for the media by a totalitarian regime will be disseminated to an audience hypnotized in front of its television screens, imprisoned in body as well as in soul.

Selected Bibliography

Baehr, Harry W., Jr. *The New York* Tribune *Since the Civil War.* New York: Dodd, Mead & Co., 1936.

Bainbridge, John. *Little Wonder; Or,* The Reader's Digest *and How It Grew.* New York: Reynal & Hitchock, 1946.

Barnouw, Erik. *A History of Broadcasting in the United States* (3 vols. *A Tower in Babel, The Golden Web, The Image Empire*). New York: The Oxford University Press, 1968.

Beebe, Lucius. *The Big Spenders.* New York: Doubleday & Co., Inc., 1966.

Bent, Silas. *Newspaper Crusaders; A Neglected Story.* New York: Whittlesey House, 1939.

——*Ballyhoo, The Voice of the Press.* New York: Horace Liveright, 1927.

Berger, Meyer. *The Story of* The New York Times *1851–1951.* New York: Simon and Schuster, 1951.

Bessie, Simon Michael. *Jazz Journalism, The Story of the Tabloid Newspapers.* New York: Dutton, 1938.

Bird, George L. and Frederic E. Merwin, Eds. *The Press and Society.* Englewood Cliffs, NJ: Prentice-Hall, Inc., 1951.

Blair, Joan and Clay Blair, Jr. *The Search for J.F.K.* New York: Berkley Publishing Co., 1976.

Bleyer, Willard Grosvenor. *Main Currents in the History of American Journalism.* Boston: Houghton Mifflin Co., 1927.

Chapman, John. *Tell It to Sweeney: The Informal History of the New York Daily News.* New York: Doubleday & Co., Inc., 1961.

Conlin, Joseph R. *The American Radical Press 1880–1960* (2 vols.). Westport, CT.: Greenwood Press, 1974.

Cook, Elizabeth Christine. *Literary Influences in Colonial Newspapers 1704–1750.* New York: Columbia University Press, 1912.

Davis, Elmer. *History of The New York Times 1851–1921.* St. Clair Shores, MI: Scholarly Press, Inc., 1971.

Downie, Leonard, Jr. *The New Muckrakers.* New York: New American Library, 1976.

Eisenschiml, Otto. *In the Shadow of Lincoln's Death.* New York: Wilfred Funk, 1940.

Emery, Edwin. *The Press and America.* Englewood Cliffs, NJ: Prentice-Hall, Inc., 1972.

Feemster, Robert M. *The Wall Street Journal: Purveyor of News to Business America.* West Chester, PA: Newcomen Society in North America, 1954.

Flumiani, C.M. *How to Read the Wall Street Journal for Pleasure and for Profit.* New York: Library of Wall Street, 1967.

Glessing, Robert, J. *The Underground Press in America.* Bloomington, IN: Indiana University Press, 1970.

Gottlieb, Robert and Irene Wolt. *Thinking Big: The Story of The Los Angeles Times, Its Publishers, and Their Influence on Southern California.* New York: G.P. Putnam's Sons, 1977.

Greer, M. Margaret. *From Trail Dust to Star Dust: The Story of Johnstown, Pennsylvania.* Ridgefield, CT: W.M. Greer, 1967.

Hohenberg, John. *The Pulitzer Prizes.* New York: Columbia University Press, 1974.

Howe, Irving. *World of Our Fathers.* New York: Simon and Schuster (Touchstone), 1976.

Hudson, Frederic. *Journalism in the United States from 1690 to 1872.* Brooklyn, N.Y.: Haskell House Publishers, Ltd., 1968.

Ireland, Alleyne. *An Adventure With a Genius: Recollections of Joseph Pulitzer.* New York: E.P. Dutton & Co., 1920.

Johnson, Willis Fletcher. *The History of the Johnstown Flood.* Philadelphia: Edgewood Publishing Co., 1889.

Juergens, George. *Joseph Pulitzer and the New York World.* Princeton, N.J.: Princeton University Press, 1966.

Kobler, John. *Luce: His* Time, Life *and* Fortune. New York: Doubleday & Co., 1968.

Lee, Alfred McClung. *The Daily Newspaper in America.* New York: Macmillan, Inc., 1947.

Lee, James Melvin. *History of American Journalism.* Boston: Houghton Mifflin, Co., 1923.

Liebling, Abbott Joseph. *The Wayward Pressman.* New York: Doubleday & Co., 1947.

———*The Press.* New York: Ballantine Books, Inc., 1961.

Lundberg, Ferdinand. *Imperial Hearst.* New York: Equinox Cooperative Press, 1936.

Lyons, Eugene. *David Sarnoff, A Biography.* New York: Harper & Row, 1966.

MacDougall, Curtis D. *Newsroom Problems and Policies.* New York: Macmillan, Inc., 1941.

Macfadden, Mary and Emile Gauvreau. *Dumbbells and Carrot Strips: The Story of Bernarr Macfadden.* New York: Holt, Rinehart & Winston, 1953.

McLean, Evalyn Walsh. *Father Struck It Rich.* Boston: Little, Brown & Co., 1936.

Merrill, John C. *The Elite Press.* Belmont, CA: Pitman Publishing, Inc., 1968.

Mott, Frank Luther. *American Journalism: A History, 1690–1960.* New York: Macmillan, Inc. 1962.

Neilson, Winthrop and Frances. *What's News—Dow Jones, Story of the* Wall Street Journal. Radnor, PA: Chilton Book Co., 1973.

Noel, Mary. *Villains Galore: The Heyday of the Popular Story Weekly.* New York: Macmillan, Inc., 1954.

O'Connor, Richard. *Johnstown the Day the Dam Broke.* Philadelphia: J.B. Lippincott Co., 1957.

Oursler, Fulton. *The True Story of Bernarr Macfadden.* New York: L. Copeland Co., 1929.

Patterson, Joseph Medill. *Confessions of a Drone.* Girard, KA: Appeal to Reason, 1906 [?].

Payne, George Henry. *History of Journalism in the United States.* New York: Appleton-Century-Crofts, 1940.

Pollock, Theodore Marvin. *The Solitary Clarinetist; A Critical Biography of Abraham Cahan.* New York: Columbia University Press, 1959.

Potter, Jeffrey. *Men, Money and Magic: The Story of Dorothy Schiff.* New York: Coward, McCann & Geoghegan, 1976.

Pound, Arthur and Samuel Taylor Moore, eds. *They Told Barron: Conversations and Revelations of an American Pepys in Wall Street.* New York: Harper & Brothers, 1930.

—— *More They Told Barron's.* New York: Harper & Brothers, 1931.

Preston, Charles, ed. *The World of the* Wall Street Journal; *Main Street and Beyond.* New York: Simon & Schuster, 1959.

Radder, Norman J. *Newspapers in Community Service.* New York: McGraw-Hill, Inc., 1926.

Roberts, Chalmers M. *The Washington* Post, *The First Hundred Years.* Boston: Houghton Mifflin Co., 1977.

Ross, Ishbel. *Ladies of the Press.* New York: Harper & Brothers, 1936.

Salmon, Lucy Maynard. *The Newspaper and the Historian.* New York: Oxford University Press, 1923.

—— *The Newspaper and Authority.* New York: Oxford University Press, 1923.

Synder, Louis L., and Richard B. Morris, eds. *A Treasury of Great Reporting.* New York: Simon and Schuster, 1949.

Stein, Leon; Abraham P. Conan, and Lynn Davision, trans. *The Education of Abraham Cahan.* New York: Jewish Publication Society of America, 1969.

Swanberg, W.A. *Citizen Hearst.* New York: Charles Scribner's Sons, 1961.

Talese, Gay. *The Kingdom and the Power.* New York: The World Publishing Co., 1969.

Tebbel, John William. *An American Dynasty.* New York: Doubleday & Co., 1947.

—— *The Compact History of the American Newspaper.* New York: Hawthorn Books, Inc., 1969.

Thomas, Dana L. *The Money Crowd.* New York: G.P. Putnam's Sons, 1972.

—— *50 Great Americans* (with Henry Thomas). New York: Doubleday & Co., 1948.

Villard, Oswald Garrison. *Some Newspapers and Newspaper-Men.* New York: Alfred A. Knopf, 1923.

Walker, James Herbert. *The Johnstown Horror.* Chicago: L.P. Miller & Co., 1889.

Wendt, Lloyd. *Chicago* Tribune, *The Rise of a Great American Newspaper*. Skokie, IL: Rand McNally & Co., 1979.

Wolseley, Roland E. *Understanding Magazines*. Ames, IA: The Iowa State University Press, 1969.

Wood, Playsted. *Of Lasting Interest: The Story of* The Reader's Digest. New York: Doubleday & Co., 1958.